NICHOLLS'S

Seamanship and Nautical Knowledge

Revised by
A. N. COCKCROFT, F.R.I.N., F.N.I., M.Phil., Extra Master

GLASGOW
BROWN, SON & FERGUSON, Ltd., Nautical Publishers
4-10 Darnley Street, G41 2SD

A

25th Edition	-	-	1983
26th Edition	-	-	1993
Revised	-	-	1995
27th Edition	-	-	1997

ISBN 0 85174 654 3 (27th Edition)
ISBN 0 85174 637 3

© 1997 BROWN, SON & FERGUSON, LTD., GLASGOW, G41 2SD
Printed and Made in Great Britain

PREFACE

FOR several decades *Nicholls's Seamanship* has served as a standard text-book for ship's officers and cadets. It is intended to cover most aspects of Seamanship to a sufficient standard for all grades of examination and to provide an introduction to Ship Construction, Stability and Cargo Work for practical requirements aboard ship. Signalling and some aspects of Shipmasters' Business are also covered.

Extensive changes have been made in this edition due to recent developments and amendments to regulations. The chapter on Life-Saving Appliances has been completely revised and the chapter on Firefighting has been changed to take account of the requirements of the IMO Safety of Life at Sea Convention and the latest regulations for U.K. ships.

Several amendments to the International Regulations for Preventing Collisions at Sea came into force in November 1989 and April 1991. The revised Regulations are incorporated in this edition. Changes have been made to other chapters where necessary.

Grateful acknowledgement is made to the following firms and organisations for information and permission to reproduce illustrations:

Blohm & Voss AG, Hamburg. (Stuelcken Derrick).
British Ropes Limited. (Wire splice).
Finn Tveten & Co. A/S, Oslo. (Velle Shipshape Crane).
Loveridge Limited. (Blocks and sheaves).
MacGregor & Co. (Naval Architects) Ltd. (Universal derrick and hatch covers).
Nu-Swift International Ltd. (Fire extinguishers).
P. & O. Steam Navigation Co. (Cargo work photographs).
R.F.D. Ltd. (Liferaft).
Pains-Wessex Limited. (Line-throwing apparatus).
Viking Life-saving Equipment Ltd. (Evacuation system).
Welin Lambie Ltd. (Lifeboat davits).
Watercraft International Ltd. (Lifeboats).

CONVERSION TABLE

Imperial to Metric Units	Metric to Imperial Units

Length

Imperial to Metric	Metric to Imperial
1 inch = 2·54 cm	1 cm = 0·394 inches
1 foot = 0·305 m	1 m = 3·28 feet
1 fathom = 1·83 m	= 0·547 fathoms
1 nautical mile = 1·85 km	1 km = 0·54 nautical miles

Weight

Imperial to Metric	Metric to Imperial
1 pound = 0·454 kg	1 kg = 2·205 lbs
1 ton = 1,016·05 kg	1 tonne = 0·984 tons
= 1·016 tonnes	= 2,204·6 lbs

Volume or Capacity

Imperial to Metric	Metric to Imperial
1 cu foot = 0·0283 m³	1 cu m = 35·315 cu ft
1 gallon = 4·546 litres	1 litre = 0·22 gallons
1 gross ton = 2·83 m³	1 cu m = 0·353 gross tons

Rope Size

Diameter of rope in mm = Circumference in inches × 8·085
Circumference of rope in inches = Diameter in mm × 0·124

CONTENTS

CONTENTS

CHAPTER XII—SHIP CONSTRUCTION

CHAPTER XIII—SHIP STABILITY

CHAPTER XIV—MISCELLANEOUS

CHAPTER XV—SIGNALLING

NICHOLLS'S
SEAMANSHIP AND NAUTICAL KNOWLEDGE

CHAPTER 1

KNOTS, BENDS, SPLICES

The Construction of Ropes

ROPE can be made from almost every pliable material, but is generally composed of vegetable fibres, synthetic fibres, steel, iron or copper wires.

The vegetable fibres used are Manila from the Philippines; Sisal from East Africa; Hemp from Europe, India and New Zealand; Cotton; Coir, often called grass line, which is manufactured from the husks of coconuts.

The fibres are combed out and formed into a continuous ribbon, spun into **Yarn** and wound on bobbins. The yarns are made into **Strands** which are **Layed** into the finished rope. The **Lay** or **Angle** at which the strands are twisted together is an important factor governing the performance of the rope. The higher the "angle of lay", the harder the rope.

Right Hand Lay or "Z" Twist signifies that the spiral shape of the strands is similar to that of a standard screw thread.

Left Hand Lay or "S" Twist is the opposite to the above.

Standard Lay is that which from experience is found to be the best angle of lay for all general work to withstand chafing and to combine pliability with strength.

Soft Lay (or Long Lay) has an angle of lay less than normal in order to increase the pliability of the rope, and to reduce elasticity.

Hard Lay (or firm or Short Lay) has an angle of lay greater than normal in order to increase elasticity and to reduce the absorbtion of water. The breaking strain and pliability are reduced, but the elasticity is increased.

The types of rope are divided into the following classes:

(1) Three-strand or Hawser-laid Rope. This construction, sometimes called "Plain Lay", is the general standard type of rope for all ordinary purposes. (Fig. 1).

(2) Four-strand or Shroud lay, provides the rope with a greater bearing surface than three strand, but its weight is greater and its strength less than three-strand rope of the same size. A core is

1

generally placed in the centre of this rope for stability. Both three and four strand ropes are normally made "right-hand". (Fig. 2).

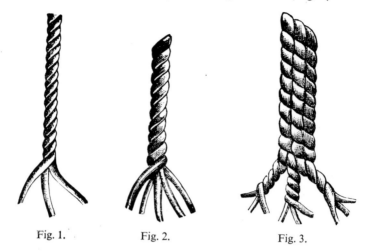

Fig. 1.   Fig. 2.   Fig. 3.

(3) Cable-laid rope (or Water Lay). This is made by laying three three-strand ropes together. It is normally made "Left Hand" but when required can be made "Right Hand". When used in conjunction with wire rope as a towing spring, it is essential that the lay of the rope is the same as that of the wire rope.

(4) Unkinkable lay. In this construction the twist of the yarn and the strands is the same, usually Left Hand, while the rope is Right Hand Lay. This provides resistance to kinking when running through sheaves and is recommended for lifeboat falls, in certain cases.

(5) Eight strand plaited rope is made by plaiting two pairs of right-hand strands with two pairs of left-hand strands. This construction give the same strength as three-strand rope of the same size but it is extremely flexible and is resistant to kinking. It grips well on winches and capstans, making it very suitable for mooring ropes. (Fig. 4).

Fig. 4.

(6) Braided rope consists of a braided sheath over a braided core. It gives greater strength than three stranded or eight-strand rope, is very flexible, does not kink and gives more grip on capstans and

warping drums because the area of contact is greater. This construction is used only for nylon ropes. (Fig. 5).

Fig. 5.

Natural Fibre Rope

Manila comes from the Abaca plant. The rope is smooth and glossy.

Sisal is relatively cheap but is not as strong as manila. It is almost white and has a hairy surface.

Hemp is used mainly for small cordage.

Coir is made from coconut fibre. It was formerly used for towing and harbour springs because it will float on water but it has low strength and has been superseded by polypropylene.

Cotton is very soft rope, used for ornamental purposes.

Synthetic Fibre Rope

Rope made from synthetic fibres is unaffected by rot and mildew and has greater strength than natural fibre rope. The following materials are used:

Polyamide (Nylon). This is the strongest of the synthetic fibre ropes. It has exceptional resistance to substantial loading. It is resistant to alkalis, oils and organic solvents but is attacked by acids.

Polyester (Terylene) is almost as strong as nylon and does not stretch as m   ther man-made fibres. It resists acids, oils and
   r   sr   att   by alkalis.

Polypropylene and Polythene. Ropes made from these fibres will float on water. They have a relatively low melting point. Both fibres are highly resistant to acids, alkalis and oils but may be affected by bleaching agents and some industrial solvents. Polypropylene is widely used as it has several advantages over natural fibre ropes, is less expensive than nylon and terylene and is stronger than polythene.

Table comparing properties of 40 mm rope made from different fibres.

	Breaking Strain (kg)	Specific Gravity	Melting Point (°C)	Extension at breaking load
Sisal	10·4	1·50	—	10–20%
Manila	11·7	1·50	—	10–20%
Polypropylene	19·4	0·91	165	25–40%
Polythene	15·4	0·95	135	27–37%
Terylene	23.9	1·38	260	23–33%
Nylon	30.0	1·14	250	33–46%

Preservation of Fibre Rope

When removing rope from a new coil take the end from the inside so that the turns can be taken off anti-clockwise for a right-hand rope, clockwise for a left-hand rope, to avoid disturbing the lay. Avoid subjecting ropes to bad nips. The diameter of sheaves to be used with fibre rope should be at least ten times the diameter of the rope. Avoid chafage. Inspect frequently to assess wear and damage.

Natural fibre should be stowed away in a well ventilated space and either hung from wooden pegs or stowed down on gratings. Do not stow in the vicinity of boilers as excessive heat will cause dryness which makes the fibre brittle. The life of manila and sisal is shortened by the action of salt water so after immersion in the sea the ropes should preferably be hosed down with fresh water. Before stowing away the ropes should be cleaned and dried.

Synthetic Fibre. Special stowage is not so important with man-made fibre ropes but they should not be stowed near boilers. They should be covered by tarpaulins when on deck as they can be harmed by exposure to sunlight.

Synthetic fibres, particularly polypropylene and polythene, have a relatively low melting point and tend to become sticky. Frictional heat is likely to develop at the warping drum which will tend to fuse the fibres so the rope should be walked back and not surged. As few turns as possible should be taken on the drum end with polypropylene rope but on whelped drums extra turns may be made to get a good grip.

Precautions when using fibre rope. When rope is under strain as few persons as necessary should remain in the vicinity. No-one should be allowed to stand in a bight of rope or across a rope under strain. Synthetic fibre rope, unlike natural fibre rope, gives no audible or visual warning when approaching the breaking point and, as the stretch will be recovered almost instantaneously when the rope parts, there may be considerable recoil.

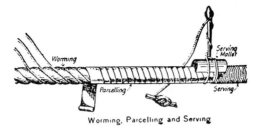

Worming, Parcelling and Serving

Fig. 6.

Protection of Rope. Some ropes have to be protected from wear by chafing. The rope is first **wormed** by filling in the lay with small stuff or lengths of spunyarn to make it nearly round, it is then **parcelled** with strips of tarred canvas about 5 cms broad and finally it is **served,** that is, spunyarn is wound tightly round the parcelling with a serving mallet or serving board, all according to the rhyme, "Worm and parcel with the lay, turn and serve the other way".

Miscellaneous Cordage

Spunyarn is made by twisting together two, three or four yarns of tarred soft hemp, usually left handed. It is used mainly for serving or seizing. Supplied in 3 kg balls.

Marline consists of two yarns of hemp, usually tarred, twisted left handed. It is used for serving and whipping ropes. (1 kg balls).

Houseline is similar to marline but is 3 ply (three yarns).

Hambroline is three stranded hemp which may be tarred. It is used for lacings and heavy servings.

Ratline is three stranded tarred hemp used mainly for heaving lines.

Point line is three stranded manila.

Bolt rope. Three stranded tarred hemp, with a soft lay for easy handling, used for sewing around the edges of sails and awnings.

Boat lacing. Polished hemp or polypropylene twine used for lacing boat covers and awnings.

Cod line is similar to boat lacing but is smaller and more tightly laid.

Seaming twine (3 ply) and **Roping twine** are made from flax or hemp.

Signal Halyard. Polythene or hemp, usually plaited.

Log line. Plaited line made from polythene or hemp.

Lead line is cable laid unpolished high grade hemp.

(1) **Whippings.** The end of a rope must always be secured in some way, or it is evident from its construction that it will, on the slightest usage, become frayed out. The commonest method is by working on an ordinary whipping, which is done as follows: First lay the end of a length of twine along the end of the rope, and then commencing at the part furthest from the rope's end take a half-dozen or more turns around both the rope and twine end (Fig. 7). Then lay the twine in the form of a loop along the rope and over the turns already taken, as in Fig. 8. To finish off take that portion of the loop designated *a*, and continue taking turns tightly round the rope and part *b* of the twine until the loop is nearly all used up; pull through the remainder snugly by part *c*, and cut off short when no end of twine will be visible as in Fig. 9.

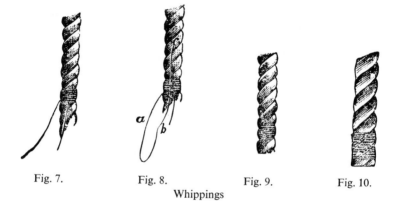

| Fig. 7. | Fig. 8. | Fig. 9. | Fig. 10. |

Whippings

(2) **A Palm and Needle Whipping** (Fig. 10) is a more permanent way of securing a rope's end from fraying than the common whipping put on by hand. First, place the needle under one of the strands and draw nearly the whole length of twine through. Take a considerable number of turns round the rope with the twine, drawing each well taut in turn, and finish up by following round with the needle between each strand, forming a series of frappings, and cut off the end of the twine short.

(3) **A West Country Whipping** is formed by middling the twine around the part of the rope to be marked and half knotting it at every half turn, so that each half knot will be on opposite sides. When a sufficient number of turns are passed, finish it off with a reef knot.

Considering that we now have at our disposal a small sized rope with the end whipped, we will at once proceed to the formation of the most elementary knots and hitches, namely, those formed by a single rope's end.

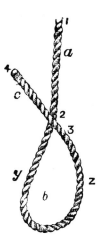

Fig. 11.
A Bight.

Fig. 12.
Overhand Knot.

Fig. 13.
Figure-of-Eight.

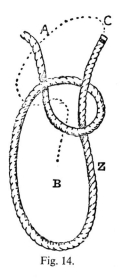

Fig. 14.

Bowline.

Fig. 15.

A Common Loop, by which most of the following knots, etc., are commenced. Note exactly how the loop lies, and let us letter its parts clearly for future reference. The part of rope extending from 1 to 2 is known as the standing part which we will call *a*, the portion included between 2 and 3 following round the loop by *y* and *z* is termed the bight which we will call *b*, and from 3 to 4 is known as the end *c*.

Then starting in each case from the position shown in Fig. 11 we make the following knots, etc.:

An Overhand Knot. Place *c* up through bight *b*, and draw taut.

A Figure-of-Eight Knot. Back *c* round behind *a*, bring over part *z* and dip down through bight *b* and haul taut.

A Bowline. Reverting to our original loop first taking part *z* in the right hand with *y* in the left, throw a loop over *c*, the end.

Secondly, lead *c* round behind part *a* and pass it down through the last made loop, as indicated by the dotted line, and haul taut as in Fig. 15.

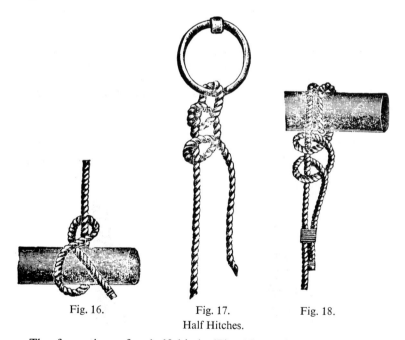

Fig. 16.   Fig. 17.   Fig. 18.

Half Hitches.

The formation of a half hitch (Fig. 16), and two half hitches (Fig. 17) is sufficiently indicated by those diagrams.

The commonest method of making a rope's end fast to a bollard, etc., is by taking a round turn and two half hitches, and stopping the end back for further security (Fig. 18).

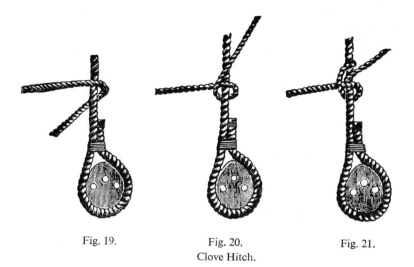

Fig. 19.   Fig. 20.   Fig. 21.
                 Clove Hitch.

A Clove Hitch is really a jamming form of two half hitches, and is principally used when a small rope has to be secured to a larger one and the end still kept free to pass along for further purposes, as in securing ratlines to the shrouds. Its formation is shown in three successive stages (Figs. 19, 20, 21).

A Rolling Hitch is commenced and finished like a clove hitch, but as will be seen from the three diagrams (Figs. 22, 23, 24), illustrating its construction, there is an intermediate round turn between the first

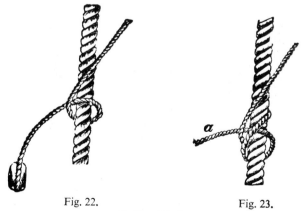

Fig. 22.   Fig. 23.
        Rolling Hitch.

and last hitches. It is principally used for securing the tail of a handy billy or snatch block to a larger rope, or when hanging off a rope with a stopper.

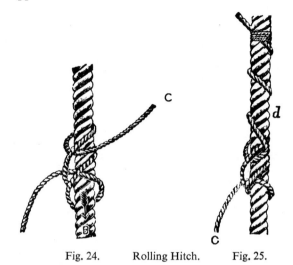

Fig. 24.   Rolling Hitch.   Fig. 25.

Note that the round turn in Fig. 23 is taken round both the standing part a and the larger rope. The great value of this hitch is its non-liability to slip in the direction B (Fig. 24). If, however, owing to an extremely severe strain or other causes the hitch is inclined to slip, the end c should be backed round part d of the first rope, that is, twisted around it in long lays in the opposite direction to that in which the hitch was formed, and the end secured by a stop (Fig. 25).

Fig. 26. Timber Hitch.

A **Timber Hitch** is a useful way of securing a rope quickly to a plank, but when there is to be a long and continuous strain, or when it is required to keep the end of a piece of timber pointed steadily in one direction, it should be supplemented with a half-hitch (Figs. 26, 27).

Fig. 27.

The timber hitch itself consists simply of a half hitch taken with a rather long end, which is used up by twisting it back around its own part of the hitch. The hitch is purposely left very loose so that its formation may be the more easily seen in the illustration (Fig. 26).

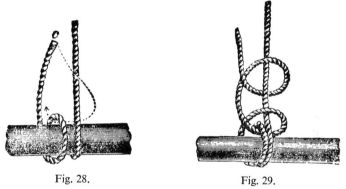

Fig. 28.   Fig. 29.

Fisherman's Bend.

A **Fisherman's Bend** is formed by taking two round turns around the object to which the rope is to be secured, and then backing the end round in the form of a half hitch under both the standing part and second round turn. The end may be further secured by taking a half hitch around its own part or by stopping it to it (Figs. 28, 29), the dotted line showing the next direction the end c must take.

A **Blackwall Hitch** is a quick way of temporarily securing a rope to a hook. As will be seen from the illustration (Fig. 30) it consists of a half hitch, the standing part a as soon as it receives the strain jamming the end part c. It holds much more firmly than would be imagined at first sight. By taking another round turn at b, before passing the end c under a, it will hold more securely.

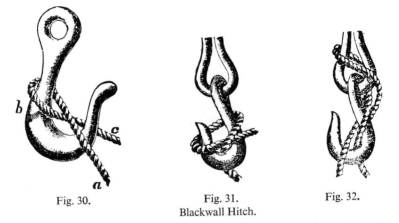

Fig. 30.   Fig. 31.   Fig. 32.
          Blackwall Hitch.

A **Midshipman's Hitch** is sometimes used instead of a Blackwall hitch, and will hold better if the rope is at all greasy. It is made by first forming a Blackwall hitch and then taking the underneath part and placing it over the bill of the hook (Fig. 31).

A **Double Blackwall Hitch** is made by taking the bight of the rope and placing it across the neck of the strop of the block, crossing it behind, then placing the under part over the hook and crossing the upper part on top of it. It holds better than either of the two preceding hitches (Fig. 32).

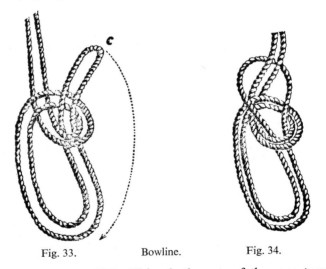

Fig. 33.   Bowline.   Fig. 34.

A **Bowline on the Bight.** Using both parts of the rope together commence as in making an ordinary bowline (Fig. 33). To finish off, open out bight *c*, and taking it in the direction indicated by the dotted line, pass the whole knot through it and haul taut, when it will appear as in Fig. 34.

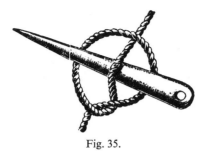

Fig. 35.

A **Marline-spike Hitch** is used for getting a purchase with a marline-spike, capstan bar, etc., when putting on a seizing or lashing. It will be seen to consist of the standing part picked through a loop laid over it, so that the spike lies under the standing part and over the sides of the loop.

A **Sheepshank** is used for shortening a rope. Gather up the amount desired in the form of Fig. 36. Then with parts *a* and *b* form a half hitch round the two parts of the bight as in Fig. 37. To render it still

Fig. 36.

Fig. 37.

Fig. 38.

Fig. 39. Sheepshank.

more dependable, the bight *a* and *b* may be seized or toggled to the standing part as in Figs. 38 and 39.

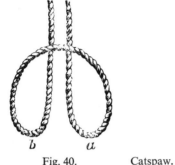

Fig. 40.   Catspaw.   Fig. 41.

A **Catspaw** is formed in a rope to make a temporary loop for hooking on the block of a tackle. First throw back a bight as in Fig. 40.

Then taking hold of *a* and *b* in either hand twist them up as in Fig. 41; bring together the two eyes *a* and *b* and hook in the tackle.

KNOTS, BENDS, AND HITCHES FOR UNITING ROPES

A **Reef Knot.** The simplest of all knots, and is always used when a common tie is required. Its formation may be easily traced in Figs. 42, 43, 44. Having constructed the knot as far as Fig. 42, be sure part *a* is kept in front of part *b* as here shown, and the end *c* led in according to the direction of the dotted line.

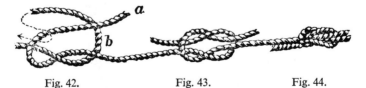

Fig. 42.   Fig. 43.   Fig. 44.

A **Common Bend or Sheet Bend.** In making a bend the ends of the two ropes are not used simultaneously as in forming a reef knot, but

an eye or loop is first formed in the end of one of the ropes as in
Fig. 45 and the other rope's end is then rove through it in various
ways according to the bend desired.

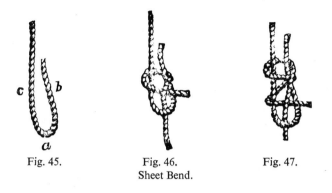

Fig. 45.   Fig. 46.   Fig. 47.
                  Sheet Bend.

To form a Sheet Bend, pass the second rope's end underneath the
eye at point *a* and bring up through the loop, then form with it a half
hitch round *c* and *b* (Fig. 46).

It will hold still better and is less likely to jamb if the end *c* is
passed round again as in Fig. 47.

Carrick Bend. For bending two hauling lines together use a **Carrick
Bend.** First form with hawser No. 1 a loop as in Fig. 48.

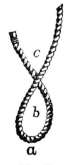

Fig. 48.   Carrick Bend.   Fig. 49.

Pass the second hawser under the first at *a*, bring up through the eye *b*, back it over the cross at *c*, and bring up again towards you through the eye *b*, and then stop the ends of each hawser to their own respective parts (Fig. 49).

A Double Carrick Bend is formed in precisely a similar manner, but a complete round turn is taken around the cross of the first hawser at *c*, and then led up again through the eye *b* and finished off as in Fig. 50.

Fig. 50.   Fig. 51.

Securing Lead Line to Lead. The lead is fitted with a goodwire grommet parcelled over. The lead line should have a long eye spliced in it, and is secured by passing the eye through the grommet and over the lead.

Fig. 52.   Fig. 53.

Mousing a Hook. All hooks in running gear should be moused as in Fig. 52.

A Spanish Windlass. To rig a Spanish Windlass (Fig. 53) take a good strand well greased in the centre. Place the strand over the two parts of the rope that are to be rove together, and bringing the ends of the strand up again place a bolt close to the strand. Take the ends of the strand and lay them up with their own parts so as to form two eyes. Take a round turn with this round the bolt, put a marline-spike through each eye and heave around.

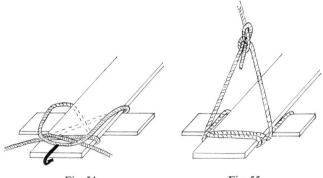

Fig. 54.   Fig. 55.

A Stage Hitch is formed by laying the bight of the rope over the stage inside the horns then crossing the two parts underneath and laying them over the stage outside the horns. The bight is then pulled over the end of the stage as shown in Fig. 54. After pulling the two parts taut use a bowline to make fast the end of the rope to the standing part (Fig. 55).

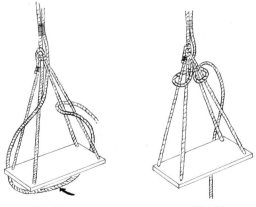

Fig. 56.   Fig. 57.

Bosun's Chair Lowering Hitch. A seaman can lower himself and secure the chair in a new position using the lowering hitch. The running part is held firmly against the standing part in one hand, or secured to it by a temporary seizing as in Fig. 56. The bight of the running part is passed through the bridge of the chair, over the man's head, and is then passed behind him and under his feet as shown in Fig. 57. The hitch which forms about the apex of the bridle is tightened and the seizing released.

Stoppers. A stopper is used to secure a mooring rope so that it may be transferred from the warping barrel of the winch to the bitts, or vice versa. Fibre stoppers should be used to secure fibre ropes, synthetic fibre stoppers for synthetic ropes and chain stoppers for wire ropes.

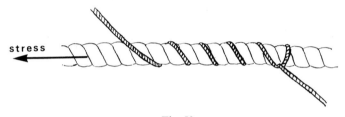

Fig. 58.

Fibre Stopper on Fibre Hawser

Fig. 59.

Chain Stopper on Wire Hawser

To pass a stopper on a fibre rope make a half hitch, or double half hitch, against the lay then back up with turns with the lay (Fig. 58). To pass a chain stopper on a wire rope make a half hitch with the lay and back up with turns against the lay (Fig. 59).

SPLICES

An Eye Splice is formed by unlaying the end of a rope for a short distance, and then, after closing up the end, to form an eye of the desired size. Lay the three strands upon the standing part, now tuck the middle strand through the strand of the standing part of the rope next to it against the lay of the rope (Fig. 60), then pass the strand on the left over the strand under which No. 1 strand is tucked, and tuck it under the next (Fig. 61), and lastly, put the remaining strand through the third strand on the other side of the rope as in Figs. 62 and 63.

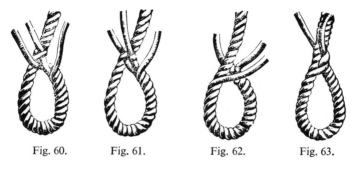

| Fig. 60. | Fig. 61. | Fig. 62. | Fig. 63. |

Now tuck each strand again alternately over a strand and under a strand of the rope, and then taper off by halving the strands before tucking the third time, and again halve them before the fourth tuck.

If the strands are tucked with the lay of the rope it is termed a Sailmaker's Splice.

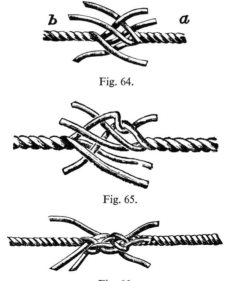

Fig. 64.

Fig. 65.

Fig. 66.

A Short Splice is used to join two ropes when it is not required to pass through a block. Unlay the two ropes the required distance, and clutch them together as in Fig. 64, that is, so that the strands of one rope go alternately between the strands of the other.

Then tuck the strands of rope *a* into the rope *b* in a similar manner to that described in an eye splice and similarly tuck the strands of *b* into *a* (Figs. 65 and 66).

A Long Splice is one of the most useful of splices, as it permits the rope to run through a block just the same as an unspliced rope.

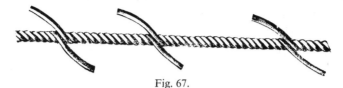

Fig. 67.

Unlay the ends of two ropes to a distance about four times the length used in a short splice, and then clutch them together as if about to commence a short splice. Now unlay one strand for a considerable distance and fill up the gap thus caused by twisting in the strand opposite to it of the other rope. Then do the same with two more strands. Let the remaining two strands stay as they were first placed. The ropes will now appear as in Fig. 67.

To finish off, tuck the ends as in a short splice, but *with* the lay of the rope, that is, so that the tuck will continually take place around the same strand, and taper off gradually by reducing the yarns in the strand.

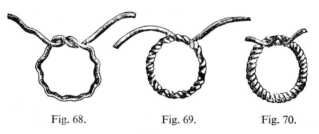

Fig. 68.   Fig. 69.   Fig. 70.

To Make a Grommet, cut a strand about three and a half times the length of the grommet required. Unlay the rope carefully and keep the turns of the strand in. Close up the strand in the form of a ring (Fig. 68), and then pass the ends round and round in their original lay until all the intervals are filled up (Fig. 69), and then finish off the two ends as in a long splice (Fig. 70).

Splices in Synthetic Fibre Rope should have at least four tucks made with each strand then two further tucks should be made with the strands first halved and then quartered. The parts of the splice containing tucks with reduced size of strands should be wrapped with adhesive tape or other suitable material.

WIRE ROPE

Wire rope used for marine purposes usually consists of six strands laid up around a central heart of fibre, or about a seventh wire strand. Each strand is made up of several wires twisted around a central fibre core, or around a single centre wire. The number of wires to the strand varies from 7 to 41, the number being governed by the size of the rope and also by the purpose for which it is required. Increasing the number of wires to the strand for the same size of rope gives greater strength and flexibility. Wire ropes are referred to by two numbers, the first indicates the number of strands, including a strand which may be used for the central heart, and the second indicates the number of wires to the strand.

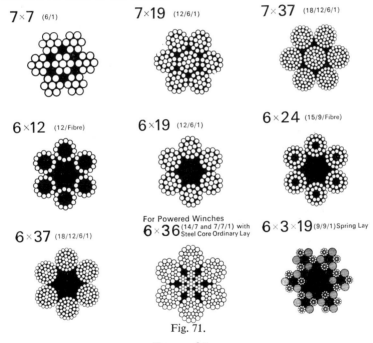

Fig. 71.

Types of Lay

Ordinary Lay. The wires are twisted in the opposite direction to the strands. Right hand rope is normally used, in which the wires are twisted left handed and the strands are twisted right handed.

Lang's lay. The direction of twist of the wires is the same as the direction of the strands. This lay provides a greater wearing surface but should only be used when both ends of the rope and the load are secured against rotation. It is not likely to be used for marine purposes.

Preformed rope. Each strand of this type of rope is preformed into a helix so that it will be easier to handle and less likely to kink.

Spring lay. This is a combined rope consisting of three galvanised wire strands and three fibre strands laid up around a central fibre core. The rope is cable laid, each main strand being made up of three fibre strands and three 19 wire strands over a fibre strand core. Spring lay rope is four times stronger than fibre ropes and 50% stronger than nylon. It is much easier to handle than ordinary wire rope and is very suitable for mooring ropes and for preventers for derrick rigs.

Application

Standing Rigging. Wire ropes used for stays, shrouds and preventers have a steel core to give extra strength. Flexibility is not important. British Standard Publication 365 recommends 7×7 construction for wires up to 28 mm in diameter, 7×19 for 32–48 mm and 7×37 for over 52 mm rope.

Cargo lashings. 6×12 ropes are recommended for sizes 8–16 mm and 6×24 construction for larger sizes.

Cargo handling. 6×24 construction is usually used but 6×19 ropes are also suitable for ropes up to 24 mm.

Mooring ropes. Wire ropes of 6×37 construction are recommended for general use but for powered winches 6×36 ropes with a wire core should be used for sizes up to 40 mm and 6×41 for sizes 44–60 mm.

Boat falls. Either 17×7 or 6×36 for ropes up to 16 mm and 6×36 for larger sizes.

HOW TO HANDLE WIRE ROPE

When uncoiling wire rope it is important that no kinks are allowed to form, as once a kink is made no amount of strain can take it out, and the rope is unsafe to work. If possible a turn-table should be employed (an old cart wheel mounted on a spindle makes an excellent one); the rope will then lead off perfectly straight without kinks.

If a turn-table is not available the rope may be rolled along the ground.

In no case must the rope be laid on the ground and the end taken over or kinks will result, and the rope will be completely spoiled.

The life of wire rope depends principally upon the diameter of drums, sheaves, and pulleys; and too much importance cannot be given to the size of the latter. Wherever possible the diameter of the sheave should be not less than 20 times the diameter of the wire rope. The diameters of drums, sheaves and pulleys should increase with the working load when the factor of safety is less than 5 to 1.

The load should not be lifted with a jerk, as the strain may equal three or four times the proper load, and a sound rope may easily be broken.

Examine ropes frequently. A new rope is cheaper than the risk of killing or maiming employees.

One-sixth of the ultimate strength of the rope should be considered a fair working load.

To increase the amount of work done, it is better to increase the working load than the speed of the rope. Experience has shown that the wear of the rope increases with the speed.

Wire rope should be greased when running or idle. Rust destroys as effectively as hard work.

Great care should be taken that the grooves of drums and sheaves are perfectly smooth, ample in diameter, and conform to the surface of the rope. They should also be in perfect line with the rope, so that the latter may not chafe on the sides of the grooves.

WIRE SPLICING

The Docks Regulations of the Factories Act require that a thimble or eye splice should have at least three tucks with the whole strand of the rope and two with half the wires cut out of each strand. The strands must be tucked against the lay of the rope. The "Liverpool Splice" is relatively quick and easy as after the first tuck each end is passed, with the lay, around the same strand four or five times, but such a splice should never be used if the end of the rope is free to rotate. If the splice is made with the lay rotation will cause the tucks to draw and the splice to pull out.

A long tapering steel marline-spike is required. After placing it under a strand do not withdraw it until the tuck is made and all the slack of the strand drawn through.

Wire splices should be parcelled with oily canvas and served with Hambro' line.

Fig. 72.

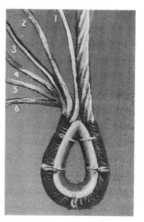

Fig. 73.

Splicing Thimbles—Under and Over Style. Ordinary type of wire rope. Serve the rope with wire or tarred yarn to suit the circumference of the thimble, bend round thimble and tie securely in place with temporary lashing till splice is finished (as in Fig. 72). Open out the strands taking care to keep the loose end of the rope to the left hand (see Fig. 73). Now insert marline-spike, lifting two strands as shown in Fig. 74, and tuck away towards the right hand (that is inserting the strand at the point, and over the spike) strand No. 1, pulling the strand well home. Next insert marline-spike through next strand to the left, only lifting one strand, the point of the spike coming out at the same place as before. Tuck away strand No. 2 as before.

Fig. 74.

Fig. 75.

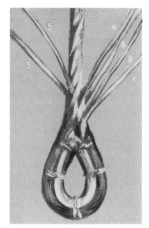

Fig. 76.

Fig. 77.

The next tuck is the locking tuck. Insert marline-spike in next strand, and, missing No. 3, tuck away strand No. 4 from the point of the spike towards the right hand. Now, without taking out the spike, tuck away strand No. 3 behind the spike towards the left hand (as shown in Fig. 75). Now insert spike in next strand, and tuck away strand No. 5 behind and over the spike. No. 6 likewise. Pull all the loose strands well down.

This completes the first series of tucks, and the splice will, if made properly, be as Fig. 76 now, starting with strand No. 1 and taking each strand in rotation, tuck away under one strand and over the next strand till all the strands have been tucked three times. The strands should at this point be split, half of the wires being tucked away as before, the other half cut close to the splice. Fig. 77 shows the finished splice ready for serving over.

It will be noticed that this style of splice possesses a plaited appearance, and the more strain applied to the rope the tighter the splice will grip, and there is no fear of the splice drawing owing to rotation of the rope.

The following illustrations of the first series of tucks for the "Five-tuck Splice" or "Boulevant Splice" are reproduced by permission of British Ropes Limited from their publication "Terminal Splicing of

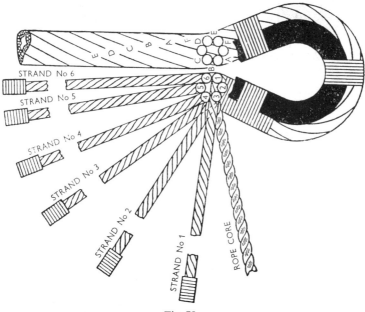

Fig. 78.

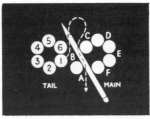

FIRST TUCK

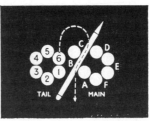

SECOND TUCK

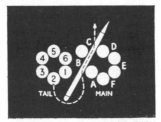

THIRD TUCK

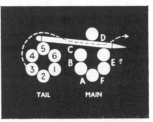

FOURTH TUCK

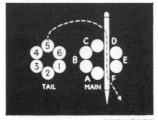

FIFTH TUCK

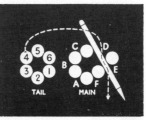

SIXTH TUCK

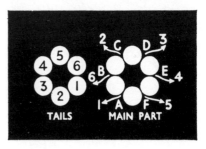

*Diagram showing emergence of tails after
the First Series is completed.*

Wire Ropes". Subsequent tucks are made against the lay, under one strand and over the next, as in the previous case.

Fig. 80. Wire Rope Grip.

Fig. 80 illustrates Bulldog grips which offer a quick and effective substitute for splicing and fastening wire ropes by unskilled labour.

HOW TO MEASURE ROPE.

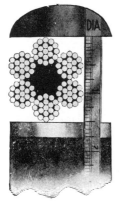 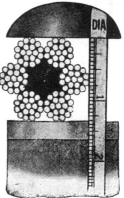

Fig. 81. Right Way.   Wrong Way.

CHAPTER II

LIFTING GEAR

THE term **stress** denotes the load put on material, and **strain** is the molecular disturbance made evident by a change of shape or a fracture of the material due to the stress which has been applied.

Stress comes before strain and the transition from stress to strain introduces another factor called the "modulus of elasticity", Young's modulus=stress divided by strain, within the limits of proportionality.

The term **breaking** or **ultimate strength** is the load or weight applied to material when testing it to destruction.

STRENGTH OF ROPE

Fibre rope is made of nylon, terylene, polypropylene, polythene, manila, sisal and coir, their relative strengths being in the order named. Splicing a rope reduces its strength by at least one tenth and knots reduce the strength by about one half.

No rigorous rule can be laid down to arrive at the ultimate breaking strengths of different sized ropes as so much depends upon the quality of the fibre and the process adopted in its manufacture. The size of a rope is expressed in terms of its diameter in millimetres (D) and an estimate of the breaking stress in tonnes is given for different types of rope by the following formulae:

Manila $\dfrac{2D^2}{300}$

Polypropylene
Polythene $\dfrac{3D^2}{300}$

Terylene $\dfrac{4D^2}{300}$

Nylon $\dfrac{5D^2}{300}$

The safe working load may be taken as one sixth of the breaking strain.

Example. Given a 40 mm diameter polypropylene rope, estimate its breaking stress and safe working load.

$$\text{Breaking stress} \quad = \frac{3D^2}{300} = \frac{3 \times 40 \times 40}{300}$$
$$= 16 \text{ tonnes}$$
$$\text{Safe working load} \quad = \frac{16}{6} = 2 \cdot 67 \text{ tonnes}$$

Example. Find the size of the smallest manila rope suitable for a load of 2 tonnes.

$$\frac{2D^2}{300} \times \frac{1}{6} = 2$$
$$D^2 = \frac{300 \times 6 \times 2}{2}$$
$$= 1800$$
$$D = 43 \text{ mm}$$

Wire Rope. The breaking stress of flexible steel wire rope in tonnes is given, approximately, by the following formulae:

$$6 \times 12, \quad \frac{15D^2}{500} \text{ tonnes}$$

$$6 \times 24, \quad \frac{20D^2}{500} \text{ tonnes}$$

$$6 \times 37, \quad \frac{21D^2}{500} \text{ tonnes}$$

D is the diameter of the rope in millimetres.

The safe working load may be taken as one sixth of the breaking stress.

Chain. The breaking stress of chain is given by the following formulae where D is the diameter in mm of the bar forming the link:

$$\text{Grade 1} \quad \frac{20D^2}{600} \text{ tonnes}$$

$$\text{Grade 2} \quad \frac{30D^2}{600} \text{ tonnes}$$

$$\text{Grade 3} \quad \frac{43D^2}{600} \text{ tonnes}$$

Example. Find the breaking stress and safe working load of a 6×24 24 mm wire rope

$$\text{Breaking stress} = \frac{20 \times 24 \times 24}{500} \text{ tonnes}$$
$$= 22 \text{ tonnes}$$
$$\text{S.W.L.} = \frac{22}{6} = 3.67 \text{ tonnes}$$

BLOCKS

A built block consists of a shell, strop, sheave, pin, shackle or hook.
The score of a block is the groove round the outside of the shell
(Fig. 1), to take the strop, rope, or wire, when one is to be fitted. The
cheeks are kept apart by two pieces of wood, one at the head and one
at the tail of the shell to form the "swallow", the name given to the
space the rope is rove through.

Fig. 1.
A Built Block.

Fig. 2.
A Clump Block is cut
out of the solid wood.

Fig. 3.
Sheave Plain Bush.

The shells of blocks are usually made of elm or oak as both kinds
of wood are good for resisting weather but they must be kept varnished
or painted.

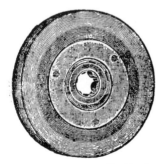

Fig. 4. Sheave, Roller Bush.

Fig. 5. Self-oiling Metal Sheave.

The strop may be of rope or wire fitted into the score round the shell and spliced as shown in the illustrations of tackles. The length of a rope strop is about one and one-third the round of the block.

Sheaves are either of lignum vitae or metal. Lignum vitae is an exceedingly hard wood dark in colour and has self-lubricating properties. The bush of the sheave may be plain, that is just a hole drilled in gun-metal (Fig. 3), or a roller bush (Fig. 4), which runs with less friction. Metal sheaves (Fig. 5) are used for heavy work. The size of a block is the length of its shell; the size of a sheave is its diameter.

An **External** bound block (Fig. 6) is one stropped with a heavy iron band, an eye being welded on it for a hook or shackle.

An **Internal** bound block is one having an iron strop inside the shell, one lug of which is sometimes extended outside the shell in the form of an eye to take the standing part of the purchase. The strop can be withdrawn from the shell for cleaning and painting; pins of blocks are scraped and rubbed with blacklead, so also are the sheaves and bush.

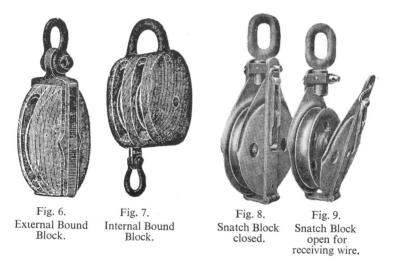

| Fig. 6.
External Bound
Block. | Fig. 7.
Internal Bound
Block. | Fig. 8.
Snatch Block
closed. | Fig. 9.
Snatch Block
open for
receiving wire. |

A **Snatch** block is a loose block having a hinged clamp at the side (Figs. 8 and 9), so that the bight of the rope may be slipped over the sheave and the clamp closed again. They are handy as portable lead blocks. Malleable iron pulley blocks (Fig. 10), are now universally used for cargo work, and Fig. 11 illustrates one of Messrs. Loveridge's derrick blocks fitted with a self-oiling sheave, the gunmetal centre, or bush, of the sheave has a large oil reservoir from which oil passes to the sheave pin. *See* groove in Fig. 5.

The simple machines are the pulley block, the wheel and axle, the lever, the wedge and the screw. All other mechanical appliances are practically a combination of one or more of those simple machines modified in form and application to meet particular requirements.

Fig. 10. Metal Block.

Fig. 11. Derrick Block.

In a simple fixed frictionless pulley (Fig. 12), if W represents a weight of 1 kg due to the downward force of gravity, and P represents a spring balance held in the hand, the balance will register 1 kg, thus demonstrating that a power or force of 1 kg has to be exerted to equalise the weight of 1 kg. If the weight of 1 kg be overcome by exerting more power at P so that W moves slowly upwards, the balance will fully register 1 kg whilst W moves up the same distance as P moves down. The downward force at C will be 2 kg. No power is gained by this system and a single pulley is only adopted in practice for convenience generally as a leading block.

Arrange the single pulley so that it is movable as in Fig. 13. Secure one end of the cord at C and attach the spring balance to the other end at P. Hang a 2 kg weight at W. The suspended weight of 2 kg is supported half by the cord at C and half by the hand at P as indicated by the balance registering 1 kg. The effort exerted by the hand at *P* is just one half of the weight to be supported. The mechanical advantage is said to be 2 because a power of 1 kg balances a weight of 2 kg. It

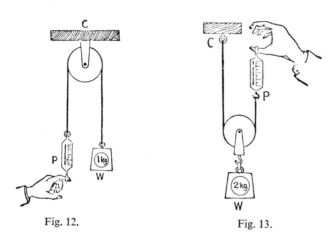

Fig. 12.   Fig. 13.

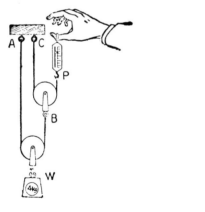

Fig. 14.   Pulley Purchases.   Fig. 15.

will be noted that there are two parts of the cord at the moving pulley and this number gives the mechanical advantage gained by this machine.

If the weight be now overcome by exerting more power at P so that W moves slowly upwards, the balance will still register 1 kg, neglecting the effect of friction, and the hand will move upwards 2 metres to raise the weight W 1 metre, because the work or power put into the machine at P is equal to the work accomplished by the machine against the resistance of the weight W.

The number of pulleys may be increased. Fig. 14 shows two movable pulleys with a 4-kg weight at W suspended from the lower pulley. The cord AB supports the 4-kg weight, 2 kg at A and 2 kg at B attached to the upper pulley. A second cord passed round the upper pulley supports the 2-kg weight at B, viz., 1 kg at C and 1 kg at the hand P holding the spring balance which will register 1 kg, neglecting the weight of the pulleys, thus a power of 1 kg supports a weight of 4 kg; the mechanical advantage of the machine is 4 because by its performance a force of 1 kg equalises a load of 4 kg.

If the load of 4 kg be now overcome by exerting more power at P so that W moves slowly upwards, the hand at P will move 4 metres to raise the load W 1 metre, again demonstrating that the work put into the machine at P is equal to the work done by the machine against the resistance at W.

The arrangement as shown in Fig. 14 is not suitable in practice so the sheaves are fitted into blocks as in Fig. 15. The principle is the same, however, and the number of parts of cord at the moving block gives the theoretical advantage or power gained by using the purchase; that is to say, the ratio between the power and the weight which, in this example, is one-quarter without friction.

There are four parts of rope holding the weight and it is evident that the pull on each part will be one-fourth part of the total weight. The load on the hook at C is equal to the weight+tackle+power exerted on the hauling part of the rope. The weight of the load and tackle is constant, but the power will depend upon whether W is at rest or being raised or lowered. When at rest $P=1$ kg, but when in motion the value of P will be increased and diminished according to the speed of raising and lowering. Needless to say, power is gained at the expense of speed. The more sheaves in the purchase the more rope must be hauled through the blocks to raise the weight a given distance, and speed is thus sacrificed to gain power. It is usual in shipwork to allow one-tenth of the weight for every sheave as an additional load due to friction.

PURCHASES

The **Mechanical Advantage** gained by using a purchase is found by counting the number of parts of rope at the moving block. This, however, is merely the theoretical advantage as friction and the weight of the block and rope are neglected.

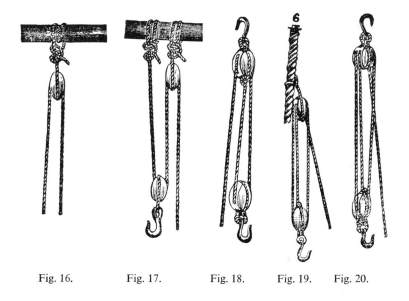

Fig. 16.   Fig. 17.   Fig. 18.   Fig. 19.   Fig. 20.

Single Whip. A rope rove through a single block fixed in any position. No power is gained (Fig. 16).

Double Whip. A rope rove through two single blocks—upper block a tail block, lower one a movable hook block. Power gained—double—that is weight of one unit on the hauling part will balance a weight of two units on the hook block (Fig. 17).

Gun Tackle. Two single blocks. Power gained two or three according to which is the movable block. If the upper block in the figure is the moving one the purchase is said to be used to advantage and the power gained is 3; but if the lower block is the moving one, the purchase is used to disadvantage and the power gained is 2 (Fig. 18).

Handy Billy or Jigger. A small tackle for general use; a double block with a tail and single block with hook (Fig. 19).

Watch Tackle or Luff Tackle. Double hook block and single hook block. If used to advantage the power gained is 4, but if used to disadvantage, the power gained is only 3 (Fig. 20).

Double Purchase. Two double blocks. Power gained is 4 or 5 depending on which is the moving block (Fig. 21).

Three-Fold Purchase. Two three-fold blocks. Power gained—six or seven times (Fig. 22).

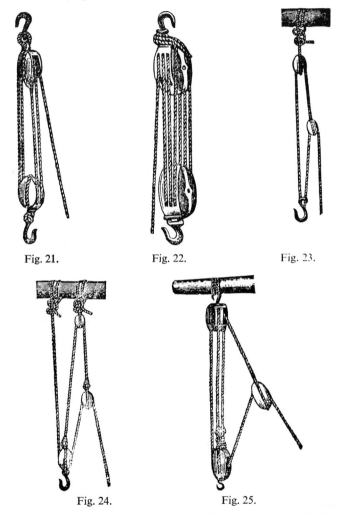

Fig. 21.   Fig. 22.   Fig. 23.

Fig. 24.   Fig. 25.

A Single Spanish Burton. Two single blocks and a hook. Power gained—three times (Fig. 23).

A Double Spanish Burton. There are two forms of this purchase— Fig. 24, by using three single blocks; Fig. 25 by using one double block and two single blocks. Power gained—five times. The disadvantage of this form of purchase is the very short travel of the lower block as the whip block comes down and meets the lower block going up.

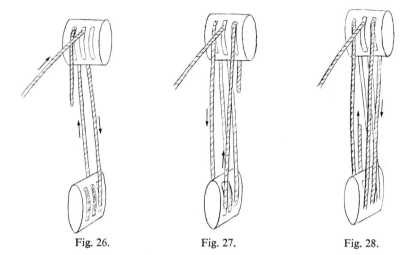

Fig. 26.   Fig. 27.   Fig. 28.

How to reeve a three-fold purchase with the hauling and standing parts of the fall in the middle sheave holes (Figs. 26, 27 and 28).

Place the two blocks on deck with the tails of the blocks towards each other. The one to take the hauling and standing parts of the fall should have a good becket or eye in the tail, and should be laid on its edge having the swallows up and down. (Call this No. 1 block.) The other one should be laid on its cheek having the swallows parallel to the deck. Lay the blocks close together and stand in line with them, having No. 1 furthest away from you.

Take the end of the fall from the coil and reeve it downwards through the middle sheavehole of No. 1 block, then from right to left through the lower sheavehole of the other block, then upwards through the left hand sheavehole of No. 1 block, and from left to right through the top sheavehole in the other block.

You should not go wrong now as there is only one vacant sheavehole in No. 1 block (the right hand one). Reeve downwards through this, then from right to left through the middle sheavehole in the other block, making the end fast to the tail of No. 1 block.

The Frictional Resistance of a purchase increases with the number of sheaves, and an allowance of about **one-tenth** of the weight to be lifted for every sheave in the purchase is usually added to the weight when estimating the additional force that must be exerted to raise the weight. The theoretical advantage is found by counting the parts of the fall at the moving block. When the single block in a luff tackle is the moving one it is said to be used to disadvantage and the power gained is three, but if the double block is the moving one it is used to advantage and the power gained is four; that is to say, a pull, or force, of 1 tonne should balance a weight of 4 tonnes. But in a luff tackle used to advantage there is the weight of the rope and blocks, also the friction of three sheaves to overcome, so $3 \times \frac{4}{10}$ tonnes $=$ 1·2 tonnes for friction and this should be added to the 4-tonne weight, making the total load on the purchase about 5·2 tonnes. The weight, however, will be distributed almost equally amongst the several parts of rope in the purchase at the moving block. There are four parts in the luff tackle when used to advantage so $\frac{5·2}{4}$ tonnes gives 1·3 tonnes as the load on each part of the purchase.

The weight+friction may be expressed as $W + \frac{nW}{10}$ where W is the weight to be lifted and n the number of sheaves, thus in the above example, $W + \frac{nW}{10} = 4 + \frac{3 \times 4}{10} = 5·2$ tonnes.

Example. A weight of 4 tonnes is to be lifted with a gun tackle, find approximately the pull on the hauling part if used to disadvantage.

Answer. There are 2 sheaves and 2 parts of rope (Fig. 18). Total load=weight+friction=$W + \frac{nW}{10} = 4 + \frac{2 \times 4}{10} = 4·8$ tonnes. Pull on hauling part $= \frac{4·8}{2} = 2·4$ tonnes.

"There is less friction with sheaves of larger diameter than of smaller diameter and with thin rope than with thick rope, so the maximum advantage is gained by using large sheaves and strong small-sized rope. Fast winding adds to the tension on each part of rope and there is less tension when lowering the weight than when it is merely hanging on the purchase."

An approximate connection between the weight being lifted and the stress on the hauling part of a purchase is given by the formula

$$S \times P = W + \frac{nW}{10}$$

where S is the stress or pull on the hauling part
P the theoretical power of the purchase
W the weight being lifted
n the number of sheaves in the purchase
$\frac{nW}{10}$ is the allowance for frictional resistance

The theoretical power or mechanical gain is equal to the number of sheaves when the hauling part of the rope comes off the standing block, but it is increased to the number of sheaves plus 1 when the hauling part comes off the moving block. In the above equation $P=n$, if the purchase is used to disadvantage, and $P=n+1$ when it is used to advantage.

Example. A 12-tonnes weight is to be lifted with a three-fold purchase used to advantage; find the tension on the hauling part of the fall and the size of manila rope to use. There is a lead block at the masthead.

S is required. $P=7$, $W=12$ tonnes, $n=7$ sheaves

$$S \times P = W + \frac{nW}{10}$$

$$S \times 7 = 12 + \frac{7 \times 12}{10} = \frac{120 + 84}{10} = \frac{204}{10}$$

$$S = \frac{204}{10} \times \frac{1}{7} = 3 \text{ tonnes, the pull on the hauling part}$$

The size of rope is given by $\dfrac{2D^2}{6 \times 300} = 3$

$$D^2 = \frac{3 \times 6 \times 300}{2}$$
$$D = \sqrt{2700}$$
$$= 52 \text{ mm.}$$

Answer. Tension on hauling part is **3 tonnes** and use a 52 mm manila rope.

Example. What resistance could be overcome with a three-fold purchase by applying a pull of 2 tonnes to the hauling part (no lead blocks)

$S=2$ tonnes, $P=6$, $n=6$ sheaves. W is required

$$S \times P = W + \frac{nW}{10}$$

$$2 \times 6 = W + \frac{6W}{10} = \frac{10W + 6W}{10} = \frac{16W}{10}$$

$$16W = 120 \therefore W = \frac{120}{16} = 7 \cdot 5 \text{ tonnes}$$

The actual weight would be 7·5 tonnes, but the total resistance (weight plus friction) would be greater. Add for friction one-tenth of the weight for each sheave, viz., 7·5 tonnes $\times \dfrac{6}{10} = 4 \cdot 5$ tonnes.

Total resistance is $7 \cdot 5 + 4 \cdot 5 = 12$ tonnes.

When a second tackle is hooked on to the hauling part of another tackle the power gained by the combination of the two purchases is approximately equal to the product of their powers.

Example. A 10-tonne load is being lifted with a two-fold purchase used to disadvantage, (power 4) with a gun tackle used to advantage (power 3) secured to its hauling part. Required the stress on the hauling part of the gun tackle.

S is required. $P=4\times3=12$. $W=10$ tonnes. $n=6$ sheaves.

$$S\times P=W+\frac{nW}{10}$$

$$S\times12=10+\frac{6\times10}{10}=16$$

$$S=\frac{16}{12}=1\cdot3 \text{ tonnes pull on the hauling part of the gun tackle.}$$

Differential pulley purchases (Fig. 29) are extremely powerful There is usually one in the engine room travelling on a heavy beam in the skylight for lifting the cylinder covers and pistons. The upper block has two sheaves rigidly attached to each other but differing slightly in diameter. An endless chain passes over the sheaves the rims being made with "snugs" to take the links of the chain to

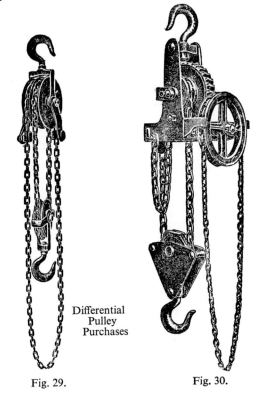

Differential
Pulley
Purchases

Fig. 29.   Fig. 30.

prevent it from slipping. The power gained is given by $\dfrac{2R}{R-r}$, where R is the radius of the larger sheave and r the radius of the smaller one in the upper block.

Screw chain hoists are sometimes used for lifting heavy weights by hand power (Fig. 30). The gearing in the system illustrated consists of pulleys of different diameters. The hauling or hand chain passing over the flywheel is endless. This flywheel has an axle with a worm screw which engages with the helical teeth of the big wheel. A sprocket is keyed to the axle of the toothed wheel and over this sprocket is seen the stout lifting chain which, in the illustration, is led through a moving block to increase the purchase, the standing end of the chain being shackled to the framework of the differential gearing.

It works as follows: the flywheel is turned by the hand chain, which turns the screw axle, which turns the toothed wheel, which turns the sprocketed axle and thus moves the stout lifting chain and raises the weight.

LOADS ON DERRICKS

Parallelogram of Forces. If two forces acting at a point be represented in magnitude and direction by the two adjacent sides of a

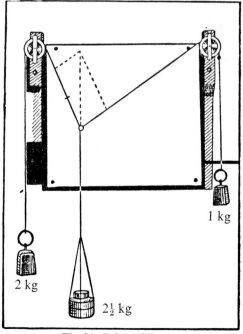

1 kg

2 kg

$2\frac{1}{2}$ kg

Fig. 31. Balanced Forces.

parallelogram drawn from the point and the parallelogram be completed then the diagonal drawn from the point of application represents the resultant force in magnitude and direction.

Cargo Spans. The tension on the pendants of a span between two masts can be readily arrived at by constructing an appropriate parallelogram of forces. Figure 31 shows the usual school apparatus for demonstrating the principle. The arrangement of pulleys and weights is obvious. A bight of cord has been led over two pulleys and a weight slung in the centre of it. The weight happens to be $2\frac{1}{2}$ kg, and it is balanced in equilibrium by a 2-kg weight at the end of the cord leading over the left-hand pulley and a 1-kg weight at the end of the cord over the right-hand pulley, thus indicating that the tension on the left-hand cord is 2 kg and on the right-hand cord 1 kg, the respective pendants making angles of 22 degrees and 53 degrees with the vertical.

By increasing or decreasing the weights relatively to each other the apparatus will illustrate very clearly the corresponding changes in the angles formed by the pendants and the tensions on the spans. It will be recognised that the greater tension will be on the span which is nearer to the vertical and that the tension on each will be at its maximum when the span is **taut,** as seamen say when the pendants form nearly a straight line between the pulleys.

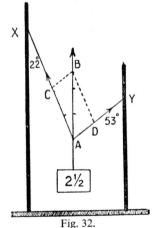

Fig. 32.

The same results may be arrived at by construction as follows:

Example. Two pendants form a span slung between two masts making angles with the vertical of 22 and 53 degrees. Find the tension on each arm, or pendant, of the span when supporting a weight of $2\frac{1}{2}$ tonnes.

Construction. Draw two parallel vertical lines to represent the masts; make angles X and Y equal to 22 and 53 degrees respectively. Points X and Y are placed anywhere on the masts and represent the positions where the ends of the pendants are made fast. The lines of the angles intersect at A. Now draw AB vertically upwards and equal in length to $2\frac{1}{2}$-tonne units from a scale of equal parts. Draw BC parallel to one span and BD parallel to the other. The length of AD represents the tension (1 tonne) on the arm from Y, and AC the tension (2 tonnes) on the arm from X.

Another Method is to give the lengths of the pendants and the heights of their standing ends above the deck as measured from the rigging plan of the ship, then draw out the facts to scale and construct the parallelogram.

Example. The horizontal distance between two vertical masts is 40 m. The end of one pendant, 30 m long, is made fast 50 m up one mast and the end of another pendant, 25 m long, is made fast 35 m up the other mast. It is intended to lift a 10-tonne boiler using the pendants as span. Find the tension on each.

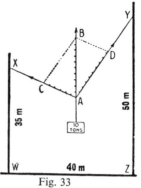
Fig. 33

Construction. Make ZW equal to 40 m, from a convenient scale, and erect perpendiculars $WX=35$ m and $ZY=50$ m. With centre X and radius 25 m on a pair of compasses describe an arc, and with centre Y and radius 30 m describe another arc cutting the first one at A. Join AX and AY. The 10-tonne weight will be suspended from A. AB is now drawn vertically upwards and made equal to 10 equal parts to represent unit-tonnes and not necessarily from the same scale as before as the parallelogram would probably be too big. BC is then drawn parallel to YA and BD parallel to XA. The length of AD measured in the same units as AB gives the tension on the pendant AY ($9\frac{1}{4}$ tonnes), and the length of AC the tension on XA (6 tonnes).

Derricks. A piece of school apparatus to demonstrate the thrust on the heel of a derrick and the tension on the span is shown in Fig. 34. A given weight is seen hanging from the end of the derrick, its heel being fitted into a circular weighing balance which registers

Fig. 34. Derrick Apparatus.

the thrust at the heel, the tension on the span being registered on a flat balance.

The thrust on the heel of a derrick and the tension on the span leading to the mast due to a weight hanging from the derrick end may be determined by means of a parallelogram.

Example. A derrick 24 m long is kept upended by means of a span 12 m long attached to a point on the mast 20 m vertically above the heel of the derrick. Find the tension on the span and the thrust on the gooseneck of the derrick when a weight of 4 tonnes is hanging from its top end.

Construction. Draw the figure to scale by making $XY=20$ m, then with centre Y and radius 12 m describe an arc, and with centre X and radius 24 m describe another arc cutting the first one at A.

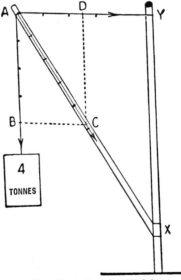

Fig. 35. A Hanging Weight.

Join AX and AY. raw DAB vertically downwards from A and make AB equal to 4 units from any convenient scale to represent the downward force of the suspended weight. Draw BC parallel to the span and CD parallel to AB; $ABCD$ is the parallelogram of forces.

The tension on the span is given by the length of AD (2·5 tonnes), and the thrust on the gooseneck by AC (4·75 tonnes).

A weight simply **hanging** from the end of a derrick is not the usual condition on board ship. The load is lifted by means of a wire fall which leads through a cargo gin at the top end of the derrick and down through a leading block at the heel of the derrick and thence to the barrel of a winch on deck. The thrust on the gooseneck of the derrick is, therefore, considerably increased as when a wire fall is used the pull exerted by the winch to hold the weight must be approximately equal to the weight itself, some allowance being made for friction at the sheaves.

The British Standard Code of Practice for Design and Operation of Ship's Derrick Rigs BS MA 48: 1976, can be used to determine the approximate loads in derrick rigs. In this publication, tables are given to show the rope tensions required for hoisting or lowering a weight, according to the number of parts of rope holding the load, assuming frictional resistance to be 6% per sheave. The following Table is based on Table 1 of the BS publication, applicable to blocks with bushed plain bearings. Table 2 of BS MA 48 should be used for blocks having sheaves with ball or roller bearings.

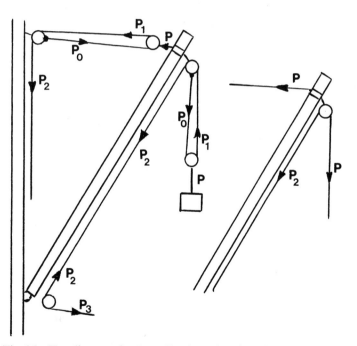

Fig. 36. Key diagrams for Rope Tensions given in Table 1

P Force acting on the lifting purchase or span tackle.

P_0 Tension in the rope at the standing part of the purchase (first rope).

P_1 Tension in the last rope in the purchase.

P_2 Tension in the rope after the first lead.

P_3 Tension in the rope after the second lead.

When determining the resultant load on the span gear, allowance should be made for the mass of the derrick boom and the mass of

Number of parts of rope holding the load	Rope Tensions (see Fig. 36)							
	P_0		P_1		P_2		P_3	
	Hoisting	Lowering	Hoisting	Lowering	Hoisting	Lowering	Hoisting	Lowering
1	—	—	—	—	1·060P	0·943P	1·124P	0·890P
2	0·485P	0·515P	0·515P	0·485P	0·545P	0·458P	0·578	0·432P
3	0·314P	0·353P	0·353P	0·314P	0·374P	0·296P	0·396P	0·280P
4	0·229P	0·272P	0·272P	0·229P	0·289P	0·216P	0·306P	0·204P
5	0·177P	0·224P	0·224P	0·177P	0·237P	0·167P	0·252P	0·158P

Table 1. Rope tensions at specified positions applicable to blocks having sheaves with bushed plain bearings (based on Table 1 BS MA 48: 1976)

the cargo gear. The BS publication gives tables for estimating the approximate mass of tubular steel derrick booms and of cargo purchases. Half the mass of the boom should be used when finding the resultant load on the span. The following examples illustrate the method of estimating loads in derrick rigs.

Example. Assuming the same conditions as in the previous example, viz. derrick 24 m long, span 12 m long, led through a span block on the mast shackled to an eyebolt 20 m above the heel of the derrick. A single fall is led down the derrick through a leading block to a winch as shown in Fig. 37. Given that the mass of the derrick boom is 1·2 tonnes and the mass of cargo gear is 0·2 tonne, find the thrust on the heel of the derrick and the loads sustained by blocks and shackles when hoisting a load of 4 tonnes.

From the Table of rope tensions, find the values of P_2 and P_3 for hoisting, for one part of rope holding the load. Multiply these values by the load, 4 tonnes, to obtain the rope tensions. Draw a figure to scale and construct parallelograms of forces as follows:—

(i) In parallelogram *ABCD*, *AB* is the load of 4·0 tonnes, *AD* is the tension in the wire fall $(P_2)=4·0\times1·06=4·24$ tonnes; *AC* is the resultant load on the derrick head cargo block 7·96 tonnes.

(ii) In parallelogram *DEFG*, *DE* is the sum of the cargo, the mass of the cargo gear and half the mass of the boom $4·0+0·2+0·6=4·8$ tonnes; *EF*, drawn parallel to the span, is the tension in the span 2·88 tonnes. $AF=AD+DF$ is the thrust on the derrick 10·0 tonnes.

(iii) In parallelogram *PQRS*, $PQ=AD$ is the tension in the wire fall between the head block and heel block (P_2) 4·24 tonnes; *PS* is the tension in the part of the fall leading to the winch

(P_3) $4.0 \times 1.124 = 4.5$ tonnes; PR is the resultant load on the heel block 6.71 tonnes.

(iv) In parallelogram $WXYZ$, $XW = EF$ is the tension in the span 2.88 tonnes; XY is the tension in the part of the span rope leading downward from the span block (P_2) = 2.88×1.06 = 3.05 tonnes; XZ is the resultant load on the span block 4.06 tonnes.

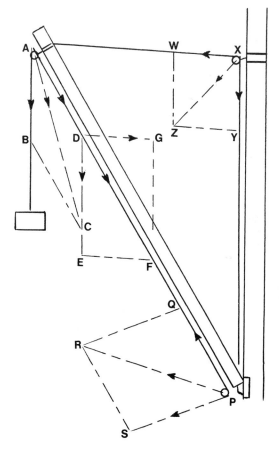

Fig. 37. Method of estimating the loads on derrick gear with a single cargo fall and a single span.

A purchase will be used to lift heavier loads, instead of a single wire fall. Less pull is required on the hauling part when a purchase is used, and this reduces the thrust on the derrick. A span tackle is also likely to be used instead of a single span rope. The following example shows how the thrust on the derrick and the loads sustained by the blocks and shackles can be determined when purchases are used.

Example. Fig. 38 shows the rig of a derrick, drawn to scale, which is being used to hoist a load of 10 tonnes. Each purchase consists of a gun tackle rove to disadvantage, the mass of the boom is 2·0 tonnes and the mass of the cargo gear is 0·5 tonne. Find (1) the load on the derrick head purchase block shackle; (2) the thrust on the derrick; (3) the load on the derrick heel block shackle; (4) the load on the span tackle block shackle.

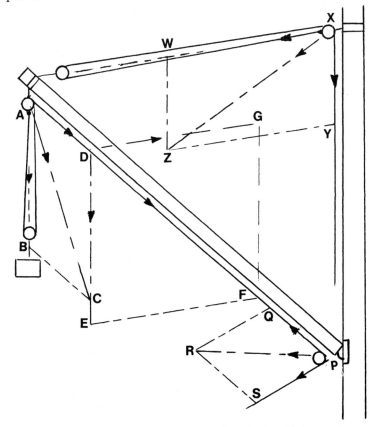

Fig. 38. Method of estimating the resultant loads with two parts in both the cargo purchase and span tackle.

From Table 1, find the values of P_2 and P_3, for hoisting, for two parts of rope holding the load. Multiply by the load, 10 tonnes, to obtain the tensions in the rope, leading out of the head block, and from the heel block to the winch. Construct parallelograms of forces as follows:

(i) In parallelogram $ABCD$, AB is the load of 10 tonnes; AD is the tension in the rope leading out of the head block (P_2) $=10\times0\cdot545=5\cdot45$ tonnes; AC is the resultant load on the derrick head cargo block 14·2 tonnes.

(ii) In parallelogram $DEFG$, DE is the sum of the cargo, the mass of the cargo gear and half the mass of the boom $10\cdot0+0\cdot5+1\cdot0=11\cdot5$ tonnes; EF is the load on the span tackle 11·5 tonnes; $AF=AD+DF$ is the thrust on the derrick 20·4 tonnes.

(iii) In parallelogram $PQRS$, $PQ=AD$ is the tension in the wire rope between the head block and heel block $(P_2)=5\cdot45$ tonnes; PS is the tension in the part of the rope leading to the winch $(P_3)=10\times0\cdot578=5\cdot78$ tonnes; PR is the resultant load on the derrick heel block shackle 9·2 tonnes.

(iv) In parallelogram $WXYZ$, $XW=EF$ is the load on the span tackle; XY is the tension in the rope leading down from the span purchase $(P_2)=11\cdot5\times0\cdot545=6\cdot267$ tonnes; XZ is the resultant load on the span tackle block shackle 13·9 tonnes.

Derrick Rigs

The Union Purchase or "married gear" is a favourite arrangement for loading and discharging. It consists of two derricks, both fixed, one guyed to plumb the hatch, the other to plumb overside. The falls from both derricks are shackled to the same cargo hook. The sling of goods in the hold is hooked on and hove up with the midship fall until it is clear of the hatch coaming. The slack of the fall from the other derrick is then run in quickly and the midship fall eased off until the load is wholly borne by the overside derrick and lowered into a lighter or on to a quay. The cargo hook is then hove back again to take the next sling.

This method, for speedy work, requires two quick acting, reliable winches and operators. It is suitable for light loads of up to 1·5 tonnes per sling, but the extra strain imposed on the falls and guys as a result of the cross pull is a disadvantage (Fig. 39).

Swinging Derrick. When there are no obstructions in its way a swinging derrick having a long reach is, perhaps, the speediest and most reliable arrangement for working heavy slings of bag cargo up to a tonne and a half in weight, especially if it be fitted with an adjustable span so that it may be regulated to plumb the hatch and also overside. It can pick up and land the goods anywhere within the radius of its swing, thus accelerating the work of handling the goods and making up the sets for slinging.

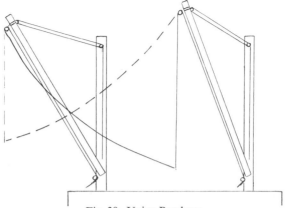

Fig. 39. Union Purchase.

The outboard guy, when discharging cargo, is usually led to a steam winch and the light derrick is sometimes pulled inboard by leading the guy through a block aloft and securing a heavy weight, a "dead man", on the end of it. There may be a prejudice against the "dead man" method of controlling the inward swing owing to the danger of someone getting hurt by the descending weight.

The Double Lift method is sometimes used for the rapid handling of mixed general cargo, viz., one derrick lifting off the quay and landing on deck, and another derrick picking off the deck and lowering into the hold, using skidboards where required.

More men are required per stevedore gang for the double handling, but rope whips substituted for wire falls and worked on the winch ends make for increased speed which may offset the increased labour cost.

Heavy Lifts

If the weight to be lifted exceeds the safe working load of the lifting gear the runner should be doubled, as shown in Fig. 40, to give mechanical advantage. If the load is greater than the safe working load of the derrick two derricks may be used together with yo-yo

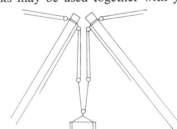

Fig. 40. Doubling up.   Fig. 41. Yo-yo gear.

gear as shown in Fig. 41. Such an arrangement would, for instance, be suitable for lifting a weight of 7 tonnes with two derricks of

Fig. 42. A Heavy Lift.

S.W.L. 5 tonnes. The heads of the derricks must be kept close together and the travelling block, which is used to equalise the load on the two derricks, must have a S.W.L. in excess of the weight to be lifted.

Derricks with a safe working load greater than 10 tonnes are usually rigged with purchases for lifting gear as well as for topping lift and guys. The hauling part of the lifting purchase is usually led through a sheave built into the derrick to a lead block on the mast or cross trees for heavy derricks with S.W.L. of 20 tonnes or more (Figures 42 and 43).

Fig. 43. Testing a Heavy Derrick.

Precautions

The vessel must have adequate stability before loading a heavy lift as when the load is suspended from the derrick its centre of gravity is virtually at the head of the derrick. The rise in the centre of gravity must not result in a negative metacentric height. Free surface effect must be reduced, if necessary by pressing up slack tanks. The vessel should be trimmed to be on even keel.

Moorings should be taut to prevent the vessel ranging along the berth, and should be tended when the weight is handled.

The mast must be adequately stayed, and if the weight is to be landed on deck it may be necessary to shore up from below. All gear must be carefully examined to see that it is in satisfactory condition. Winches and guys should be controlled by competent men.

The operation of loading or discharging a heavy lift must be carried out slowly and evenly. Steadying lines should be attached to the load. When the weight is being landed on the quay the vessel will list over towards the shore. As the weight is landed the vessel will right herself suddenly, tending to drag the load sideways towards the ship, so the lifting purchase and guy should be slacked down at this moment.

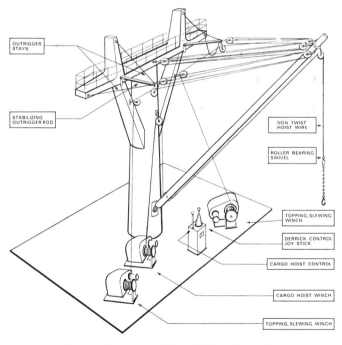

Fig. 44. MacGregor/Hallen Universal Derrick.

Patent Derricks or Ship Cranes

Several types of patent derricks are being fitted on modern vessels including the Hallen, Velle, Thompson and Speedcrane. Most of these derricks are provided with three winches, two for topping and slewing and a third for hoisting and lowering the cargo. All three are usually controlled by one winchman using two levers (Figs. 44 and 45).

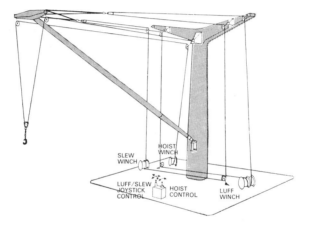

Fig. 45. Velle Crane.

The Stuelcken derrick may have a safe working load of up to 300 tonnes. The derrick is positioned between two posts and, with some types, may be used to serve two hatches by swinging between the posts in a fore and aft direction. Three or four winches are provided for each derrick, two of which are used for topping. These winches are controlled by using a portable control box which has two hand levers so only one operator is required (Figs. 46, 47 and 48).

Fig. 46. Blue Star Cargo Liner with Stuelcken Derrick.

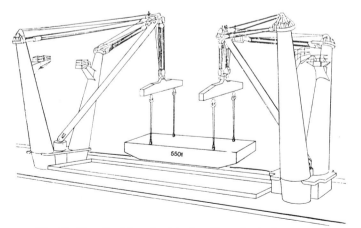

Fig. 47. Two Stuelcken derricks handling a load of 550 tonnes.

Fig. 48. General arrangements of the 300 tonne Stuelcken Derrick.

CHAPTER III

LIFESAVING APPLIANCES

Requirements. The life-saving appliances to be carried by ships must be in accordance with the IMO Safety of Life at Sea (SOLAS) Convention, Chapter III, and with any additional requirements of the national administration. Ships registered in the United Kingdom must be fitted with appliances in accordance with the Merchant Shipping (Life-Saving Appliances) Regulations.

IMO requirements for cargo ships of over 500 tons gross.

1. Survival Craft for ships built after 1st July 1986.

(a) One or more totally enclosed lifeboats on each side to accommodate the total number of persons on board. The Administration may permit cargo ships, except tankers and gas carriers, to carry partially enclosed lifeboats. In addition one or more rigid or inflatable liferafts capable of being launched on either side of the ship and of such aggregate capacity to accommodate all persons on board. If the liferaft(s) cannot be readily transferred the capacity on each side shall be sufficient to accommodate all persons on board.

(b) In lieu of the above, one or more totally enclosed lifeboats capable of being free-fall launched over the stern of the ship of aggregate capacity to accommodate all persons on board. In addition one or more rigid or inflatable liferafts on each side of the ship of aggregate capacity to accommodate all persons on board. The liferafts on at least one side to be served by launching appliances.

(c) In lieu of the above cargo ships of less than 85 m. in length, other than tankers and gas carriers, may carry one or more liferafts of aggregate capacity to accommodate all persons on board. If the liferafts cannot readily be transferred for launching on either side additional liferafts shall be provided so that the capacity on each side will accommodate 150% of all persons on board, the rescue boat may be included in this capacity if it is also a lifeboat. In the event of any one survival craft being lost or rendered unserviceable there shall be sufficient survival craft available for use on each side to accommodate all persons on board.

(d) Where survival craft are stowed more than 100 m. from the stem or stern an addition liferaft shall be stowed as far forward or aft, or one as far forward and another as far aft, as is reasonable and practicable. Such liferaft need not be fitted with a float free arrangement but may be securely fastened so as to permit manual release and need not be launched from a launching device.

(e) With the exception of survival craft boarded from a position on deck less than 4·5 m. above the waterline all survival craft shall be capable of being launched with their full complement of persons and equipment within 10 minutes from the time the abandon ship signal is given.

(f) Chemical tankers and gas carriers carrying cargoes emitting toxic vapours or gases shall carry totally enclosed lifeboats with a self-contained air support system.

(g) Oil tankers, chemical tankers and gas carriers carrying cargoes having a flashpoint not exceeding 60° C shall carry totally enclosed lifeboats with a self-contained air support system and which are fire-protected.

2. Rescue Boats.

Cargo ships shall carry at least one rescue boat. A lifeboat may be accepted as a rescue boat if it complies with the requirements for a rescue boat.

3. Survival Craft for ships built before 1st July 1986.

On each side of the ship one or more lifeboats (not necessarily enclosed) of sufficient capacity to accommodate all persons on board, including at least one motor lifeboat. In addition one or more rigid or inflatable liferafts with float-free arrangement of aggregate capacity to accommodate all persons on board. Paragraph 1(d) above also applies.

4. Radio equipment.

Ships constructed before 1st February 1992 shall be provided with either portable radio equipment and a survival craft emergency position-indicating radio beacon (EPIRB) or a satellite EPIRB and at least one radar transponder on each side of the ship.

Ships completed after 1st Februuary 1992 shall be provided with either a satellite EPIRB or a survival craft EPIRB. All ships shall be provided with a satellite EPIRB after 1st August 1993 and with at least one radar transponder on each side after 1st February 1995.

5. Two-way radiotelephone apparatus.

Waterproofed two-way radiotelephone sets shall be provided for communication between survival craft, between survival craft and ship and between survival craft and rescue unit. At least three sets shall be provided, of which at least one shall be portable.

6. Lifebuoys.

The minimum number of lifebuoys to be carried by ships built after 1st July 1986 is as follows:—

Length of ship in metres	Minimum number of lifebuoys
Under 100	8
100 and under 150	10
150 and under 200	12
200 and over	14

7. Lifejackets.

A lifejacket shall be carried for every person on board. In addition a sufficient number shall be carried for persons on watch and for use at remotely located survival craft stations. Lifejackets suitable for children must be provided for each child passenger on board.

8. Line-throwing appliance.

A line-throwing appliance shall be provided.

9. Immersion suits.

An immersion suit of an appropriate size shall be provided for every person assigned to crew the rescue boat.

10. Distress flares.

Not less than 12 rocket parachute flares shall be carried and stowed on or near the navigating bridge.

LIFEBOATS

Glass reinforced plastic (GRP) lifeboats are now generally carried on ships but lifeboats made of wood or metal are also permitted to be used. Boats constructed from GRP have a longer life and require less maintenance than boats built of wood. GRP is fire resistant, rot proof, non corrosive and impervious to electrolytic action. Holes and small damage may be easily repaired but the material gives poor resistance to abrasion. Buoyancy is usually provided by blocks of expanded plastic foam which are often built in and enclosed with fibre glass to form sidebenches. Wood is used for thwarts, lower seats and bottom boards.

Fig. 1.—Watercraft Mark V Totally enclosed lifeboat.

Open lifeboats may still be carried on ships built before 1st July 1986 but most ships are now equipped with totally enclosed boats. A totally enclosed boat must be provided with a rigid watertight enclosure which completely encloses the boat. Access is provided by hatches capable of being closed from both inside and outside.

The stability of a totally enclosed lifeboat shall be such that it is inherently or automatically self-righting when loaded with its full or a partial complement of persons and equipment and all entrances and openings are closed watertight and the persons are secured with safety belts.

All lifeboats on ships built after 1st July 1986 shall be capable of being launched and towed when the ship is making headway at a speed of 5 knots in calm water. They shall not accommodate more than 150 persons.

The number of persons which a lifeboat is permitted to carry shall be the lesser of:—

1. the number of persons (average mass 75 kg.) wearing lifejackets that can be seated without interfering with the means of propulsion or the operation of lifeboat equipment, or

2. the number of spaces that can be provided on the seating arrangements.

Every lifeboat shall be powered by a compression ignition engine. The speed of a lifeboat when proceeding ahead in calm water when loaded with its full complement of persons and equipment shall be at least 6 knots and at least 2 knots when towing a 25 person liferaft loaded with its full complement of persons and equipment.

Fig. 2.—Watercraft partially enclosed lifeboat.

Fig. 3.—Welin Lambie gravity davits.

DAVITS

On ships built after 1st July 1986 a launching appliance shall not depend on any means other than gravity, or stored mechanical power which is independent of the ship's power supplies, to launch the survival craft or rescue boat it serves in the fully loaded or light condition. Gravity davits are generally used. On ships built before 1st July 1986 luffing type davits may be fitted for boats weighing not more than 2·3 tonnes in their turning out condition. Luffing davits require the boat to be taken from inboard to outboard by the manual turning of a worm screw or telescopic screw.

Fig. 4.—Welin Lambie gravity davits.

Each launching appliance together with all its launching and recovery gear shall be so arranged that the fully equipped survival craft or rescue boat it serves can be safely lowered against a trim of up to 10° and a list of up to 20° either way. Launching appliances for oil tankers, chemical tankers and gas carriers with a final angle

Fig. 5—Viking Marine Evacuation System.

of heel greater than 20° but not greater than 30° shall be capable of operating at the final angle on the lower side of the ship.

The speed at which the survival craft or rescue boat is lowered into the water shall be not less than that obtained from the formula:—

$$S = 0·4 + (0·02 \times H)$$

where   S   =   speed of lowering in metres per second
and   H   =   height in metres from davit head to the waterline at lightest seagoing condition.

Every launching appliance shall be fitted with brakes capable of stopping the descent of the survival craft or rescue boat and holding it securely when loaded with its full complement of persons and equipment.

Every rescue boat launching appliance shall be capable of hoisting the rescue boat when loaded with its full rescue boat complement of persons and equipment at a rate of not less than 0·3 m/s.

LIFERAFTS

Every liferaft shall be so constructed as to be capable of withstanding exposure for 30 days afloat in all sea conditions and so that when it is dropped into the water from a height of 18 m. the liferaft and its equipment will operate satisfactorily. It must be capable of being towed at a speed of 3 knots in calm water when loaded with its full complement of persons and equipment and with one of its sea-anchors streamed.

The liferaft shall have a canopy to protect the occupants from exposure which is automatically set in place when the liferaft is launched and waterborne. The canopy shall provide insulation against heat and cold. Each entrance shall be clearly indicated and provided with efficient adjustable closing arrangements which can be easily and quickly opened from inside and outside the liferaft so as to permit ventilation but exclude seawater wind and cold.

Unless the liferaft is to be launched by an approved launching appliance and is not required to be portable the total mass of the liferaft its container and its equipment shall be not more than 185 kilogrammes. The carrying capacity shall be not less than six persons.

The liferaft shall be fitted with a painter of length equal to not less than twice the distance from the stowed position to the waterline in the lightest sea-going condition or 15 m. whichever is the greater. The painter system shall provide a connection between the ship and the liferaft to ensure that the liferaft when released is not dragged under by the sinking ship.

The buoyancy chamber of an inflatable liferaft shall be divided into not less than two separate compartments. If one compartment is damaged or fails to inflate the intact compartments shall be able to support the number of persons the liferaft is permitted to accommodate.

Inflation shall be completed within a period of 1 minute at an ambient temperature between 18° and 20°C and within 3 minutes at an ambient temperature of —30°C. A non-toxic gas shall be used for inflation. A topping-up pump or bellows shall be provided for maintaining the working pressure.

Fig. 6.—RFD Surviva 10 person liferaft.

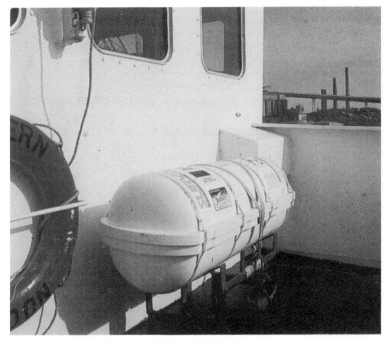

Fig. 7.—RFD Surviva liferaft container.

The number of persons which an inflatable liferaft is permitted to carry shall be the lesser of:—

1. the greatest number obtained by dividing the volume in cubic metres by 0·096, or

2. the greatest number obtained by dividing the floor area in square metres by 0·372, or

3. the number of persons (average mass 75 kg.) wearing life-jackets that can be seated without interfering with the operation of the equipment.

The floor of the inflatable liferaft shall be waterproof and capable of being sufficiently insulated against cold either by means of one or more inflatable compartments or by other equally efficient means not dependent on inflation.

An inflatable liferaft shall be packed in a container capable of withstanding conditions encountered at sea and of sufficient buoyancy to pull the painter from within and to operate the inflation mechanism should the ship sink.

The buoyancy of a rigid liferaft shall be provided by approved inherently buoyant material placed as near as possible to the periphery of the liferaft. The buoyant material shall be fire-retardant or protected by a fire-retardant covering. A rigid liferaft shall be capable of operating safely whichever way up it is floating, if not it shall be either self-righting or readily righted in a seaway in calm water by one person.

EQUIPMENT FOR LIFEBOATS AND LIFERAFTS

The following items of equipment shall be provided on a lifeboat and on a liferaft:—

a buoyant bailer;

a sea anchor;

one buoyant rescue quoit attached to not less than 30 metres of buoyant line;

watertight receptacles containing 3 litres of fresh water for each person, of which 1 litre per person may be replaced by a de-salting apparatus capable of producing an equal amount of water in 2 days;

a rust proof drinking vessel (3 for UK ships) and rust proof dipper;

food rations, not less than 10,000 kj. for each person, kept in airtight packaging and stowed in a watertight container;

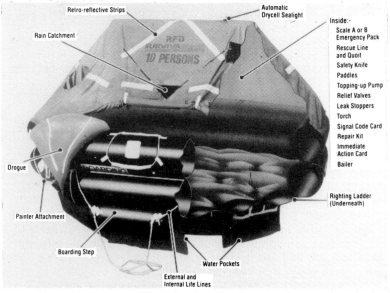

Fig. 8.—RFD Surviva liferaft location of equipment and accessories.

four rocket parachute flares; six hand flares;
two buoyant smoke signals;
one waterproof electric torch suitable for signalling, with one set
of spare batteries and one spare bulb in a waterproof container;
one daylight signalling mirror;
one whistle or equivalant sound signal;
one knife; three tin openers;
a first aid outfit in a waterproof case;
an efficient radar reflector;
one set of fishing tackle;
six doses of anti-seasickness medicine and one seasickness bag
for each person;
survival instructions and lifesaving signals table.

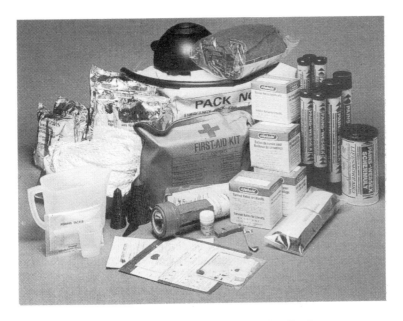

Fig. 9.—RFD Surviva Emergency pack for liferafts.

In addition to the above equipment a lifeboat shall also be
provided with:—
sufficient buoyant oars to make headway in calm seas; thole pins
crutches or equivalent arrangements shall be provided for each oar;
two boat hooks;
two buckets;
two hatchets;

two painters;

a binnacle containing an efficient compass;

a manual pump;

a searchlight;

a portable fire extinguisher (2 for UK ships);

an additional buoyant rescue quoit.

In addition to the equipment listed above for a lifeboat and a liferaft a liferaft shall also be provided with:—

two buoyant paddles;

two sponges;

an additional sea anchor.

LIFEBUOYS

A lifebuoy shall be constructed of inherently buoyant material. It shall not depend upon rushes, cork shavings, granulated cork, any other loose granulated material or any air compartment which depends on inflation for buoyancy. The materials shall be rot-proof, corrosion-resistant and not be unduly affected by seawater, oil or fungal attack.

A lifebuoy shall be capable of supporting not less than 14·5 kg. of iron in fresh water for a period of 24 hours. It shall have a mass of not less than 2·5 kg. The outer diameter shall be not more than 800 mm. and the inner diameter not less than 400 mm. It shall be constructed to withstand a drop into water from the height at which it is stowed above the waterline in the lightest seagoing condition, or 30 m., whichever is the greater without impairing its operating capability.

Lifebuoys shall be of highly visible colour and shall be marked in block capitals of the Roman alphabet with the name and port of registry of the ship. They shall be fitted with retro-reflective material to assist in detection.

A lifebuoy shall be fitted with a grabline not less than 9·5 mm. in diameter and not less than 4 times the outside diameter of the buoy. The grabline shall be secured at 4 equidistant points around the circumference of the buoy to form 4 equal loops.

At least half the lifebuoys shall be provided with self-igniting lights and not less than two of these shall also be provided with self-activating smoke signals and be capable of quick release from the bridge. In tankers the lights shall be of an electric battery type. The lights shall be capable of burning continuously with a lumious intensity of not less than 2 candela in all directions for a period of at least 2 hours.

One lifebuoy on each side of the ship shall be fitted with a buoyant lifeline of length not less than twice the height at which it is stowed above the waterline in light condition, or 30 m., whichever is the greater. The lifebuoy with lines shall not have a self-igniting light attached.

LIFEJACKETS

Lifejackets shall be so placed as to be readily accessible and their position shall be plainly indicated.

A lifejacket shall be so constructed that after demonstration a person can correctly don it within a period of 1 minute without assistance. It shall be capable of being worn inside-out or clearly capable of being worn in only one way and as far as possible cannot be donned incorrectly. It shall allow the wearer to jump from a height of at least 4·5 m. into the water without injury and without dislodging or damaging the lifejacket.

A lifejacket shall have sufficient buoyancy and stability in calm fresh water to lift the mouth of an exhausted or unconscious person not less than 120 mm. clear of the water with the body inclined backwards at an angle of not less than 20° and not more than 50° from the vertical position, also to turn the body of an unconscious person in the water from any position to one where the mouth is clear of the water in not more than 5 seconds. The buoyancy shall not be reduced by more than 5% after 24 hours submersion in fresh water.

A lifejacket shall not sustain burning or continue melting after being totally enveloped in a fire for a period of 2 seconds. It shall be rot-proof, corrosion-resistant and not be unduly affected by seawater, oil or fungal attack.

A Lifejacket shall be of highly visible colour and shall be fitted with retro-reflective material.

A lifejacket which depends on inflation for buoyancy shall have not less than two separate compartments and shall inflate automatically on immersion. It shall be provided with a device to permit inflation by a single manual motion and be capable of being inflated by mouth. In the event of loss of buoyancy in any one compartment it shall be capable of complying with the above requirements for buoyancy.

Each lifejacket shall be fitted with a light which shall have a luminous intensity of not less than 0·75 candela for a period of at least 8 hours.

LINE-THROWING APPLIANCES AND PYROTECHNICS

A line-throwing appliance shall be capable of throwing a line with reasonable accuracy. It shall include not less than four projectiles and four lines. The projectiles shall be capable of carrying the lines at least 230 m. in calm weather with a lateral deflection which does not exceed 10 per cent. The lines shall have a breaking strength of not less than 2 kilonewtons.

A rocket parachute flare shall be contained in a water-resistant casing. A rocket shall, when fired vertically, reach an altitude of not less than 300 m. At or near the top of its trajectory the rocket shall eject a parachute flare which shall burn with a bright red colour for not less than 40 seconds. The flare shall burn uniformly with an average luminous intensity of not less than 30,000 candela and have a rate of descent of not more than 5 m. per second. The rocket shall be capable of functioning when fired at an angle of 45° to the horizontal.

A hand flare shall be contained in a water-resistant casing and have a self-contained means of ignition. It shall burn uniformly with a bright red colour with an average luminous intensity of not less than 15,000 candela for a period of not less than one minute. It shall be so designed as not to cause discomfort to the person holding the casing and not to endanger the survival craft by burning or glowing residues when used in accordance with the manufacturer's operating instructions.

A buoyant smoke signal shall emit smoke of a highly visible colour at a uniform rate for a period of not less than 3 minutes when floating in calm water and shall continue to emit smoke when submerged in water for a period of 10 seconds under 100 mm. of water.

EPIRB

"Satellite EPIRB" means an emergency position-indicating radio beacon, being an earth station in the mobile-satellite service, the emissions of which are intended to facilitate search and rescue operations and is capable of:—

(a) floating free if the ship sinks,

(b) being automatically activated when afloat;

(c) being manually activated, and

(d) being carried by one person.

"Survival craft EPIRB" means an emergency position-indicating radio beacon, being a station in the mobile service, for carriage in survival craft, the emissions of which are intended to facilitate search and rescue operations.

LOWERING A LIFEBOAT

The gripes and securing hooks or pins are released. The brake is lifted so that the boat moves down under its own weight until the tricing-in pendants tighten and cause the boat to swing alongside the embarkation deck. The boat is then held in to the ship's side by bowsing tackles and the tricing-in pendants slipped.

The lifeboat painter is taken forward clear of everything and secured. The plug is checked. When the boat has its full complement on board the bowsing tackles are released and the brake lever lifted to lower the boat into the water.

If the ship is making any headway it is essential to keep the painter tight and to release the after fall first so that the boat does not broach to.

LIFEBOAT ENGINE

Starting Instructions for Diesel Engines

When a maker's Instruction manual is available it should be carefully studied, but in the absence of this, the following routine should be followed:—

(*a*) By means of the dip stick, check the oil level in the engine, also in the reverse gear and in the reducing gear if these are lubricated separately.

(*b*) Turn on sea-cock. If fresh water cooling is fitted, check the level in the water header tank.

(*c*) Make sure that the fuel is turned on. This should never be turned off in the case of a diesel engine as the slightest leak in any fuel pipe connection is likely to let air into the system.

(*d*) Check that the reverse lever is in neutral.

(*e*) If starting a sea-water-cooled engine with the boat in the davits, it is advisable to turn the water pump greasers as the pump will be running dry.

(*f*) Set the throttle at least two-thirds open and if starting from cold, trip the excess fuel device which is fitted to the fuel pump on some engines.

(*g*) For hand-starting, set the valve decompression lever to the decompressed position. If the engine is fitted with electric starting, it is not usually necessary to use the decompressor.

(*h*) Engage starting handle and swing engine briskly. When it is turning at the maximum speed, pull the decompressed lever back to full compression whilst continuing to swing as fast as possible.

(*i*) As soon as the engine starts, close the throttle.

(*j*) Check that the oil pressure is showing on the pressure gauge and if the engine is sea water cooled and the boat is afloat, see that the cooling water is flowing through the engine.

If a diesel engine fails to start, it is nearly always due to one of the following reasons:—

(i) Air in the fuel system or faulty injection.

(ii) Lack of compression.

(iii) Lubricating oil too heavy.

To check for air in the system or faulty injectors, turn the engine over slowly decompressed when each injector should be heard as it comes into operation. If air is suspected, bleed the fuel filter and fuel pump at the vent plugs provided. If the injectors are suspected, clean or fit spares which are usually provided.

Lack of compression can be caused by either gummed up piston rings of faulty valves. The former can be checked by trying to turn the engine over on full compression when any blow past the pistons will be heard. If the leaking is past the valves, the cylinder head should be removed and the valves ground in.

With regard to lubricating oil, it is particularly important that the correct grade be used. If it is too heavy it will cause a heavy drag and prevent the engine being turned fast enough to get it sharply over compression.

SAILING A LIFEBOAT

On ships built after the 1st July 1986 all lifeboats must be motor boats and are not required to be provided with a mast and sails.

For ships built before 1st July 1986 the equipment of an open lifeboat includes a mast with galvanized wire stays together with orange coloured sails. The rig is a standing lug and jib.

The illustration (Fig. 10) shows a boat fitted with a standing lug and jib. The yard and sail remain always on one side of the mast and so they are to windward of the mast when the boat is on one tack and to leeward when on the other. The tack of the standing lug is secured in a position close to the mast by means of a tack lashing or a small tackle. This may lead to an eyebolt in the keelson close to the heel of the mast, or may be secured to the mast itself, or around the mast thwart. The yard is kept close to the mast by the traveller, which is an iron ring round the mast with a hook attached for the strop of the yard. The traveller slides up and down when the yard is hoisted and lowered.

The lugsail is a free-footed sail (no boom). When sailing with the wind well aft, a boom would spread the foot of the sail out and thereby increase its efficiency. If a boom is used for boat sailing the foot of the sail may be laced along it, but it is best to have a clew lashing only, there is then a clear space between the boom and the foot of the sail, and any sea or heavy spray that was shipped in the sail would immediately clear itself. Fitting a boom is better than the common practice of holding the clew out with a boat hook, which may easily be let go and lost.

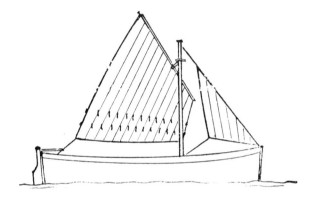

Fig. 10. Standing Lug and Jib.

One or two rows of reef points are put in the sail with corresponding reef cringles on the luff-rope for the tack, and on the leech for the sheet. These, of course, only come into use when the sail is reefed.

The jib is set by means of a halyard and sheet, the tack being secured at the stem head. It is most important that the luff of the jib is always set tight.

When a vessel is sailing close to the wind she is said to be **close-hauled**. If she has the wind abeam or abaft the beam she is said to be **"free"**.

In small vessels, when steering with a tiller, the order **"up helm"** means that the tiller is to be moved towards the wind (to windward), the rudder, of course, canting to leeward, and the vessel's head paying off.

The term **"down helm"** means exactly the opposite to "up helm"; that is, the tiller is to be moved away from the wind (to leeward), the rudder is then canted to windward, and the vessel's head comes up towards the wind.

When under sail the terms "up helm" and "down helm" are used more than "port" or "starboard".

When the wind is right aft the order "up helm" or "down helm" is understood according to which side of the wheel the man is steering from.

The term **luff** is used by seamen to indicate the act of bringing a close-hauled boat up in the wind by easing the helm down, and thereby causing the sails to shake. This may be done to ease the pressure on the sails and gear in a squall, or to take the wind out of a sail so that a better pull can be got on a sheet or halyards, or for the purpose of checking a boat's way through the water without quite stopping her.

When the helm is put up again, and her head is canting away from the wind she is said to be **"paying off"** or **"filling"**, and when the sails are quite steady again she is said to be **"full"**.

When a vessel has the wind **free**, and it is required to bring her nearer to the wind, the term **"luff"** is not generally used. The order would be "let her come **up** a point", "let her come **to** a point" or whatever alteration of course was required.

Tacking is to bring the boat's head to wind so as to change from close-hauled on one tack to close-hauled on the other.

Wearing is keeping the boat's head off the wind so as to change from close-hauled on one tack to close-hauled on the other by bringing the wind round the stern.

Gybing is altering course so as to bring the wind round the stern from one quarter to the other.

When sailing a ship's boat with a fair wind, there is nothing to do but steer for your objective and haul in or slacken off the sheet of the sail should the wind alter in direction and always, in an open boat, to be on the alert and ready to slack off the sheet quickly when a gust or squall comes along. The sail is like a bag full of wind. The sheet acts in the same way as a lashing on the mouth of a bag, you must let go the lashing before the bag can be emptied. Similarly, let go the sheet to empty or "spill" the wind out of the sail. It will flap and make a noise because the pressure is off the canvas but the boat will remain upright. The particular danger when sailing an open boat in squally weather is her lurching and dipping the lee gunwale under water; even if she is well ballasted she may not come upright as the lurching tends to throw the weight of the crew to the lee side and their weight heels her over still further. Never hesitate to slack off the sheet when a puff of wind comes along, it is easy hauled in again.

The science of a boat beating to windward is an application of simple mechanics. A boat with lugsail will make headway when 4 points, 45 degrees, from the wind, and she will zig-zag her way into the wind's eye tack for tack; she will not make good the direction she is heading as ship's boats are flat-bottomed things and make a lot of leeway.

In the figure the arrow and dotted line represent a North wind blowing down the page. *A* is a boat close-hauled

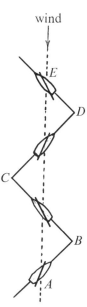

wind

on the port tack heading N.E. She tacks at *B* and heads N.W. towards *C* on the starboard tack. She tacks at *C* and heads N.E. for *D* on the port tack. She changes again from port to starboard tack at *D* and heads N.W. for *E*. The distance made good to windward is from *A* to *E*. If *AB* is one mile, *BC* 2 miles, *CD* 2 miles and *DE* 1 mile the boat sails 6 miles in all. It will be found on looking up the Traverse Table with 45° as a course and these distances in the Distance column that the Difference of Latitude column gives 4·2 miles which is the length of *AE*, so that the boat has sailed 6 miles to make good 4·2 miles against the wind. She would actually have to do more as there is always some leeway to make up.

The trim of a boat is a vital factor in determining her sailing qualities. When a boat is down by the head she will try to bring herself head to wind and when down by the stern she wants to put her stern into the wind. The deep or heavy end of the boat tends to hang windward; this, of course, may be counteracted with the rudder but the angled rudder would retard the boat's speed. Immediately on getting under way the position of the members of the crew should be changed about until the best sailing balance or trim of the boat is found. The person steering can tell this by the feel of the tiller because when the boat is in nice trim, she requires very little helm.

The knack of sailing a boat can only be acquired from experience and no opportunity should be witheld from, or rejected by, responsible members of a ship's crew of getting practice whenever possible.

The crew of the s.s. *Trevassa* got two hours' notice to prepare for a trip of 1700 miles in open boats when their ship suddenly and mysteriously foundered in the middle of the Indian Ocean in 1923. It was fortunate for the crew that the captain and the chief officer had previous experience in handling a boat under sail.

CHAPTER IV

ANCHORS AND CABLES

THE principal parts of both stocked and stockless anchors are shown in Figs. 1–4. Merchant vessels are generally required to carry two bower anchors and a spare bower, which are invariably of the stockless type for easy stowage. The head of a stockless anchor is generally made of cast steel and the shank of forged steel. A stream anchor, of about one third the required weight of the bower, may also be carried for use at the stern.

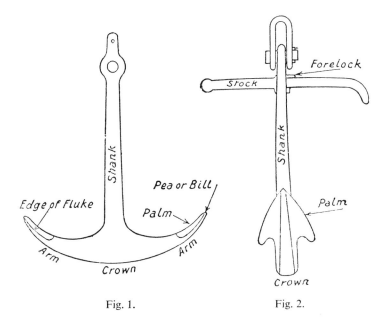

Fig. 1.   Fig. 2.

The Stocked or Common Anchor

This type is difficult to stow but it may be carried in some merchant ships for use as a stream or kedge anchor.

The stock must weigh one quarter of the weight of the remainder of the anchor. Its purpose is to assist the arm and fluke to bite into

79

the ground. Should the anchor fall with its arms flat the stock will be upright and when stress is applied through the cable the stock being heavier and longer than the arms will turn the anchor. There are no moving parts.

The upper fluke does not contribute to the holding power and may be caught in the bight of the cable when the ship swings with the tide.

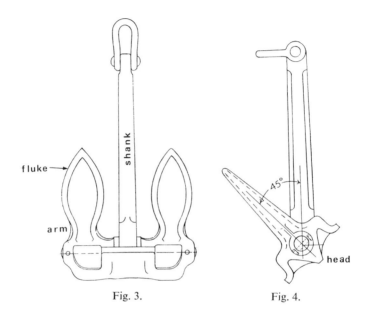

Fig. 3.   Fig. 4.

The Stockless Anchor

This type can be hove up into the hawse pipe. The head, which must weigh at least 60 per cent of the weight of the anchor, pivots about the end of the shank so that the arms will open to an angle of 45° as shown in Fig. 4. When the anchor strikes the sea bed the tripping palms tilt the flukes downwards so that they dig in. The disadvantages are that there are moving parts which may become choked, the anchor is relatively unstable and is liable to rotate when dragged under severe loading conditions, and the flukes may fail to re-trip when the anchor is dislodged. The holding power is about four times the weight of the anchor in good holding ground.

Fig. 5. Patent Stockless Anchor.

High Holding Power Anchors

In 1950, after carrying out a series of tests on anchors of different designs, the Admiralty produced the AC 14 which has a holding power of approximately twelve times the weight of the anchor in good holding ground. The improvement in efficiency is due to increasing the fluke area, using unribbed flukes and providing stabilizing fins which cause the anchor to bury evenly with an equal pull on each fluke. Other similar types of high holding power anchors which have been approved by classification societies include the Stokes, the Pool, the Meon and the Byers High Holding Power Anchor.

A reduction of weight of 25 per cent is permitted by the classification societies when a high holding power anchor is fitted but the cable is required to be of special quality and a more powerful windlass will normally be required. Anchors of this type are being fitted to some ships, particularly large vessels and warships.

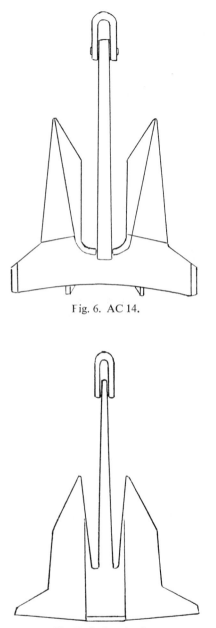

Fig. 6. AC 14.

Fig. 7. Stokes Anchor.

Permanent Mooring Anchors for buoys and beacons in shallow water have usually one fluke only and the anchor is lowered to the

Fig. 8. One Fluke Mooring Anchor.

bottom fluke downwards, by means of a slip rope rove through a shackle in the crown.

Bow Stoppers are provided between the hawsepipe and the windlass or capstan to relieve the strain on the windlass when the ship is at anchor, to secure the anchor when the ship is at sea and to hold the cable and anchor temporarily when the inboard part of the cable

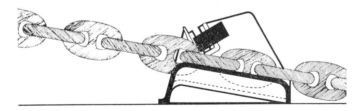

Fig. 9. Track Bowstopper.

has to be handled. There are several types in use. Fig. 9 shows the Clarke Chapman self holding and automatically releasing track bowstopper. When heaving in the anchor in heavy weather this type automatically accepts any excess of strains outside the hawsepipe due to the rise and fall of the vessel as the chain cable lifts the lever link by link.

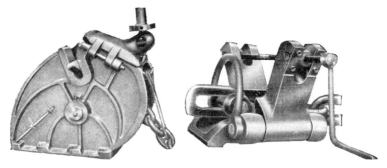

Fig. 10. Bow Stoppers.

CABLES

Chain cable is measured by the diameter of the bar from which the link is made. Studs are fitted in the links to keep the chain from kinking. They also give increased strength. Cable is usually made of mild steel, electrically welded. Special quality steel cable of increased strength must be used with high holding power anchors and may be used with ordinary stockless anchors. A lower diameter of cable is permitted when Grade U3, special quality, cable is used, and this results in a saving of weight.

Anchor cable is made in lengths of 27·5 m (15 fathoms) called "shackles". The shackles which connect these lengths are placed in the cable with the bow, or round end of the shackle, forward so that the lugs will not foul any projection when the cable runs out.

SHACKLES

The shackles which join the lengths of cable together differ slightly from those used for shackling it to the anchor. In the joining shackles the pin does not project beyond the width of the shackle, and is secured by a hard wood plug passing through the pin and one lug of the shackle. The anchor shackle is larger than the joining shackles and the usual method of attaching the cable to the anchor is by a "D" type shackle. Another method is to use a permanent attachment of two or more links on the bower anchor and the cable is then attached by a patent lugless shackle.

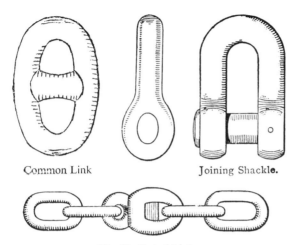

Common Link   Joining Shackle.

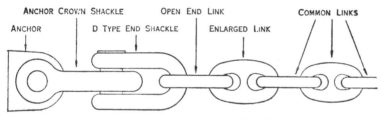

Fig. 11. Swivel Link.

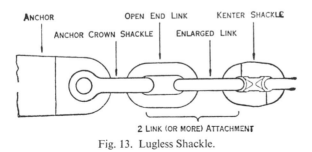

ANCHOR CROWN SHACKLE   OPEN END LINK   COMMON LINKS

ANCHOR   D TYPE END SHACKLE   ENLARGED LINK

Fig. 12. "D" Type End Shackle.

ANCHOR   OPEN END LINK   KENTER SHACKLE

          ANCHOR CROWN SHACKLE   ENLARGED LINK

2 LINK (OR MORE) ATTACHMENT
Fig. 13. Lugless Shackle.

The inboard end of the cable is generally shackled to a good eyebolt in the collision bulkhead at the bottom of the chain locker. A simple method is to secure the cable by a bolt through the open end link and a clench as shown below.

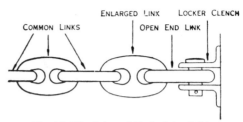

Fig. 14. The Inboard End of the Cable.

The lengths of cables are marked in succession as follows: At the first shackle (15 fathoms) by a piece of seizing wire on the stud of the first link abaft the shackle; at the second shackle (30 fathoms) by a

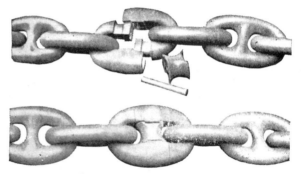

Fig. 15. Kenter Lugless Shackle.

piece of wire on the second studded link abaft the shackle; at the third shackle (45 fathoms) by a piece of wire on the third studded link, and so on.

Usually all the marked links are painted white forward as well as abaft the shackle so that they may be more easily noted when the cable is running out.

INSPECTION OF ANCHORS AND CABLES

Vessels undergo a periodical survey every four years by one of the classification societies, such as Lloyd's, under which British vessels are registered. The hull, machinery and deck equipment are then inspected. The chain cables are ranged for inspection and anchors and chains examined and placed in good working order. If any length of chain cable is found to be reduced in mean diameter by 10 per cent of its original size at its most worn part it is to be renewed. The chain locker is examined internally.

The cable is ranged in long lengths up and down the bottom of the dry dock, pins of shackles knocked out and examined, coated with white lead and tallow and replaced with new wooden holding pins driven into the pins of the connecting shackles. The links are sounded by tapping with a hammer to hear if they give out a clear ring. It is desirable to occasionally replace the two or three lengths next the anchor with two or three lengths from the bottom of the locker as all chain gets fatigued and brittle when lying idle. This also gives an opportunity of cleaning out the locker. When dirty cable is being hove up from a muddy bottom it should be hosed down as it enters the hawsepipe. It may be remarked here that at each survey the masts, spars, rigging and general deck equipment are inspected, including hatch covers and supports, tarpaulins, cleats and battens, ventilator coamings and covers.

The Anchors and Chain Cables Act 1967 requires that anchors and chain cable for use aboard ships registered in the United Kingdom should be subjected to certain tests. Details of the tests are given in the Anchor and Chain Cables Rules (1970) for anchors of over 76 kg and for cable of 12·5 mm or more in diameter. Application for tests must be made to a Certifying Authority which means the Department of Transport or other authority authorised by the DTp such as the Classification Societies.

An anchor must be tested by being subjected to a specified proof load on a testing machine. The proof loads are given in a table from which the following examples are taken:

Weight of anchor in tonnes	1	5	10	30
Proof load in tonnes	20·3	67·4	103·0	203·0

The Supervisor of Tests must be satisfied that there is no material deformation flaw or weakness after the test has been carried out.

Cables must also be subjected to load tests on verified testing machines. Three links are taken from each length and subjected to a tensile breaking load test. If this test is satisfactory every length must be separately subjected to a proof load test. In each case the loads are specified according to the size and grade of the cable. No deformation, flaw or weakness must be found after the load tests have been completed. Special quality (Grade U3) cable is subjected to additional mechanical tests to determine the ultimate tensile strength, elongation and impact value.

Chain cable accessories such as shackles must also be subjected to the proof load test and samples are subjected to the breaking load test.

Marking of Anchors and Cables

When an anchor has passed the test prescribed in the Anchor and Chain Cables Rules it must be permanently stamped in a conspicuous place with a circle giving the particulars indicated in Fig. 16.

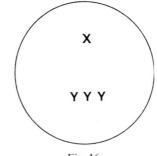

Fig. 16.

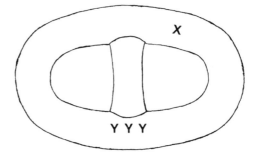

X Number of Certificate.
Y Letters indicating Certifying Authority.

Fig. 17.

Chain cable is marked as shown in Fig. 17 at each end and at intervals of not more than 30 m. Each cable accessory must also be marked in this way.

Certificate

If a request is made within one month of the marking of the anchor or cable the Certifying Authority must issue a certificate giving the serial number, names and marks of the Certifying Authority and testing establishment and the name of the Supervisor of Tests. The Anchor Certificate must show the type of anchor, weight in kilogrammes, length of shank and arm and diameter of trend in millimetres and the proof load in tonnes. The Chain Cable Certificate must show the type and grade of cable, length, diameter, total weight, length and breadth of link, breaking and proof loads applied and number and type of accessories included.

CHAPTER V

INTERNATIONAL REGULATIONS FOR PREVENTING COLLISIONS AT SEA (1972)

(as amended by Resolutions A464(XII), A626(15), A678(16) and A736(18))

Amended version formally adopted by the United Kingdom from 1st May 1996, applicable internationally from 4th November, 1995.

PART A. GENERAL

RULE 1

Application

(*a*) These Rules shall apply to all vessels upon the high seas and in all waters connected therewith navigable by seagoing vessels.

(*b*) Nothing in these Rules shall interfere with the operation of special rules made by an appropriate authority for roadsteads, harbours, rivers, lakes or inland waterways connected with the high seas and navigable by seagoing vessels. Such special rules shall conform as closely as possible to these Rules.

(*c*) Nothing in these Rules shall interfere with the operation of any special rules made by the Government of any State with respect to additional station or signal lights, shapes or whistle signals for ships of war and vessels proceeding under convoy, or with respect to additional station or signal lights or shapes for fishing vessels engaged in fishing as a fleet. These additional station or signal lights, shapes or whistle signals shall, so far as possible, be such that they cannot be mistaken for any light, shape or signal authorized elsewhere under these Rules.

(*d*) Traffic separation schemes may be adopted by the Organization for the purpose of these Rules.

(*e*) Whenever the Government concerned shall have determined that a vessel of special construction or purpose cannot comply fully with the provisions of any of these Rules with respect to the number, position, range or arc of visibility of lights or shapes, as well as to the disposition and characteristics of sound-signalling appliances, such vessel shall comply with such other provisions in regard to the number, position, range or arc of visibility of lights or shapes, as well as to the disposition and characteristics of sound-signalling appliances, as her Government shall have determined to be the closest possible compliance with these Rules in respect of that vessel.

RULE 2

Responsibility

(*a*) Nothing in these rules shall exonerate any vessel, or the owner, master or crew thereof, from the consequences of any neglect to comply with these Rules or of the neglect of any precaution which may be required by the ordinary practice of seamen, or by the special circumstances of the case.

(*b*) In construing and complying with these Rules due regard shall be had to all dangers of navigation and collision and to any special circumstances, including the limitations of the vessels involved, which may make a departure from these rules necessary to avoid immediate danger.

RULE 3

General definitions

For the purpose of these Rules, except where the context otherwise requires.

(*a*) The word ''vessel'' includes every description of water craft, including non-displacement craft and seaplanes, used or capable of being used as a means of transportation on water.

(*b*) The term ''power-driven vessel'' means any vessel propelled by machinery.

(*c*) The term ''sailing vessel'' means any vessel under sail provided that propelling machinery, if fitted, is not being used.

(*d*) The term ''vessel engaged in fishing'' means any vessel fishing with nets, lines, trawls or other fishing apparatus which restrict manoeuvrability, but does not include a vessel fishing with trolling lines or other fishing apparatus which do not restrict manoeuvrability.

(*e*) The word ''seaplane'' includes any aircraft designed to manoeuvre on the water.

(*f*) The term ''vessel not under command'' means a vessel which through some exceptional circumstance is unable to manoeuvre as required by these Rules and is therefore unable to keep out of the way of another vessel.

(g)   The term "vessel restricted in her ability to manoeuvre" means a vessel which from the nature of her work is restricted in her ability to manoeuvre as required by these Rules and is therefore unable to keep out of the way of another vessel.

The term "vessels restricted in their ability to manoeuvre" shall include but not be limited to:

   (i) a vessel engaged in laying, servicing or picking up a navigation mark, submarine cable or pipeline;
   (ii) a vessel engaged in dredging, surveying or underwater operations;
   (iii) a vessel engaged in replenishment or transferring persons, provisions or cargo while underway;
   (iv) a vessel engaged in the launching or recovery of aircraft;
   (v) a vessel engaged in mineclearance operations;
   (vi) a vessel engaged in a towing operation such as severely restricts the towing vessel and her tow in their ability to deviate from their course.

(h)   The term "vessel constrained by her draught" means a power-driven vessel, which because of her draught in relation to the available depth and width of navigable water, is severely restricted in her ability to deviate from the course she is following.

(i)   The word "underway" means that a vessel is not at anchor, or made fast to the shore, or aground.

(j)   The words "length" and "breadth" of a vessel mean her length overall and greatest breadth.

(k)   Vessels shall be deemed to be in sight of one another only when one can be observed visually from the other.

(l)   The term "restricted visibility" means any condition in which visibility is restricted by fog, mist, falling snow, heavy rainstorms, sandstorms or any other similar causes.

PART B. STEERING AND SAILING RULES

Section I. Conduct of vessels in any condition of visibility

RULE 4

Application

Rules in this Section apply in any condition of visibility.

Rule 5

Look-out

Every vessel shall at all times maintain a proper look-out by sight and hearing as well as by all available means appropriate in the prevailing circumstances and conditions so as to make a full appraisal of the situation and the risk of collision.

Rule 6

Safe speed

Every vessel shall at all times proceed at a safe speed so that she can take proper and effective action to avoid collision and be stopped within a distance appropriate to the prevailing circumstances and conditions.

In determining a safe speed the following factors shall be among those taken into account.

(*a*) By all vessels:
  (i) the state of visibility;
  (ii) the traffic density including concentrations of fishing vessels or any other vessels;
  (iii) the manoeuvrability of the vessel with special reference to stopping distance and turning ability in the prevailing conditions;
  (iv) at night the presence of background light such as from shore lights or from back scatter of her own lights;
  (v) the state of wind, sea and current, and the proximity of navigational hazards;
  (vi) the draught in relation to the availabe depth of water.

(*b*) Additionally, by vessels with operational radar:
  (i) the characteristics, efficiency and limitations of the radar equipment;
  (ii) any constraints imposed by the radar range scale in use;
  (iii) the effect on radar detection of the sea state, weather and other sources of interference;
  (iv) the possibility that small vessels, ice and other floating objects may not be detected by radar at an adequate range;
  (v) the number, location and movement of vessels detected by radar;
  (vi) the more exact assessment of the visibility that may be possible when radar is used to determine the range of vessels or other objects in the vicinity.

Rule 7

Risk of collision

(*a*) Every vessel shall use all available means appropriate to the prevailing circumstances and conditions to determine if risk of collision exists. If there is any doubt such risk shall be deemed to exist.

(*b*) Proper use shall be made of radar equipment if fitted and operational, including long-range scanning to obtain early warning of risk of collision and radar plotting or equivalent systematic observation of detected objects.

(*c*) Assumptions shall not be made on the basis of scanty information, especially scanty radar information.

(*d*) In determining if risk of collision exists the following considerations shall be among those taken into account:

    (i) such risk shall be deemed to exist if the compass bearing of an approaching vessel does not appreciably change;

    (ii) such risk may sometimes exist even when an appreciable bearing change is evident, particularly when approaching a very large vessel or a tow or when approaching a vessel at close range.

Rule 8

Action to avoid collision

(*a*) Any action taken to avoid collision shall, if the circumstances of the case admit, be positive, made in ample time and with due regard to the observance of good seamanship.

(*b*) Any alteration of course and/or speed to avoid collision shall, if the circumstances of the case admit, be large enough to be readily apparent to another vessel observing visually or by radar; a succession of small alterations of course and/or speed should be avoided.

(*c*) If there is sufficient sea room, alteration of course alone may be the most effective action to avoid a close-quarters situation provided that it is made in good time, is substantial and does not result in another close-quarters situation.

(*d*) Action taken to avoid collision with another vessel shall be such as to result in passing at a safe distance. The effectiveness of the action shall be carefully checked until the other vessel is finally past and clear.

(*e*) If necessary to avoid collision or allow more time to assess the situation, a vessel shall slacken her speed or take all way off by stopping or reversing her means of propulsion.

(*f*)   (i) A vessel which, by any of these Rules, is required not to impede the passage or safe passage of another vessel shall, when required by the circumstances of the case, take early action to allow sufficient sea room for the safe passage of the other vessel.

(ii)   A vessel required not to impede the passage or safe passage of another vessel is not relieved of this obligation if approaching the other vessel so as to involve risk of collision and shall, when taking action, have full regard to the action which may be required by the Rules of this Part.

(iii)   A vessel whose passage is not to be impeded remains fully obliged to comply with the Rules of this Part when the two vessels are approaching one another so as to involve risk of collision.

Rule 9

Narrow channels

(*a*) A vessel proceeding along the course of a narrow channel or fairway shall keep as near to the outer limit of the channel or fairway which lies on her starboard side as is safe and practicable.

(*b*) A vessel of less than 20 metres in length or a sailing vessel shall not impede the passage of a vessel which can safely navigate only within a narrow channel or fairway.

(*c*) A vessel engaged in fishing shall not impede the passage of any other vessel navigating within a narrow channel or fairway.

(*d*) A vessel shall not cross a narrow channel or fairway if such crossing impedes the passage of a vessel which can safely navigate only within such channel or fairway. The latter vessel may use the sound signal prescribed in Rule 34 (*d*) if in doubt as to the intention of the crossing vessel.

(*e*) (i) In a narrow channel or fairway when overtaking can take place only if the vessel to be overtaken has to take action to permit safe passing, the vessel intending to overtake shall indicate her intention by sounding the appropriate signal prescribed in Rule 34 (*c*) (i). The vessel to be overtaken shall, if in agreement, sound the appropriate signal prescribed in Rule 34 (*c*) (ii) and take steps to permit safe passing. If in doubt she may sound the signals prescribed in Rule 34 (*d*).

(ii) This rule does not relieve the overtaking vessel of her obligation under Rule 13.

(*f*) A vessel nearing a bend or an area of a narrow channel or fairway where other vessels may be obscured by an intervening obstruction shall navigate with particular alertness and caution and shall sound the appropriate signal prescribed in Rule 34 (*e*).

(*g*) Any vessel shall, if the circumstances of the case admit, avoid anchoring in a narrow channel.

RULE 10

Traffic separation schemes

(*a*) This Rule applies to traffic separation schemes adopted by the Organization and does not relieve any vessel of her obligation under any other Rule.

(*b*) A vessel using a traffic separation scheme shall:
  (i) proceed in the appropriate traffic lane in the general direction of traffic flow for that lane;
  (ii) so far as practicable keep clear of a traffic separation line or separation zone;
  (iii) normally join or leave a traffic lane at the termination of the lane, but when joining or leaving from either side shall do so at as small an angle to the general direction of traffic flow as practicable.

(*c*) A vessel shall, so far as practicable, avoid crossing traffic lanes but if obliged to do so shall cross on a heading as nearly as practicable at right angles to the general direction of traffic flow.

(*d*)   (i) A vessel shall not use an inshore traffic zone when she can safely use the appropriate traffic lane within the adjacent traffic separation scheme. However, vessels of less than 20 metres in length, sailing vessels and vessels engaged in fishing may use the inshore traffic zone.
  (ii) Notwithstanding subparagraph (*d*)(i), a vessel may use an inshore traffic zone when en route to or from a port, offshore installation or structure, pilot station or any other place situated within the inshore traffic zone or to avoid immediate danger.

(*e*) A vessel other than a crossing vessel or a vessel joining or leaving a lane shall not normally enter a separation zone or cross a separation line except:
  (i) In cases of emergency to avoid immediate danger;
  (ii) to engage in fishing within a separation zone.

(*f*) A vessel navigating in areas near the terminations of traffic separation schemes shall do so with particular caution.

(*g*) A vessel shall so far as practicable avoid anchoring in a traffic separation scheme or in areas near its terminations.

(*h*) A vessel not using a traffic separation scheme shall avoid it by as wide a margin as is practicable.

(*i*) A vessel engaged in fishing shall not impede the passage of any vessel following the traffic lane.

(*j*) A vessel of less than 20 metres in length or a sailing vessel shall not impede the safe passage of a power-driven vessel following a traffic lane.

(*k*) A vessel restricted in her ability to manoeuvre when engaged in an operation for the maintenance of safety of navigation in a traffic separation scheme is exempted from complying with this Rule to the extent necessary to carry out the operation.

(*l*) A vessel restricted in her ability to manoeuvre when engaged in an operation for the laying, servicing or picking up of a submarine cable, within a traffic separation scheme, is exempted from complying with this Rule to the extent necessary to carry out the operation.

Section II. Conduct of vessels in sight of one another

RULE 11

Application

Rules in this Section apply to vessels in sight of one another.

RULE 12

Sailing vessels

(*a*) When two sailing vessels are approaching one another, so as to involve risk of collision, one of them shall keep out of the way of the other as follows:

(i) when each has the wind on a different side, the vessel which has the wind on the port side shall keep out of the way of the other;

(ii) when both have the wind on the same side, the vessel which is to windward shall keep out of the way of the vessel which is to leeward;

(iii) if a vessel with the wind on the port side sees a vessel to windward and cannot determine with certainty whether the other vessel has the wind on the port or on the starboard side, she shall keep out of the way of the other.

(*b*) For the purposes of this Rule the windward side shall be deemed to be the side opposite to that on which the mainsail is carried or, in the case of a square-rigged vessel, the side opposite to that on which the largest fore-and-aft sail is carried.

RULE 13

Overtaking

(*a*) Notwithstanding anything contained in the Rules of Part B, Sections I and II, any vessel overtaking any other shall keep out of the way of the vessel being overtaken.

(*b*) A vessel shall be deemed to be overtaking when coming up with another vessel from a direction more than 22·5 degrees abaft her beam, that is, in such a position with reference to the vessel she is overtaking, that at night she would be able to see only the sternlight of that vessel but neither of her sidelights.

(*c*) When a vessel is in doubt as to whether she is overtaking another, she shall assume that this is the case and act accordingly.

(*d*) Any subsequent alteration of the bearing between the two vessels shall not make the overtaking vessel a crossing vessel within the meaning of these Rules or relieve her of the duty of keeping clear of the overtaken vessel until she is finally past and clear.

RULE 14

Head-on situation

(*a*) When two power-driven vessels are meeting on reciprocal or nearly reciprocal courses so as to involve risk of collision each shall alter her course to starboard so that each shall pass on the port side of the other.

(*b*) Such a situation shall be deemed to exist when a vessel sees the other ahead or nearly ahead and by night she could see the masthead lights of the other in a line or nearly in a line and/or both sidelights and by day she observes the corresponding aspect of the other vessel.

(*c*) When a vessel is in any doubt as to whether such a situation exists she shall assume that it does exist and act accordingly.

RULE 15

Crossing situation

When two power-driven vessels are crossing so as to involve risk of collision, the vessel which has the other on her own starboard side shall keep out of the way and shall, if the circumstances of the case admit, avoid crossing ahead of the other vessel.

RULE 16

Action by give-way vessel

Every vessel which is directed to keep out of the way of another vessel shall, so far as possible, take early and substantial action to keep well clear.

RULE 17

Action by stand-on vessel

(a) (i) Where one of the two vessels is to keep out of the way the other shall keep her course and speed.

(ii) The latter vessel may however take action to avoid collision by her manoeuvre alone, as soon as it becomes apparent to her that the vessel required to keep out of the way is not taking appropriate action in compliance with these Rules.

(b) When, from any cause, the vessel required to keep her course and speed finds herself so close that collision cannot be avoided by the action of the give-way vessel alone, she shall take such action as will best aid to avoid collision.

(c) A power-driven vessel which takes action in a crossing situation in accordance with sub-paragraph (a) (ii) of this Rule to avoid collision with another power-driven vessel shall, if the circumstances of the case admit, not alter course to port for a vessel on her own port side.

(d) This rule does not relieve the give-way vessel of her obligation to keep out of the way.

RULE 18

Responsibilities between vessels

Except where Rules 9, 10 and 13 otherwise require:

(a) A power-driven vessel underway shall keep out of the way of:

(i) a vessel not under command;

    (ii) a vessel restricted in her ability to manoeuvre;

    (iii) a vessel engaged in fishing;

    (iv) a sailing vessel;

(b) A sailing vessel underway shall keep out of the way of:

    (i) a vessel not under command;

    (ii) a vessel restricted in her ability to manoeuvre;

    (iii) a vessel engaged in fishing.

(c) A vessel engaged in fishing when underway shall, so far as possible, keep out of the way of:

    (i) a vessel not under command;

    (ii) a vessel restricted in her ability to manoeuvre.

(d) (i) Any vessel other than a vessel not under command or a vessel restricted in her ability to manoeuvre shall, if the circumstances of the case admit, avoid impeding the safe passage of a vessel constrained by her draught, exhibiting the signals in Rule 28.

    (ii) A vessel constrained by her draught shall navigate with particular caution having full regard to her special condition.

(e) A seaplane on the water shall, in general, keep well clear of all vessels and avoid impeding their navigation. In circumstances, however, where risk of collision exists, she shall comply with the Rules of this Part.

Section III. Conduct of vessels in restricted visibility

RULE 19

Conduct of vessels in restricted visibility

(a) This Rule applies to vessels not in sight of one another when navigating in or near an area restricted of visibility.

(b) Every vessel shall proceed at a safe speed adapted to the prevailing circumstances and conditions of restricted visibility. A power-driven vessel shall have her engines ready for immediate manoeuvre.

(c) Every vessel shall have due regard to the prevailing circumstances and conditions of restricted visibility when complying with the Rules of Section I of this Part.

(d) A vessel which detects by radar alone the presence of another vessel shall determine if a close-quarters situation is developing and/or risk of collision exists. If so, she shall take avoiding action in ample time, provided that when such action consists of an alteration of course, so far as possible the following shall be avoided.

(i) an alteration of course to port for a vessel forward of the beam, other than for a vessel being overtaken;

(ii) an alteration of course towards a vessel abeam or abaft the beam.

(*e*) Except where it has been determined that a risk of collision does not exist, every vessel which hears apparently forward of her beam the fog signal of another vessel, or which cannot avoid a close-quarters situation with another vessel forward of her beam, shall reduce her speed to the minimum at which she can be kept on her course. She shall if necessary take all her way off and in any event navigate with extreme caution until danger of collision is over.

PART C. LIGHTS AND SHAPES

RULE 20

Application

(*a*) Rules in this part shall be complied with in all weathers.

(*b*) The Rules concerning lights shall be complied with from sunset to sunrise, and during such times no other lights shall be exhibited, except such lights as cannot be mistaken for the lights specified in these Rules or do not impair their visibility or distinctive character, or interfere with the keeping of a proper look-out.

(*c*) The lights prescribed by these Rules shall, if carried, also be exhibited from sunrise to sunset in restricted visibility and may be exhibited in all other circumstances when it is deemed necessary.

(*d*) The Rules concerning shapes shall be complied with by day.

(*e*) The lights and shapes specified in these Rules shall comply with the provisions of Annex I to these Regulations.

RULE 21

Definitions

(*a*) "Masthead light" means a white light placed over the fore and aft centreline of the vessel showing an unbroken light over an arc of the horizon of 225 degrees and so fixed as to show the light from right ahead to 22·5 degrees abaft the beam on either side of the vessel.

(*b*) "Sidelights" means a green light on the starboard side and a red light on the port side each showing an unbroken light over an arc of the horizon of 112·5 degrees and so fixed as to show the light from right ahead to 22·5 degrees abaft the beam on its respective side. In a vessel of less than 20 metres in length the sidelights may be combined in one lantern carried on the fore and aft centreline of the vessel.

(c) "Sternlight" means a white light placed as nearly as practicable at the stern showing an unbroken light over an arc of the horizon of 135 degrees and so fixed as to show the light 67·5 degrees from right aft on each side of the vessel.

(d) "Towing light" means a yellow light having the same characteristics as the "sternlight" defined in paragraph (c) of this Rule.

(e) "All round light" means a light showing an unbroken light over an arc of the horizon of 360 degrees.

(f) "Flashing light" means a light flashing at regular intervals at a frequency of 120 flashes or more per minute.

Rule 22

Visibility of lights

The lights prescribed in these Rules shall have an intensity as specified in Section 8 of Annex I to these Regulations so as to be visible at the following minimum ranges:

(a) In vessels of 50 metres or more in length:
—a masthead light, 6 miles;
—a sidelight, 3 miles;
—a sternlight, 3 miles;
—a towing light, 3 miles;
—a white, red, green or yellow all-round light, 3 miles.

(b) In vessels of 12 metres or more in length but less than 50 metres in length;
—a masthead light, 5 miles; except that where the length of the vessel is less than 20 metres, 3 miles;
—a sidelight, 2 miles;
—a sternlight, 2 miles;
—a towing light, 2 miles;
—a white, red, green or yellow all-round light, 2 miles.

(c) In vessels of less than 12 metres in length:
—a masthead light, 2 miles;
—a sidelight, 1 mile;
—a sternlight, 2 miles;
—a towing light, 2 miles;
—a white, red, green or yellow all-round light, 2 miles.

(*d*) In inconspicuous, partly submerged vessels or objects being towed:
—a white all-round light, 3 miles.

RULE 23

Power-driven vessels underway

(*a*) A power-driven vessel underway shall exhibit:
   (i) a masthead light forward;
   (ii) a second masthead light abaft of and higher than the forward one; except that a vessel of less than 50 metres in length shall not be obliged to exhibit such light but may do so;
   (iii) sidelights;
   (iv) a sternlight.
(*b*) An air-cushion vessel when operating in the non-displacement mode shall, in addition to the lights prescribed in paragraph (*a*) of this Rule, exhibit an all-round flashing yellow light.
(*c*)   (i) A power-driven vessel of less than 12 metres in length may in lieu of the lights prescribed in paragraph (*a*) of this Rule exhibit an all-round white light and sidelights;
   (ii) a power-driven vessel of less than 7 metres in length whose maximum speed does not exceed 7 knots may in lieu of the lights prescribed in paragraph (*a*) of this Rule exhibit an all-round white light and shall, if practicable, also exhibit sidelights;
   (iii) the masthead light or all-round white light on a power-driven vessel of less than 12 metres in length may be displaced from the fore and aft centreline of the vessel if centreline fitting is not practicable, provided that the sidelights are combined in one lantern which shall be carried on the fore and aft centreline of the vessel or located as nearly as practicable in the same fore and aft line as the masthead light or the all-round white light.

RULE 24

Towing and pushing

(*a*) A power-driven vessel when towing shall exhibit:
   (i) instead of the lights prescribed in Rule 23 (*a*) (i) or (*a*) (ii), two masthead lights in a vertical line. When the length of the tow, measuring from the stern of the towing vessel to the

after end of the tow exceeds 200 metres, three such lights in a vertical line.

(ii) sidelights;

(iii) a sternlight;

(iv) a towing light in a vertical line above the sternlight;

(v) when the length of the tow exceeds 200 metres, a diamond shape where it can best be seen.

(b) When pushing a vessel and a vessel being pushed ahead are rigidly connected in a composite unit they shall be regarded as a power-driven vessel and exhibit the lights prescribed in Rule 23.

(c) A power-driven vessel when pushing ahead or towing alongside, except in the case of a composite unit, shall exhibit:

(i) instead of the light prescribed in Rule 23 (a) (i) or (a) (ii), two masthead lights in a vertical line;

(ii) sidelights;

(iii) a sternlight.

(d) A power-driven vessel to which paragraph (a) or (c) of this Rule applies shall also comply with Rule 23 (a) (ii).

(e) A vessel or object being towed, other than those mentioned in paragraph (g) of this Rule, shall exhibit:

(i) sidelights;

(ii) a sternlight;

(iii) when the length of the tow exceeds 200 metres, a diamond shape where it can best be seen.

(f) Provided that any number of vessels being towed alongside or pushed in a group shall be lighted as one vessel.

(i) a vessel being pushed ahead, not being part of a composite unit, shall exhibit at the forward end, sidelights;

(ii) a vessel being towed alongside shall exhibit a sternlight and at the forward end, sidelights.

(g) An inconspicuous, partly submerged vessel or object, or combination of such vessels or objects being towed, shall exhibit:

(i) if it is less than 25 metres in breadth, one all-round white light at or near the forward end and one at or near the after end except that dracones need not exhibit a light at or near the forward end;

(ii) if it is 25 metres or more in breadth, two additional all-round white lights at or near the extremities of its breadth;

(iii) if it exceeds 100 metres in length, additional all-round white lights between the lights prescribed in sub-paragraphs (i) and (ii) so that the distance between the lights shall not exceed 100 metres;

(iv) a diamond shape at or near the aftermost extremity of the last vessel or object being towed and if the length of the tow exceeds 200 metres an additional diamond shape where it can best be seen and located as far forward as is practicable.

(*h*) Where from any sufficient cause it is impracticable for a vessel or object being towed to exhibit the lights or shapes prescribed in paragraph (*e*) or (*g*) of this rule, all possible measures shall be taken to light the vessel or object towed or at least to indicate the presence of such vessel or object.

(*i*) Where from any sufficient cause it is impracticable for a vessel not normally engaged in towing operations to display the lights prescribed in paragraph (*a*) or (*c*) of this Rule, such vessel shall not be required to exhibit those lights when engaged in towing another vessel in distress or otherwise in need of assistance. All possible measures shall be taken to indicate the nature of the relationship between the towing vessel and the vessel being towed as authorized by Rule 36, in particular by illuminating the towline.

RULE 25

Sailing vessels underway and vessels under oars

(*a*)   A sailing vessel underway shall exhibit:
(i) sidelights;
(ii) a sternlight.

(*b*) In a sailing vessel of less than 20 metres in length the lights prescribed in paragraph (*a*) of this Rule may be combined in one lantern carried at or near the top of the mast where it can best be seen.

(*c*) A sailing vessel underway may, in addition to the lights prescribed in paragraph (*a*) of this Rule, exhibit at or near the top of the mast, where they can best be seen, two all-round lights in a vertical line, the upper being red and the lower green, but these lights shall not be exhibited in conjunction with the combined lantern permitted by paragraph (*b*) of this Rule.

(*d*)   (i)   A sailing vessel of less than 7 metres in length shall, if practicable, exhibit the lights prescribed in paragraphs (*a*) or (*b*) of this Rule, but if she does not, she shall have ready at hand an electric torch or lighted lantern showing a white light which shall be exhibited in sufficient time to prevent collision.

(ii)   A vessel under oars may exhibit the lights prescribed in this Rule for sailing vessels, but if she does not, she shall have ready at hand an electric torch or lighted lantern showing a white light which shall be exhibited in sufficient time to prevent collision.

(*e*) A vessel proceeding under sail when also being propelled by machinery shall exhibit forward where it can best be seen a conical shape, apex downwards.

Rule 26

Fishing vessels

(*a*) A vessel engaged in fishing, whether underway or at anchor, shall exhibit only the lights and shapes prescribed in this Rule.

(*b*) A vessel when engaged in trawling, by which is meant the dragging through the water of a dredge net or other apparatus used as a fishing appliance, shall exhibit:

> (i) two all-round lights in a vertical line, the upper being green and the lower white, or a shape consisting of two cones with their apexes together in a vertical line one above the other.

> (ii) a masthead light abaft and higher than the all-round green light; a vessel of less than 50 metres in length shall not be obliged to exhibit such a light but may do so;

> (iii) when making way through the water, in addition to the lights prescribed in this paragraph, sidelights and a sternlight.

(*c*) A vessel engaged in fishing, other than trawling, shall exhibit:

> (i) two all-round lights in a vertical line, the upper being red and the lower white, or a shape consisting of two cones with apexes together in a vertical line one above the other.

> (ii) when there is outlying gear extending more than 150 metres horizontally from the vessel, an all-round white light or a cone apex upwards in the direction of the gear;

> (iii) when making way through the water, in addition to the lights prescribed in this paragraph, sidelights and a sternlight.

(*d*) The additional signals described in Annex II to these Regulations apply to a vessel engaged in fishing in close proximity to other vessels engaged in fishing.

(*e*) A vessel when not engaged in fishing shall not exhibit the lights or shapes prescribed in this Rule, but only those prescribed for a vessel of her length.

Rule 27

Vessels not under command or restricted in their ability to manoeuvre

(*a*)   A vessel not under command shall exhibit:
   (i) two all-round red lights in a vertical line where they can best be seen;
   (ii) two balls or similar shapes in a vertical line where they can best be seen;
   (iii) when making way through the water, in addition to the lights prescribed in this paragraph, sidelights and a sternlight.

(*b*)   A vessel restricted in her ability to manoeuvre, except a vessel engaged in mineclearance operations, shall exhibit:

   (i) three all-round lights in a vertical line where they can best be seen. The highest and lowest of these lights shall be red and the middle light shall be white;

   (ii) three shapes in a vertical line where they can best be seen. The highest and lowest of these shapes shall be balls and the middle one a diamond;

   (iii) when making way through the water, a masthead light or lights, sidelights and a sternlight, in addition to the lights prescribed in sub-pargraph (i);

   (iv) when at anchor, in addition to the lights or shapes prescribed in sub-paragraphs (i) and (ii), the light, lights or shape prescribed in Rule 30.

(*c*) A power-driven vessel engaged in a towing operation such as severely restricts the towing vessel and her tow in their ability to deviate from their course shall, in addition to the lights or shapes prescribed in Rule 24 (*a*), exhibit the lights or shapes prescribed in sub-paragraphs (*b*) (i) and (ii) of this Rule.

(*d*) A vessel engaged in dredging or underwater operations, when restricted in her ability to manoeuvre, shall exhibit the lights and shapes prescribed in sub-paragraphs (*b*) (i), (ii) and (iii) of this Rule and shall in addition, when obstruction exists, exhibit:

   (i) two all-round red lights or two balls in a vertical line to indicate the side on which the obstruction exists;

   (ii) two all-round green lights or two diamonds in a vertical line to indicate the side on which another vessel may pass;

   (iii) when at anchor, the lights or shapes prescribed in this paragraph instead of the lights or shape prescribed in Rule 30.

(*e*) Whenever the size of a vessel engaged in diving operations makes it impracticable to exhibit all lights and shapes prescribed in paragraph (*d*) of this Rule, the following shall be exhibited:
    (i) three all-round lights in a vertical line where they can best be seen. The highest and lowest of these lights shall be red and the middle light shall be white;
    (ii) a rigid replica of the International Code flag ''A'' not less than 1 metre in height. Measures shall be taken to ensure its all round visibility.

(*f*) A vessel engaged in mineclearance operations shall in addition to the lights prescribed for a power-driven vesssel in Rule 23 or to the lights or shape prescribed for a vessel at anchor in Rule 30 as appropriate, exhibit three all-round green lights or three balls. One of these lights or shapes shall be exhibited near the foremast head and one at each end of the fore yard. These lights or shapes indicate that it is dangerous for another vessel to approach within 1000 metres of the mineclearance vessel.

(*g*) Vessels of less than 12 metres in length, except those engaged in diving operations, shall not be required to exhibit the lights and shapes prescribed in this Rule.

(*h*) The signals prescribed in this Rule are not signals of vessels in distress and requiring assistance. Such signals are contained in Annex IV to these regulations.

Rule 28

Vessels constrained by their draught

A vessel constrained by her draught may, in addition to the lights prescribed for power-driven vessels in Rule 23, exhibit where they can best be seen three all-round red lights in a vertical line, or a cylinder.

Rule 29

Pilot vessels

(*a*) A vessel engaged on pilotage duty shall exhibit:
    (i) at or near the masthead, two all-round lights in a vertical line, the upper being white and the lower red;
    (ii) when underway, in addition, sidelights and a sternlight;
    (iii) when at anchor, in addition to the lights prescribed in sub-paragraph (i), the light, lights or shape prescribed in Rule 30 for vessels at anchor.

(*b*) A pilot vessel when not engaged on pilotage duty shall exhibit the lights or shapes prescribed for a similar vessel of her length.

RULE 30

Anchored vessels and vessels aground

(*a*) A vessel at anchor shall exhibit where it can best be seen:
  (i) in the fore part, an all-round white light or one ball;
  (ii) at or near the stern and at a lower level than the light prescribed in sub-paragraph (i), an all-round white light.

(*b*) A vessel of less than 50 metres in length may exhibit an all-round white light where it can best be seen instead of the lights prescribed in paragraph (*a*) of this Rule.

(*c*) A vessel at anchor may, and a vessel of 100 metres and more in length shall, also use the available working or equivalent lights to illuminate her decks.

(*d*) A vessel aground shall exhibit the lights prescribed in paragraphs (*a*) or (*b*) of this Rule and in addition, where they can best be seen:
  (i) two all-round red lights in a vertical line;
  (ii) three balls in a vertical line.

(*e*) A vessel of less than 7 metres in length, when at anchor, not in or near a narrow channel, fairway or anchorage, or where other vessels normally navigate, shall not be required to exhibit the lights or shapes prescribed in paragraphs (*a*) and (*b*) of this Rule.

(*f*) A vessel of less than 12 metres in length, when aground, shall not be required to exhibit the lights or shapes prescribed in sub-paragraphs (*d*) (i) and (ii) of this Rule.

RULE 31

Seaplanes

Where it is impracticable for a seaplane to exhibit lights and shapes of the characteristics or in the positions prescribed in the Rules of this Part she shall exhibit lights and shapes as closely similar in characteristics and position as is possible.

PART D—SOUND AND LIGHT SIGNALS

RULE 32

Definitions

(*a*) The word "whistle" means any sound signalling appliance capable of producing the prescribed blasts and which complies with the specifications in Annex III to these regulations.

(*b*) The term "short blast" means a blast of about one second's duration.

(*c*) The term "prolonged blast" means a blast of from four to six seconds' duration.

RULE 33

Equipment for sound signals

(*a*) A vessel of 12 metres or more in length shall be provided with a whistle and a bell and a vessel of 100 metres or more in length shall, in addition, be provided with a gong, the tone and sound of which cannot be confused with that of the bell. The whistle, bell and gong shall comply with the specifications in Annex III to these regulations. The bell or gong or both may be replaced by other equipment having the same respective sound characteristics, provided that manual sounding of the prescribed signals shall always be possible.

(*b*) A vessel of less than 12 metres in length shall not be obliged to carry the sound signalling appliances prescribed in paragraph (*a*) of this Rule but if she does not, she shall be provided with some other means of making an efficient sound signal.

RULE 34

Manoeuvring and warning signals

(*a*) When vessels are in sight of one another, a power-driven vessel underway, when manoeuvring as authorized or required by these Rules, shall indicate that manoeuvre by the following signals on her whistle:

—one short blast to mean "I am altering my course to starboard";

—two short blasts to mean "I am altering my course to port";

—three short blasts to mean "I am operating astern propulsion".

(*b*) Any vessel may supplement the whistle signals prescribed in paragraph (*a*) of this Rule by light signals, repeated as appropriate, whilst the manoeuvre is being carried out:

> (i) these light signals shall have the following significance:
> —one flash to mean "I am altering my course to starboard";
> —two flashes to mean "I am altering my course to port";
> —three flashes to mean "I am operating astern propulsion".

> (ii) the duration of each flash shall be about one second, the interval between flashes shall be about one second, and the interval between successive signals shall be not less than ten seconds;

> (iii) the light used for this signal shall, if fitted, be an all-round white light, visible at a minimum range of 5 miles, and shall comply with the provisions of Annex I to these Regulations.

(*c*) When in sight of one another in a narrow channel or fairway:

> (i) a vessel intending to overtake another shall in compliance with Rule 9 (*e*) (i) indicate her intention by the following signals on her whistle:
> —two prolonged blasts followed by one short blast to mean "I intend to overtake you on your starboard side";
> —two prolonged blasts followed by two short blasts to mean "I intend to overtake you on your port side".

> (ii) the vessel about to be overtaken when acting in accordance with Rule 9 (*e*) (i) shall indicate her agreement by the following signal on her whistle:
> —one prolonged, one short, one prolonged and one short blast, in that order.

(*d*) When vessels in sight of one another are approaching each other and from any cause either vessel fails to understand the intentions or actions of the other, or is in doubt whether sufficient action is being taken by the other to avoid collision, the vessel in doubt shall immediately indicate such doubt by giving at least five short and rapid blasts on the whistle. Such signal may be supplemented by a light signal of at least five short and rapid flashes.

(*e*) A vessel nearing a bend or an area of a channel or fairway where other vessels may be obscured by an intervening obstruction shall sound one prolonged blast. Such signal shall be answered with a prolonged blast by any approaching vessel that may be within hearing around the bend or behind the intervening obstruction.

(*f*) If whistles are fitted on a vessel at a distance apart of more than 100 metres, one whistle only shall be used for giving manoeuvring and warning signals.

Rule 35

Sound signals in restricted visibility

In or near an area of restricted visibility, whether by day or night, the signals prescribed in this Rule shall be used as follows:

(*a*) A power-driven vessel making way through the water shall sound at intervals of not more than 2 minutes one prolonged blast.

(*b*) A power-driven vessel underway but stopped and making no way through the water shall sound at intervals of not more than 2 minutes two prolonged blasts in succession with an interval of about 2 seconds between them.

(*c*) A vessel not under command, a vessel restricted in her ability to manoeuvre, a vessel constrained by her draught, a sailing vessel, a vessel engaged in fishing and a vessel engaged in towing or pushing another vessel shall, instead of the signals prescribed in paragraphs (*a*) or (*b*) of this Rule, sound at intervals of not more than 2 minutes three blasts in succession, namely one prolonged followed by two short blasts.

(*d*) A vessel engaged in fishing, when at anchor, and a vessel restricted in her ability to manoeuvre when carrying out her work at anchor, shall instead of the signals prescribed in paragraph (*g*) of this Rule, sound the signal prescribed in paragraph (*c*) of this Rule.

(*e*) A vessel towed or if more than one vessel is towed the last vessel of the tow, if manned, shall at intervals of not more than 2 minutes sound four blasts in succession, namely one prolonged followed by three short blasts. When practicable, this signal shall be made immediately after the signal made by the towing vessel.

(*f*) When a pushing vessel and a vessel being pushed ahead are rigidly connected in a composite unit they shall be regarded as a power-driven vessel and shall give the signals prescribed in paragraphs (*a*) or (*b*) of this Rule.

(*g*) A vessel at anchor shall at intervals of not more than one minute ring the bell rapidly for about 5 seconds. In a vessel of 100 metres or more in length the bell shall be sounded in the forepart of the vessel and immediately after the ringing of the bell the gong shall be sounded rapidly for about 5 seconds in the after part of the vessel. A vessel at anchor may in addition sound three blasts in succession, namely one short, one prolonged and one short blast, to give warning of her position and of the possibility of collision to an approaching vessel.

(h) A vessel aground shall give the bell signal and if required the gong signal prescribed in paragraph (g) of this Rule and shall, in addition, give three separate and distinct strokes on the bell immediately before and after the rapid ringing of the bell. A vessel aground may in addition sound an appropriate whistle signal.

(i) A vessel of less than 12 metres in length shall not be obliged to give the above-mentioned signals but, if she does not, shall make some other efficient sound signal at intervals of not more than 2 minutes.

(j) A pilot vessel when engaged on pilotage duty may in addition to the signals prescribed in paragraphs (a), (b) or (g) of this Rule sound an identity signal consisting of four short blasts.

Rule 36

Signals to attract attention

If necessary to attract the attention of another vessel any vessel may make light or sound signals that cannot be mistaken for any signal authorized elsewhere in these Rules, or may direct the beam of her searchlight in the direction of the danger, in such a way as not to embarrass any vessel. Any light to attract the attention of another vessel shall be such that it cannot be mistaken for any aid to navigation. For the purpose of this Rule the use of high intensity intermittent or revolving lights, such as strobe lights, shall be avoided.

Rule 37

Distress signals

When a vessel is in distress and requires assistance she shall use or exhibit the signals prescribed in Annex IV to these Regulations.

PART E—EXEMPTIONS

Rule 38

Exemptions

Any vessel (or class of vessels) provided that she complies with the requirements of the International Regulations for

Preventing Collisions at Sea, 1960, the keel off which is laid or which is at a corresponding stage of construction before the entry into force of these Regulations may be exempted from compliance therewith as follows:

(*a*)   The installation of lights with ranges prescribed in Rule 22, until four years after the date of entry into force of these Regulations.

(*b*)   The installation of lights with colour specifications as prescribed in Section 7 of Annex I to these Regulations, until four years after the date of entry into force of these Regulations.

(*c*)   The repositioning of lights as a result of conversion from Imperial to metric units and rounding off measurement figures, permanent exemption.

(*d*)   (i)   The repositioning of masthead lights on vessels of less than 150 metres in length, resulting from the prescriptions of Section 3 (*a*) of Annex I to these Regulations, permanent exemption.

      (ii)   The repositioning of masthead lights on vessels of 150 metres or more in length, resulting from the prescriptions of Section 3 (*a*) of Annex I to these Regulations, until nine years after the date of entry into force of these Regulations.

(*e*)   The repositioning of masthead lights resulting from the prescriptions of Section 2 (*b*) of Annex I , to these Regulations until nine years after the date of entry into force of these Regulations.

(*f*)   The repositioning of sidelights resulting from the prescriptions of Sections 2 (*g*) and 3 (*b*) of Annex I to these Regulations until nine years after the date of entry into force of these Regulations

(*g*)   The requirements for sound signal appliances prescribed in Annex III, to these Regulations until nine years after the date of entry into force of these Regulations.

(*h*)   The repositioning of all-round lights resulting from the prescription of Section 9 (*b*) of Annex I to these Regulations, permanent exemption.

ANNEX I

Positioning and technical details of lights and shapes

1.   *Definition.*
The term "height above the hull" means height above the

uppermost continuous deck. This height shall be measured from the position vertically beneath the location of the light.

2. *Vertical positioning and spacing of lights.*

(*a*) On a power-driven vessel of 20 metres or more in length the masthead lights shall be placed as follows:

> (i) the forward masthead light, or if only one masthead light is carried, then that light, at a height above the hull of not less than 6 metres, and, if the breadth of the vessel exceeds 6 metres, then at a height above the hull not less than such breadth, so however that the light need not be placed at a greater height above the hull than 12 metres;
>
> (ii) when two masthead lights are carried the after one shall be at least 4·5 metres vertically higher than the forward one.

(*b*) The vertical separation of masthead lights of power-driven vessels shall be such that in all normal conditions of trim the after light will be seen over and separate from the forward light at a distance of 1,000 metres from the stem when viewed from sea level.

(*c*) The masthead light of a power-driven vessel of 12 metres but less than 20 metres in length shall be placed at a height above the gunwale of not less than 2·5 metres.

(*d*) A power-driven vessel of less than 12 metres in length may carry the uppermost light at a height of less than 2·5 metres above the gunwale. When, however, a masthead light is carried in addition to sidelights and a sternlight or the all-round light prescribed in Rule 23 (*c*) (i) is carried in addition to sidelights, then such masthead light or all-round light shall be carried at least 1 metre higher than the sidelights.

(*e*) One of the two or three masthead lights prescribed for a power-driven vessel when engaged in towing or pushing another vessel shall be placed in the same position as either the forward masthead light or the after masthead light; provided that, if carried on the aftermast, the lowest after masthead light shall be at least 4·5 metres vertically higher than the forward masthead light.

(*f*) (i) The masthead light or lights prescribed in Rule 23 (*a*) shall be so placed as to be above and clear of all other lights and obstructions except as described in sub-paragraph (ii).

> (ii) When it is impracticable to carry the all-round light prescribed by Rule 27 (*b*) (i) or Rule 28 below the masthead lights, they may be carried above the after masthead light(s) or vertically in between the forward masthead light(s) and after masthead light(s), provided that in the latter case the requirement of Section 3 (*c*) of this Annex shall be complied with.

(*g*) The sidelights of a power-driven vessel shall be placed at a height above the hull not greater than three-quarters of that of the forward masthead light. They shall not be so low as to be interfered with by deck lights.

(*h*) The sidelights, if in a combined lantern and carried on a power-driven vessel of not less than 20 metres in length, shall be placed not less than 1 metre below the masthead light.

(*i*) When the Rules prescribe two or three lights to be carried in a vertical line, they shall be spaced as follows:

(i) on a vessel of 20 metres in length or more such lights shall be spaced not less than 2 metres apart, and the lowest of these lights shall, except where a towing light is required, be placed at a height of not less than 4 metres above the hull.

(ii) on a vessel of less than 20 metres in length such lights shall be spaced not less than 1 metre apart, and the lowest of these lights shall, except where a towing light is required, be placed at a height of not less than 2 metres above the gunwale.

(iii) when three lights are carried they shall be equally spaced.

(*j*) The lower of the two all-round lights prescribed for a vessel when engaged in fishing shall be at a height above the sidelights not less than twice the distance between the two vertical lights.

(*k*) The forward anchor light prescribed in Rule 30 (*a*) (i), when two are carried, shall not be less than 4·5 metres above the after one. On a vessel of 50 metres or more in length this forward anchor light shall be placed at a height of not less than 6 metres above the hull.

3.   *Horizontal positioning and spacing of lights.*

(*a*) When two masthead lights are prescribed for a power-driven vessel, the horizontal distance between them shall not be less than one-half of the length of the vessel but need not be more than 100 metres. The forward light shall be placed not more than one-quarter of the length of the vessel from the stem.

(*b*) On a power-driven vessel of 20 metres or more in length the sidelights shall not be placed in front of the forward masthead lights. They shall be placed at or near the side of the vessel.

(*c*) When the lights prescribed in Rule 27 (*b*) (i) or Rule 28 are placed vertically between the forward masthead light(s) and the after masthead light(s) these all-round lights shall be placed at a horizontal distance of not less than 2 metres from the fore and aft centreline of the vessel in the athwartship direction.

(*d*) When only one masthead light is prescribed for a power-driven vessel, this light shall be exhibited forward of amidships, except that a vessel of less than 20 metres in length need not exhibit this light forward of amidships but shall exhibit it as far forward as is practicable.

4. *Details of location of direction-indicating lights for fishing vessels, dredgers and vessels engaged in underwater operations.*

(*a*) The light indicating the direction of the outlying gear from a vessel engaged in fishing as prescribed in Rule 26 (*c*) (ii) shall be placed at a horizontal distance of not less than 2 metres and not more than 6 metres away from the two all-round red and white lights. This light shall be placed not higher than the all-round white light prescribed in Rule 26 (*c*) (i) and not lower than the sidelights.

(*b*) The lights and shapes on a vessel engaged in dredging or underwater operations to indicate the obstructed side and/or the side on which it is safe to pass, as prescribed in Rule 27 (*d*) (i) and (ii), shall be placed at the maximum practical horizontal distance, but in no case less than 2 metres, from the lights or shapes prescribed in Rule 27 (*b*) (i) and (ii). In no case shall the upper of these lights or shapes be at a greater height than the lower of the three lights or shapes prescribed in Rule 27 (*b*) (i) and (ii).

5. *Screens for sidelights.*

The sidelights of vessels of 20 metres or more in length shall be fitted with inboard screens painted matt black, and meeting the requirements of Section 9 of this Annex. On vessels of less than 20 metres in length the sidelights, if necessary to meet the requirements of Section 9 of this Annex, shall be fitted with inboard matt black screens. With a combined lantern, using a single vertical filament and a very narrow division between the green and red sections, external screens need not be fitted.

6. *Shapes.*

(*a*) Shapes shall be black and of the following sizes:
  (i) a ball shall have a diameter of not less than 0·6 metre;
  (ii) a cone shall have a base diameter of not less than 0·6 metre and a height equal to its diameter;
  (iii) a cylinder shall have a diameter of at least 0·6 metre and a height of twice its diameter;
  (iv) a diamond shape shall consist of two cones as defined in (ii) above having a common base.

(*b*) The vertical distance between shapes shall be at least 1·5 metres.

(*c*) In a vessel of less than 20 metres in length shapes of lesser dimensions but commensurate with the size of the vessel may be used and the distance apart may be correspondingly reduced.

7. *Colour specification of lights.*

The chromaticity of all navigation lights shall conform to the following standards, which lie with the boundaries of the area of the diagram specified for each colour by the International Commission on Illumination (CIE).

The boundaries of the area for each colour are given by indicating the corner co-ordinates, which are as follows:

(i) *White*

x	0·525	0·525	0·452	0·310	0·310	0·443
y	0·382	0·440	0·440	0·348	0·283	0·382

(ii) *Green*

x	0·028	0·009	0·300	0·203
y	0·385	0·723	0·511	0·356

(iii) *Red*

x	0·680	0·660	0·735	0·721
y	0·320	0·320	0·265	0·259

(iv) *Yellow*

x	0·612	0·618	0·575	0·575
y	0·382	0·382	0·425	0·406

8.   *Intensity of lights.*

(*a*) The minimum luminous intensity of lights shall be calculated by using the formula:

$$I = 3·43 \times 10^6 \times T \times D^2 \times K^D$$

where I is luminous intensity in candelas under service conditions,
   T is threshold factor 2×10^{-7} lux,
   D is range of visibility (luminous range) of the light in nautical miles,
   K is atmospheric transmissivity.
   For prescribed lights the value of K shall be 0·8, corresponding to
      a meteorological visbility of approximately 13 nautical miles.

(*b*) A selection of figures derived from the formula is given in the following table:

Range of visibility (luminous range) of light in nautical miles D	Luminous intensity of light in candelas for K = 0·8 I
1	0·9
2	4·3
3	12
4	27
5	52
6	94

Note: The maximum luminous intensity of navigation lights should be limited to avoid undue glare. This shall not be achieved by a variable control of the luminous intensity.

9.   *Horizontal sectors.*

(*a*) (i) In the forward direction, sidelights as fitted on the vessel shall show the minimum required intensities. The intensities must decrease to reach practical cut-off between 1 degree and 3 degrees outside the prescribed sectors.

(ii) For sternlights and masthead lights and at 22·5 degrees abaft the beam for sidelights, the minimum required intensities shall be maintained over the arc of the horizon upto 5 degrees within the limits of the sectors prescribed in Rule 21. From 5 degrees within the prescribed sectors the intensity may decrease by 50 per cent up to the prescribed limits, it shall decrease steadily to reach practical cut-off at not more than 5 degrees outside the prescribed sectors.

(*b*) (i) All-round lights shall be so located as not to be obscured by masts, topmasts or structures within angular sectors of more than 6 degrees, except anchor lights prescribed in Rule 30, which need not be placed at an impractical height above the hull.

(*b*) (ii) If it is impracticable to comply with paragraph (*b*) (i) of this section by exhibiting only one all-round light, two all-round lights shall be used suitably positioned or screened so that they appear, as far as practicable, as one light at a distance of one mile.

10.   *Vertical sectors.*

(*a*) The vertical sectors of electric lights as fitted, with the exception of lights on sailing vessels underway shall ensure that:

      (i) at least the required minimum intensity is maintained at all angles from 5 degrees above to 5 degrees below the horizontal;

      (ii) at least 60 per cent of the required minimum intensity is maintained from 7·5 degrees above to 7·5 degrees below the horizontal;

(*b*) In the case of sailing vessels underway the vertical sectors of electric lights as fitted shall ensure that:

      (i) at least the required minimum intensity is maintained at all angles from 5 degrees above to 5 degrees below the horizontal;

      (ii) at least 50 per cent of the required minimum intensity is maintained from 25 degrees above to 25 degrees below the horizontal.

(*c*) In the case of lights other than electric these specifications shall be met as closely as possible.

11.   *Intensity of non-electric lights.*

Non-electric lights shall so far as practicable comply with the minimum intensities, as specified in the Table given in Section 8 of this Annex.

12. Manoeuvring light.

Notwithstanding the provisions of paragraph 2 (*f*) of this Annex the manoeuvring light described in Rule 34 (*b*) shall be placed in the same fore and aft vertical plane as the masthead light or lights and, where practicable, at a minimum height of 2 metres vertically above the forward masthead light, provided that it shall be carried not less than 2 metres vertically above or below the after masthead light. On a vessel where only one masthead light is carried, the manoeuvring light, if fitted, shall be carried where it can best be seen, not less than 2 metres vertically apart from the masthead light.

13. High speed craft.

The masthead light of high speed craft with a length to breadth ratio of less than 3.0 may be placed at a height related to the breadth of the craft lower than that prescribed in paragraph 2(*a*) (i) of this Annex, provided that the base angle of the isosceles triangles formed by the sidelights and masthead light when seen in end elevation is not less than 27°.

14. Approval.

The construction of lights and shapes and the installation of lights on board the vessel shall be to the satisfaction of the appropriate authority of the State whose flag the vessel is entitled to fly.

ANNEX II

Additional signals for fishing vessels fishing in close proximity

1. General.

The lights mentioned herein shall, if exhibited in pursuance of Rule 26 (*d*) be placed where they can best be seen. They shall be at least 0·9 metre apart but at a lower level than lights prescribed in Rule 26 (*b*) (i) and (*c*) (i). The lights shall be visible all round the horizon at a distance of at least 1 mile but at a lesser distance than the lights prescribed by these Rules for fishing vessels.

2. Signals for trawlers.

(*a*) Vessels of 20 metres or more in length when engaged in trawling, whether using demersal or pelagic gear, shall exhibit:
    (i) when shooting their nets:
        two white lights in a vertical line;
    (ii) when hauling their nets:
        one white light over one red light in a vertical line;
    (iii) when the net has come fast upon an obstruction:
        two red lights in a vertical line.

(b) Each vessel of 20 metres or more in length engaged in pair trawling shall exhibit:
  (i) by night, a searchlight directed forward and in the direction of the other vessel of the pair;
  (ii) when shooting or hauling their nets or when their nets have come fast upon an obstruction, the lights prescribed in 2 (a) above.

(c) A vessel of less than 20 metres in length engaged in trawling, whether using demersal or pelagic gear or engaged in pair trawling, may exhibit the lights prescribed in paragraphs (a) or (b) of this section as appropriate.

3. *Signals for purse seiners.*
Vessels engaged in fishing with purse seine gear may exhibit two yellow lights in a vertical line. These lights shall flash alternately every second and with equal light and occultation duration. These lights may be exhibited only when the vessel is hampered by its fishing gear.

ANNEX III

Technical details of sound signal appliances

1. *Whistles.*
  (a) *Frequencies and range of audibility.*
The fundamental frequency of the signal shall lie within the range 70-700Hz.
The range of audibility of the signal from a whistle shall be determined by those frequencies, which may include the fundamental and/or one or more higher freqencies, which lie within the range 180-700 Hz (± 1 per cent) and which provide the sound pressure levels specified in paragraph 1 (c) below.
  (b) *Limits of fundamental frequencies.*
To ensure a wide variety of whistle characteristics, the fundamental frequency of a whistle shall be between the following limits:
  (i) 70-200 Hz, for a vessel 200 metres or more in length;
  (ii) 130-350 Hz, for a vessel 75 metres but less than 200 metres in length;
  (iii) 250-700 Hz, for a vessel less than 75 metres in length.
  (c) *Sound signal intensity and range of audibility.*
A whistle fitted in a vessel shall provide, in the direction of maximum intensity of the whistle and at a distance of 1 metre from it, a sound pressure level in at least one 1/3rd-octave band within the range of frequencies 180-700 Hz (± 1 per cent) of not less than the appropriate figure given in the following table.

Length of vessel in metres	1/3rd octave band level at 1 metre in dB referred to 2×10^{-5} N/m²	Audibility range in nautical miles
200 or more	143	2
75 but less than 200	138	1·5
20 but less than 75	130	1
Less than 20	120	0·5

The range of audibility in the table above is for information and is approximately the range at which a whistle may be heard on its forward axis with 90 per cent probability in conditions of still air on board a vessel having average background noise level at the listening posts (taken to be 68 dB in the octave band centred on 250 Hz and 63 dB in the octave band centred on 500 HZ).

In practice the range in which a whistle may be heard is extremely variable and depends critically on weather conditions; the values given can be regarded as typical but under conditions of strong wind or high ambient noise level at the listening post the range may be much reduced.

(d) *Directional properties.*

The sound pressure level of a directional whistle shall be not more than 4 dB below the prescribed sound pressure level on the axis at any direction in the horizontal plane within ± 45 degrees of the axis. The sound pressure level at any other direction in the horizontal plane shall be not more than 10 dB below the prescribed sound pressure level on the axis, so that the range in any direction will be at least half the range on the forward axis. The sound pressure level shall be measured in that 1/3rd-octave band which determines the audibility range.

(e) *Positioning of whistles.*

When a directional whistle is to be used as the only whistle on a vessel, it shall be installed with its maximum intensity directed straight ahead.

A whistle shall be placed as high as practicable on a vessel, in order to reduce interception of the emitted sound by obstructions and also to minimize hearing damage risk to personnel. The sound pressure level of the vessel's own signal at listening posts shall not exceed 110 dB (A) and so far as practicable should not exceed 100 dB (A).

(*f*) *Fitting of more than one whistle.*

If whistles are fitted at a distance apart of more than 100 metres, it shall be so arranged that they are not sounded simultaneously.

(*g*) *Combined whistle systems.*

If due to the presence of obstructions the sound field of a single whistle or of one of the whistles referred to in paragraph 1 (*f*) above is likely to have a zone of greatly reduced signal level, it is recommended that a combined whistle system be fitted so as to overcome this reduction. For the purposes of the Rules a combined whistle system is to be regarded as a single whistle. The whistles of a combined system shall be located at a distance apart of not more than 100 metres and arranged to be sounded simultaneously. The frequency of any one whistle shall differ from those of the others by at least 10 Hz.

2. *Bell or gong.*

(*a*) *Intensity of signal.*

A bell or gong, or other device having similar sound characteristics shall produce a sound pressure level of not less than 110 dB at a distance of 1 metre from it.

(*b*) *Construction.*

Bells and gongs shall be made of corrosion-resistant material and designed to give a clear tone. The diameter of the mouth of the bell shall be not less than 300 mm for vessels of 20 metres or more in length, and shall be not less than 200 mm for vessels of 12 metres or more but of less than 20 metres in length. Where practicable, a power-driven bell striker is recommended to ensure constant force but manual operation shall be possible. The mass of the striker shall be not less than 3 per cent of the mass of the bell.

3. *Approval.*

The construction of sound signal appliances, their performance and their installation on board the vessel shall be to the satisfaction of the appropriate authority of the State whose flag the vessel is entitled to fly.

ANNEX IV

Distress signals

1.   The following signals, used or exhibited either together or separately, indicate distress and need of assistance:

(a)   a gun or other explosive signal fired at intervals of about a minute;

(b) a continuous sounding with any fog-signalling apparatus;
(c) rockets or shells, throwing red stars fired one at a time at short intervals;
(d) a signal made by radiotelegraphy or by any other signalling method consisting of the group . . . – – – . . . (SOS) in the Morse Code;
(e) a signal sent by radiotelephony consisting of the spoken word ''Mayday'';
(f) the International Code Signal of distress indicated by N.C.;
(g) a signal consisting of a square flag having above or below it a ball or anything resembling a ball;
(h) flames on the vessel (as from a burning tar barrel, oil barrel, etc.);
(i) a rocket parachute flare or a hand flare showing a red light;
(j) a smoke signal giving off orange-coloured smoke;
(k) slowly and repeatedly raising and lowering arms outstretched to each side;
(l) the radiotelegraph alarm signal;
(m) the radiotelephone alarm signal;
(n) signals transmitted by emergency position-indicating radio beacons.
(o) approved signals transmitted by radiocommunication systems, including survival craft radar transponders.

2.   The use or exhibition of any of the foregoing signals except for the purpose of indicating distress and need of assistance and the use of other signals which may be confused with any of the above signals is prohibited.

3.   Attention is drawn to the relevant sections of the International Code of Signals, the Merchant Ship Search and Rescue Manual and the following signals:
(a) a piece of orange coloured canvas with either a black square and circle or other appropriate symbol (for identification from the air);
(b) a dye marker.

THE STEERING AND SAILING RULES

Rules 4 to 19

Safe Speed. Every vessel is required to proceed at a safe speed in any condition of visibility. In clear visibility full speed would normally be accepted as safe in the open sea but not in areas where there are numerous small craft or where the water is relatively very shallow. In restricted visibility a power-driven vessel is required to have her engines ready for immediate manoeuvre which usually means that the speed will have to be reduced. A safe speed in some circumstances may be considered to be a speed at which the vessel could be stopped within half the range of visibility but a vessel making proper use of radar in the open sea may be justified in proceeding at almost full speed in poor visibility if there is no indication of a close quarters situation developing with other vessels.

Risk of Collision. Proper use of radar, if fitted and operational, is required to obtain warning of risk of collision in all conditions of visibility. The radar can sometimes be used to advantage in clear visibility to assess the situation by determining distances.

Risk of collision does not necessarily apply at long ranges even if the compass bearing is not appreciably changing.

Narrow Channels. The Courts have considered passages up to about two miles wide to be narrow channels.

Traffic Separation Schemes for the Dover Straits, Straits of Gibraltar and other areas were first recommended for use by IMO in 1967. All vessels must now comply with Rule 10 of the Collision Regulations which applies to traffic separation schemes adopted by IMO. Information about traffic separation schemes is given in the IMO publication "Ships' Routeing".

CONDUCT OF VESSELS IN SIGHT OF ONE ANOTHER

Rule 14 requires each of two power-driven vessels, meeting on reciprocal or nearly reciprocal courses so as to involve risk of collision, to take avoiding action. The other Rules governing conduct of vessels in sight of one another assign the main responsibility for keeping out of the way to one of the two vessels involved, which is referred to as the give-way vessel. The other vessel, known as the stand-on vessel, is initially required to keep her course and speed when risk of collision exists.

Action by the give-way vessel. Every vessel which is directed to keep out of the way of another vessel must take early and substantial action to keep well clear. When two power-driven vessels are crossing the vessel with the other on her own starboard side shall, if the circumstances of the case admit, avoid crossing ahead, but no guidance is given as to the action to be taken in other cases.

The 1960 Rules required every give-way vessel in a crossing or overtaking situation in clear visibility to avoid crossing ahead. Although this is not specifically required for all cases by the 1972

Rules action taken to avoid collision must result in a safe passing distance and there must be due regard to the observance of good seamanship (Rule 8).

Action by the stand-on vessel. The stand-on vessel is initially required to keep her course and speed when risk of collision exists but she may take action as soon as it becomes apparent that the other vessel is not acting in compliance with the Rules. A power-driven vessel which takes such action must not alter course to port for a vessel on the port side, unless there are special circumstances. No action should be taken which would conflict with the most likely form of avoiding action for the give-way vessel.

A stand-on vessel should not take avoiding action of this kind without first determining that risk of collision does in fact exist. It may be dangerous to turn to starboard to cross ahead of a vessel crossing from the port bow if the bearing is closing on the bow.

When collision cannot be avoided by the give-way vessel alone the stand-on vessel must take such action as will best aid to avoid collision. An alteration to port for a vessel on the port side is permitted at this stage and may be the best action to take in certain circumstances.

CONDUCT OF VESSELS IN RESTRICTED VISIBILITY

No vessel is required to stand-on if risk of collision exists with another vessel which has not been visually sighted. Every vessel is required to take avoiding action if a close quarters situation is developing, or risk of collision exists, with a vessel detected by radar alone. Rule 19 effectively requires an alteration of course to be to starboard for a vessel forward of the beam and on the port quarter, and to port for a vessel on the starboard beam or starboard quarter. A reduction of speed may be preferable to an alteration to starboard in order to avoid a vessel which is on the port bow and drawing ahead.

If a fog signal is heard apparently forward of the beam, speed must be reduced to bare steerage way unless it has been determined that risk of collision does not exist. A power-driven vessel is not specifically required to stop her engines but this may be necessary in order to bring the speed down quickly. All way must be taken off if circumstances require it. This would apply if a fog signal is heard apparently ahead.

LIGHTS

Significance of Lights in Diagrams 1 to 19

1. Rule 23—A power-driven vessel of less than 50 m. in length, seen from directly ahead, showing a masthead light and sidelights.

2. Rule 23—A power-driven vessel under way seen from the starboard side.

3. Rule 23—A power-driven vessel under way seen from the port side.

4. Rule 23—A power-driven vessel, probably more than 50 m. in length, under way, seen from ahead; or a power-driven vessel of less than 50 m. in length engaged in towing, seen from ahead, when the length of tow is less than 200 m.

5. Rule 24—A power-driven vessel, of less than 50 m. in length, towing another vessel, with length of tow less than 200 m., seen from the starboard side.

6. Rule 24—A power-driven vessel, probably more than 50 m. in length, towing another vessel, with length of tow exceeding 200 m., seen from the starboard side.

7. Rule 26—A vessel engaged in trawling, probably more than 50 m. in length, seen from the starboard side.

8. Rule 25—A sailing vessel under way, seen from directly ahead, showing sidelights and the optional all-round lights at or near the top of the mast.

9. Rule 26—A vessel engaged in fishing, but not trawling, either with gear extending more than 150 m. horizontally, not making through the water, with the lower white light indicating the direction of the gear, or with gear extending not more than 150 m. and making way through the water showing a stern light. In the second case the vessel is being seen from more than $22\frac{1}{2}°$ abaft the port beam.

10. Rule 27—A vessel not under command making way through the water and approaching end-on.

11. Rule 27—A vessel restricted in her ability to manoeuvre not making way through the water.

12. Rule 27—A vessel restricted in her ability to manoeuvre making way through the water seen from the starboard side.

13. Rule 27—Vessels engaged in a towing operation which are unable to deviate from their course, with length of tow exceeding 200 m. seen from the starboard side.

14. Rule 27—A vessel engaged in dredging or underwater operations, not making way through the water, with an obstruction on the side indicated by the two red lights. The two green lights indicate the side on which it is safe to pass.

15. Rule 28—A vessel constrained by her draught seen from the starboard side.

16. Rule 29—A vessel engaged on pilotage duty, under way, seen from directly ahead.

17. Rule 29—A vessel of less than 50 m. in length engaged on pilotage duty, at anchor, or a vessel engaged on pilotage duty under way seen from more than $22\frac{1}{2}^{\circ}$ abaft the port beam.

18. Rule 30—A vessel at anchor, which is probably over 50 m. in length, seen from the starboard side.

19. Rule 30—A vessel aground seen from the starboard side.

DAY SIGNALS
(See Page 130)
Significance of Shapes in Diagrams 20 to 28.

20. Rule 24—A diamond shape exhibited by both the towing vessel and the vessel, or vessels, being towed when the length of tow exceeds 200 m.

21. Rule 25—A vessel under sail which is also being propelled by machinery.

22. Rule 26—A vessel fishing with nets extending more than 150 m. horizontally.

23. Rule 27—A vessel not under command.

24. Rule 27—A vessel restricted in her ability to manoeuvre.

25. Rule 27—A vessel engaged in minesweeping.

26. Rule 28—A vessel constrained by her draught.

27. Rule 30—A vessel at anchor.

28. Rule 30—A vessel aground.

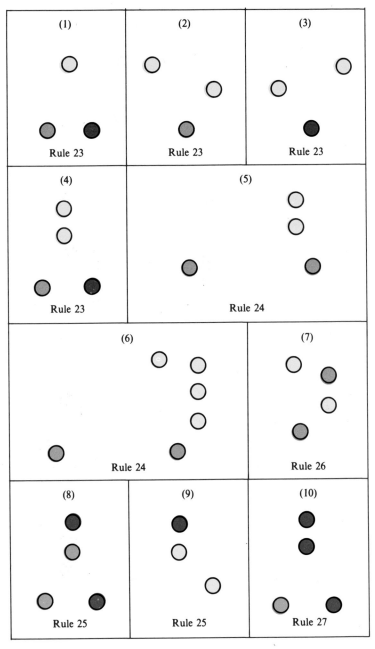

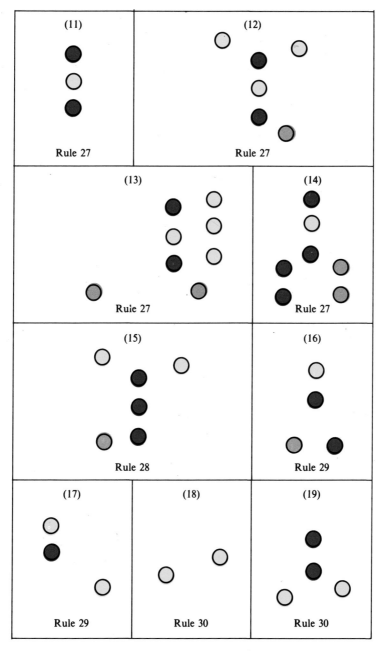

(11)

Rule 27

(12)

Rule 27

(13)

Rule 27

(14)

Rule 27

(15)

Rule 28

(16)

Rule 29

(17)

Rule 29

(18)

Rule 30

(19)

Rule 30

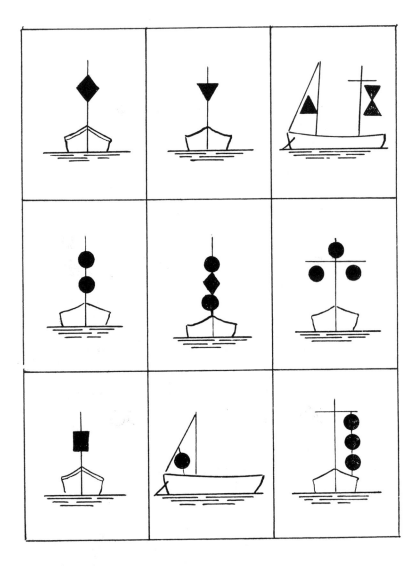

CHAPTER VI

SAFETY INFORMATION

THE following publications contain information on safety:

Merchant Shipping Notices issued by the Department of Transport give information to mariners, mainly relating to safety aboard ship. They may be obtained from Mercantile Marine Offices and Customs Houses and are issued free of charge. The notices are issued whenever it is considered necessary. Several notices have been issued after shipping casualties or accidents aboard ship. A list of notices remaining in force is issued annually.

Notices to Mariners give information to enable mariners to keep charts, Sailing Directions, Light Lists, etc., corrected up to date. The Annual Summary of Notices to Mariners contains the important notices which usually do not change much from year to year. Included amongst these are notices concerned with distress and rescue at sea, firing practice areas and submarines.

The Mariners Handbook. One chapter of this book is devoted to navigational hazards. Information is given on lights and signals shown by warships, deep draught vessels, hovercraft and flexible oil barges.

Sailing Directions amplify the information given on charts and give general information to the mariner. Information about the closing of ports in times of emergency and on signals shown by vessels navigating stern foremost is given in the Sailing Directions for the United Kingdom.

The Code of Safe Working Practices issued by the Stationery Office gives information about safety aboard ship. There are sections for owners and masters and for deck, engineering and catering officers and ratings.

INTERNATIONAL ASSOCIATION OF LIGHTHOUSE AUTHORITIES MARITIME BUOYAGE SYSTEM

The IALA Maritime Buoyage System is being extended to countries throughout the world on a regional basis. The system uses both lateral marks, whereby the port and starboard sides of a channel or

131

route are indicated, and cardinal marks, whereby one or more buoys are laid out in the quadrant of the compass to indicate where the danger lies in relation to the mark.

The world is considered to be divided into two regions using different versions of the buoyage system for lateral buoys, these are known as Region A and Region B. In Region A the colour red is used to mark the port hand of a channel. This region includes Europe, Africa, Australia, New Zealand and some Asian countries. In Region B the colour red is used to mark the starboard side of a channel. Region B includes North, Central and South America, Japan, Korea and the Philippines. Only the lateral marks differ between the two regions, the other four types of mark are used in both.

IALA MARITIME BUOYAGE SYSTEM

1. GENERAL

1.1   Scope

This system applies to all fixed and floating marks (other than lighthouses, sector lights, leading lights, lightships and large navigation buoys) serving to indicate:

1.1.1   The lateral limits of navigable channels

1.1.2   Natural dangers and other obstructions such as wrecks

1.1.3   Other areas or features of importance to the mariner

1.1.4   New dangers

1.2 Types of marks

The system of buoyage provides five types of marks which may be used in any combination:

1.2.1   Lateral marks used in conjunction with a conventional direction of buoyage, generally used for well defined channels. These marks indicate the port and starboard sides of the route to be followed. Where a channel divides a modified lateral mark may be used to indicate the preferred route.

1.2.2   Cardinal marks, used in conjunction with the mariners' compass, indicate where the mariner may find navigable water

1.2.3   Isolated Danger Marks indicating isolated dangers of limited size that have navigable water all around them

1.2.4   Safe water marks indicating that there is navigable water all around that position, e.g. mid-channel mark

1.2.5   Special marks not primarily intended to assist navigation but indicating an area or feature referred to in nautical documents

1.3 Method of characterising marks

The significance of the mark depends upon one or more of the following features:

    1.3.1 By night—colour and rhythm of light

    1.3.2 By day—colour, shape, topmark

For charting of IALA buoys whose shape is unknown, a pillar shape will be used.

2. LATERAL MARKS

2.1 Definition of conventional direction of buoyage

The conventional direction of buoyage which must be indicated on appropriate nautical documents, may be defined where required, in one of two ways:

    2.1.1 The general direction taken by the mariner when approaching a harbour, river estuary or other waterway from seaward: or

    2.1.2 In other areas it should be determined in detail by the appropriate authority in consultation with neighbouring countries. In principle it should follow a clockwise direction around land masses   (See fig. 3, page 139)
        In all cases the conventional direction must be indicated in appropriate nautical documents

2.2 Buoyage Regions

There are two international Buoyage Regions A and B where lateral marks differ in that the red and green colours of marks and lights are reversed. These buoyage regions are indicated in Figure 4.

2.3.1 Description of Lateral Marks

	Port hand		Starboard hand	
	Region A	Region B	Region A	Region B
Colour:	Red	Green	Green	Red
Shape (Buoys):	Cylindrical (can), pillar or spar	Cylindrical (can), pillar or spar	Conical, pillar or spar	Conical, pillar or spar
Topmark (if any):	Single red cylinder (can)	Single green cylinder (can)	Single green cone, point upward	Single red cone, point upward
Light (when fitted): Colour:	Red	Green	Green	Red
Rhythm:	Any, other than that described in Section 2.3.2.			

2.3.2   At the point where a channel divides, when proceeding in the conventional direction of buoyage, a preferred channel may be indicated by a modified Port or Starboard lateral mark as follows:

	Preferred Channel to Starboard		Preferred Channel to Port	
	Region A	Region B	Region A	Region B
Colour:	Red with one broad green horizontal band	Green with one broad red horizontal band	Green with one broad red horizontal band	Red with one broad green horizontal band
Shape (Buoys):	Cylindrical (can), pillar or spar	Cylindrical (can), pillar or spar	Conical, pillar or spar	Conical, pillar or spar
Topmark (if any):	Single red cylinder (can)	Single green cylinder (can)	Single green cone point upward	Single red cone point upward
Light (when fitted):	Red	Green	Green	Red
Rhythm:	Composite group flashing Fl(2+1)R	Composite group flashing Fl(2+1)G	Composite group flashing Fl(2+1)G	Composite group flashing Fl(2+1)R

2.5 General Rules for Lateral Marks

2.5.1   Shapes
Where lateral marks do not rely upon cylindrical (can) or conical buoy shapes for identification they should. where practicable, carry the appropriate topmark.

2.5.2   Numbering or lettering
If marks at the sides of a channel are numbered or lettered, the numbering or lettering shall follow the conventional direction of buoyage.

CARDINAL MARKS

3.1 Definition of cardinal quadrants and marks

3.1.1   The four quadrants (North, East, South and West) are bounded by the true bearings NW-NE, NE-SE, SE-SW, SW-NW taken from the point of interest

3.1.2   A cardinal mark is named after the quadrant in which it is placed

3.1.3   The name of a cardinal mark indicates that it should be passed to the named side of the mark

3.2 Use of Cardinal Marks

A Cardinal Mark may be used, for example:

3.2.1   To indicate that the deepest water in that area is on the named side of the mark

3.2.2   To indicate the safe side on which to pass a danger

3.2.2   To draw attention to a feature in a channel such as a bend, a junction, a bifurcation, or the end of a shoal

3.3 Description of Cardinal marks

3.3.1   North cardinal marks

Topmark[b]   —2 black cones, one above the other, points upward
Colour   —Black above yellow
Shape   —Pillar or spar
Light (when fitted):
    Colour—White
    Rhythm—VQ or Q

3.3.2 East Cardinal mark

Topmark[b]   ·   —2 black cones, one above the other, base to base
Colour   —Black with a single broad horizontal yellow band
Shape   —Pillar or spar

(b)   The double cone topmark is the most important feature of every Cardinal Mark by day, and should be used wherever practicable and be as large as possible with a clear separation between the cones.

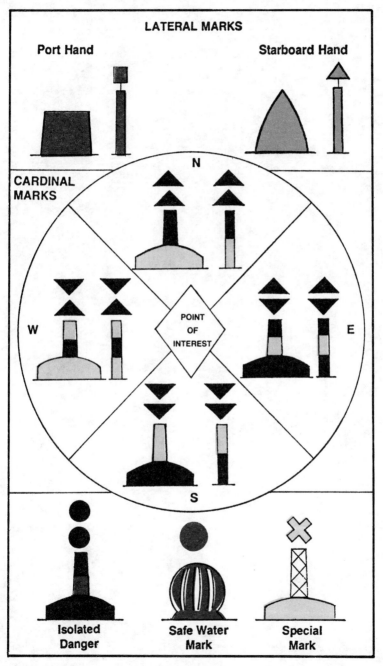

System A Buoys.

Light (when fitted):
Colour—White
Rhythm—VQ (3) every 5 sec. or Q (3) every 10 sec.

3.3.3   South Cardinal Mark

Topmark[b]   —2 black cones, one above the other, points downward
Colour   —Yellow above black
Shape   —Pillar or spar
Light (when fitted):
Colour—White
Rhythm—VQ (6)+Long flash every 10 sec.
    or Q (6)+Long flash every 15 sec.

3.3.4   West Cardinal Mark

Topmark[b]   —2 black cones, one above the other, point to point
Colour   —Yellow with a single broad horizontal black band
Shape   —Pillar or spar
Light (when fitted):
Colour—White
Rhythm—VQ (9) every 10 sec. or Q (9) every 15 sec.

4.   ISOLATED DANGER MARKS

4.1 Definition of Isolated Danger Marks

An Isolated Danger Mark is a mark erected on, or moored on or above, an isolated danger which has navigable water all around it.

4.2 Description of Isolated Danger Marks

Topmark[f]   —2 black spheres, one above the other
Colour   —Black with one or more broad horizontal red bands
Shape   —Optional but not conflicting with lateral marks. Pillar or spar preferred
Light (when fitted):
Colour—White
Rhythm—Group flashing (2) or Morse "A"

5.   SAFE WATER MARKS

5.1 Definition of Safe Water Marks

Safe water marks serve to show that there is navigable water all round the mark; these include centre line marks and mid-channel marks. Such a mark may also be used as an alternative to a Cardinal or a Lateral mark to indicate a landfall.

(f)   The double sphere topmark is the most important feature of every isolated danger mark by day, and should be used wherever practicable and be as large as possible with a clear separation between the spheres.

5.2 Description of Safe Water Marks

Colour	—Red and White vertical stripes
Shape	—Spherical, pillar with spherical top-mark or spar
Topmark (if any)	—Single red sphere

Light (when fitted):
Colour—White
Rhythm—Isophase, Occulting, one long flash every 10 secs. or Morse "A"

6. SPECIAL MARKS

6.1 Definition of Special Marks

Marks not primarily intended to assist navigation but which indicate a special area or feature referred to in appropriate nautical documents, for example:

6.1.1   Ocean Data Acquisition Systems (ODAS) marks

6.1.2   Traffic Separation Marks where use of conventional channel may cause confusion

6.1.3   Spoil Ground Marks

6.1.4   Military exercise zone marks

6.1.5   Cable or pipe line marks

6.1.6   Recreation zone marks

6.2 Description of special marks

Colour	—Yellow
Shape	—Optional but not conflicting with navigational marks
Topmark (if any)	—Single yellow 'X' shape

Light (when fitted):
Colour—Yellow
Rhythm—Any, other than those described in Sections 3, 4 or 5

6.3 Additional Special Marks

Special marks other than those listed in paragraph 6.1 and described in paragraph 6.2 may be established by the responsible administration to meet exceptional circumstances. These additional marks shall not conflict with navigational marks and shall be promulgated in appropriate nautical documents and the International Association of Lighthouse Authorities notified as soon as practicable.

7. NEW DANGERS

7.1 Definition of New Dangers

The term "New Danger" is used to describe newly discovered hazards not yet indicated in nautical documents. "New Dangers"

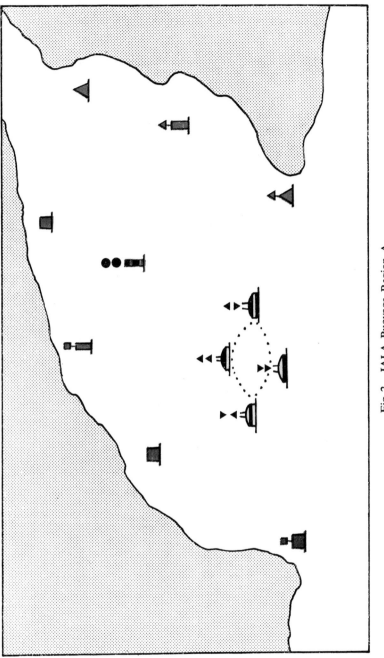

Fig 2. IALA Buoyage Region A

include naturally occurring obstructions such as sandbanks or rocks or man made dangers such as wrecks.

7.2 Marking of New Dangers

7.2.1   New Dangers shall be marked in accordance with these rules. If the appropriate Authority considers the danger to be especially grave at least one of the marks shall be duplicated as soon as practicable

7.2.2   Any lighted mark used for this purpose shall have an appropriate cardinal or lateral VQ or Q light character

7.2.3   Any duplicate mark shall be identical to its partner in all respects

7.2.4   A New Danger may be marked by a racon, coded Morse "D", showing a signal length of 1 nautical mile on the radar display

7.2.5   The duplicate mark may be removed when the appropriate Authority is satisfied that information concerning the new danger has been sufficiently promulgated

Fig. 3. Conventional Direction of Buoyage for U.K. Waters

8.   INTERNATIONAL BUOYAGE REGIONS A AND B.

There are two International Buoyage Regions A and B where Lateral marks differ as described in Section 2. The geographical divisions of these two Regions are indicated in Fig. 4.

CLOSING OF PORTS

(Sailing directions for U.K.)

If it becomes necessary to control the entrance and movement of ships in United Kingdom ports, the following signals will be displayed from some conspicuous position near the port entrance, or by an Examination or Traffic Control Vessel:

(*a*) Entrance to the port prohibited.
    (1) Three red balls in vertical line by day.
    (2) Three flashing red lights in vertical line by night.

(*b*) Entrance permitted.
    (1) Three green lights in vertical line.

(*c*) Movement of shipping prohibited.
    (1) A blue flag by day.
    Three lights—red, green, red—vertically disposed by night.

Masters are advised to communicate with any Government or Port Authority vessel to ascertain the approach route and are warned not to enter.

An examination vessel shows a special flag with white over red horizontal bands surrounded by a blue border.

SUBMARINES

(Annual Summary of Notices to Mariners)

British vessels fly the International Code Group "NE2" to denote that submarines, which may be submerged, are in the vicinity. Vessels are cautioned to steer so as to give a wide berth to any vessel flying this signal. If for any reason it is necessary to approach such a vessel a good look-out must be kept for submarines whose presence may be indicated only by their periscopes or by masts showing above the water.

The following signals are used by submerged submarines:

White smoke candle (with or without flame) may be accompanied by yellowish green fluorescent dye. Yellow smoke candles. Green flares launched approx. 60-90 metres into the air burning for about 5 seconds.	Indicates position in response to request from ship or aircraft as required.
Red flares (grenades) (characteristics as for green flares above).	Emergency surfacing. Keep clear. Do not stop propellers. Clear area immediately. Stand by to give assistance.
Two white or yellow smoke candles released singly about 3 minutes apart.	Keep clear. Submarine surfacing. Do not stop propellers. Clear the immediate vicinity.

Submarines may have their forward steaming light lower than the side lights and the after steaming light may be forward of the mid-point. The stern light will be very low and may be partially obscured by spray and wash.

When anchored submarines display an all round white light amidships in addition to normal anchor lights. Some submarines are fitted with a yellow quick flashing light above the after steaming light showing 90 flashes per minute. This should not be confused with the similar light used by hovercraft which makes 120 flashes per minute.

A submarine which is unable to surface will try to indicate her position by the following methods:

(a) Releasing an indicator buoy which may show a light flashing approximately once per second. The buoy carries a vertical whip aerial and is marked with a serial number for identification. It is attached to a line 1000 metres in length.

(b) Firing yellow or white smoke candles on the approach of other vessels.

(c) Pumping out oil fuel.

(d) Blowing out air.

If an indicator buoy is sighted it should be reported to the Navy or Coastguard, if possible giving the serial number of the buoy. If the buoy is attached to a submarine the vessel should remain in position and should indicate to those trapped in the submarine that help is at hand by running the echosounder and/or banging on the shell plating below the waterline with a hammer at frequent intervals.

WARSHIPS' LIGHTS
(Mariners' Handbook)

Aircraft carriers have steaming lights permanently off the centre line of the ship with reduced horizontal separation. Their side lights may be on either side of the hull or on either side of the island structure; in the latter case the port side light may be as much as 30 m from the port side of the ship. When at anchor they may exhibit 4 white lights. The two forward lights will be in the same horizontal plane not less than 1·5 m below the flight deck and will show over an arc of at least 180° from one point on the opposite bow to one point from right astern on their own side. The two after lights will be not less than 5 m below the forward ones, showing from one point on the opposite quarter to one point from right ahead on their own side.

Certain warships of 50 m in length or over may not have a second steaming light or may have a reduced separation between steaming lights.

VESSELS ENGAGED IN SEISMIC SURVEYS
(Mariners' Handbook)

These vessels generally show the signals described in Rule 27(b) of the Regulations for Preventing Collisions at Sea (1972). They may also show signals "PO" and "IR". Such vessels may work in pairs. The shooting vessel may show flag "B" or at night a single red light. Survey vessels are unable to manoeuvre freely and mariners are urged to give them a wide berth—at least 2 miles.

HOVERCRAFT
(Mariners' Handbook)

Hovercraft, whether airborne or waterborne, will comply, as far as practicable, with the Regulations for Preventing Collisions at Sea as though they were power-driven vessels. They are capable of very high speeds but they are subject to wind effects so the navigation lights may not indicate their direction of travel. In an emergency they can stop extremely quickly by alighting on the water.

Sound signals may not be heard from some types of hovercraft because of the noise of operation and they may not be able to hear sound signals made by other vessels.

Hovercraft must comply with the Rules concerning lights as closely as circumstances permit and they must also show an all round yellow light flashing at approximately 120 times per minute, visible at least 5 miles, when operating fully or partly airborne. (Rule 23).

VESSELS NAVIGATING STERN FOREMOST
(U.K. Sailing Directions)

Vessels fitted with a bow rudder and being navigated stern foremost when entering or leaving certain ports in the English Channel display two black balls, each 0·6 m in diameter, at least 2·4 m apart on an athwartships horizontal jackyard and at least 1·8 m higher than the funnel top.

TRAFFIC SEPARATION SCHEME
(M 1448)

The DTp has introduced a special two letter signal "YG", with the meaning "You appear not to be complying with the traffic separation scheme". The master of any vessel receiving the signal should take immediate action to check his course and position and take any further steps which appear to him appropriate in the circumstances.

PRACTICE AREA
(Annual Summary of Notices to Mariners)

Firing and bombing practices and defence exercises take place in a number of areas off the coast of the British Commonwealth. Warning signals usually consist of red flags by day and red fixed or flashing lights at night. They are shown from shortly before practice starts until it ceases. Ships and aircraft carrying out night exercises may illuminate with bright red or orange flares. Remote control craft carry not under control shapes and lights as well as normal navigation lights.

PILOTS

Caution. In view of the danger and difficulty often attending the shipping and discharging of pilots in exposed positions, the attention of masters is directed to the necessity of observing every precaution in manoeuvring their ships when a pilot is either boarding or leaving, especially in cases where a vessel is in ballast and strong winds are prevailing. The master or officer in charge of the bridge should take care to satisfy himself, on dropping the pilot, that the latter is well clear of the ship and particularly of the counter before the propeller is moved.

LIGHTVESSELS IN THE UNITED KINGDOM

Regulations. The following Regulations have been established respecting the several lightvessels on the coasts of the United Kingdom, viz.:

A white light is exhibited from the forestay of each lightvessel, at a height of 2 m above the rail, for the purpose of showing in which direction the vessel is riding, when at her station.

Lightvessels under the jurisdiction of the Corporation of Trinity House when not in their correct position as a safe guide to shipping will continue the present practice of not showing their characteristic light or sounding their fog signal, will exhibit the following special signals, viz.:

By Day. The characteristic topmark will be struck if practicable. Two large black globes or shapes will be exhibited one forward and one aft. The International Code Signal "LO" will be flown.

By Night. Two red lights will be exhibited one forward and one aft. Two flares, one red and the other white, will be shown simultaneously at least every quarter of an hour or if the use of flares be impracticable a red light and a white light will be displayed simultaneously.

Watch buoys are can buoys painted red, with "Watch" preceded by lightvessel's name in white letters. They are moored near the vessel to mark position.

If from any cause the lightvessel be unable to exhibit her usual lights whilst at her station, the riding light only will be shown.

The mouths of fog horns, which are not fitted to distribute the sound equally all round, are pointed to windward.

At lightvessels where a hand horn is used, the intervals will be shortened as vessels approach, and should a vessel come dangerously close the sound will be continuous until she has passed.

When, from any of the lightvessels or from Trinity House Lighthouse a vessel is seen standing into danger, the two signal flags N F of the International Code, "You are standing into danger", will be hoisted and kept flying until answered. In addition to the above flag signal the light vessel will fire a gun or rocket signal, and repeat it at short intervals until observed by the vessel.

It should be remembered that lightvessels are liable to be withdrawn for repairs, without notice, and in some cases not replaced by relief vessels.

COLLISIONS WITH LIGHTVESSELS

Caution. In consequence of lightvessels being from time to time run into and seriously damaged by vessels navigating in their vicinity, the Corporation of Trinity House deem it desirable to warn mariners that when passing a lightvessel, and particularly when attempting to cross her bows, they should make due allowance for the set of the tide and take every other precaution desirable in the circumstances in order to avoid striking the lightvessel.

SUBMARINE CABLES

Should a submarine cable be lifted to the surface by a vessel heaving up anchor she should pass the end of a 40 mm fibrerope (do not use wire) under the cable, make the end fast inboard, haul the rope tight and hang the cable on the bight of the rope, then lower the anchor clear of the cable which can then be slipped The fouling of a cable together with the position as accurately as possible should be reported to the nearest cable station.

Skippers of trawlers are urged to exercise care when trawling near telegraph cables, and if a cable is fouled great caution should be exercised in attempting to clear it. It is advisable to sacrifice the gear rather than to exert force in freeing it. Compensation for loss of gear is made on a sworn declaration being made and upheld.

FLEXIBLE OIL BARGES

Oil barges known as "Dracones" consist of a sausage-shaped envelope of strong woven nylon fabric coated with synthetic rubber. Since they float by reason of the buoyancy of their oil cargo they are almost entirely submerged. A typical tow would be 30 m long on 200-metre tow line.

"Dracones" are unable to carry normal navigation lights. When they are in tow the following special signals are displayed:

By Day. The vessel towing will exhibit a *Black Diamond Shape*. The "Dracone" will tow a float also exhibiting a *Black Diamond Shape*, thus indicating the length of the tow.

By Night. The float towed by the "Dracone" will exhibit an all round *White Light*, visible three miles.

The lights and shapes for Dracones are prescribed by Rule 24(g) of the Collision Regulations.

CHAPTER VII

DISTRESS AND RESCUE

ASSISTANCE may be given to a ship or aircraft in distress off the coast of the United Kingdom by the following authorities: (Notice 4 Annual Summary of Notices to Mariners).

(1) **Coast Radio Stations** keep continuous watch on the distress frequencies of 500 kHz and 2,182 kHz. On receiving a distress signal, the Coast Radio Station will notify the Coastguard and other authorities and will transmit the distress call to ships at sea.

(2) **H.M. Coastguard** is the authority responsible for initiating and co-ordinating search and rescue measures for vessels in distress off the coast of the United Kingdom up to approximately 1,000 miles from the shore.

(3) **The Royal National Lifeboat Institution** maintains 120 lifeboats round the coast of the United Kingdom and Eire and also has a large fleet of inshore lifeboats. Lifeboats are equipped with radio sets which operate on 2,182 kHz. They are also fitted with FM/VHF. A quick-flashing blue light showing at least 120 flashes every minute is exhibited from the masthead of RNLI lifeboats.

(4) **The Royal Navy** may assist using ships and aircraft including helicopters.

(5) **The Royal Air Force** is responsible for providing rescue facilities for aircraft but may also give assistance to ships in distress.

(6) **Air Traffic Control Services** may assist by communicating with aircraft engaged in search and rescue operations.

Statutory Obligations

The Master of a British ship on receiving a distress signal that a vessel or aircraft is in distress must proceed with all speed to give assistance, unless he is unable, or in special circumstances considers it unreasonable or unnecessary, or unless he is released from the obligation. Every distress signal received must be entered in the official log book.

After a collision the Master, or person in charge, is required to render such assistance as may be practicable and necessary to save the passengers and crew from danger, and to stay by the other vessel until assistance is no longer required.

The master of the other vessel should be informed of the name and port of registry of own vessel, also of the names of the port of departure and port to which she is bound. A statement should be made in the official log book as soon as possible after the collision.

Use of Distress Signals

The statutory distress signals are listed in Annex IV of the International Regulations for preventing Collisions at Sea (1972). Experience has shown that a "continuous sounding with any fog-signal apparatus" and

146

"flames on the vessel" may give rise to misunderstanding. It is therefore recommended that the continuous sounding should be made by repeating the Morse signal "SOS" on the whistle or fog horn. Rockets or flares should be used rather than flames on the vessel.

Global Maritime Distress and Safety System (GMDSS)

The GMDSS will be fully implemented by 1 February 1999. Vessels built after 1 February 1995 must comply with all applicable GMDSS requirements. Descriptions of the operational procedures to be observed by ships fitted with GMDSS equipment are contained in the Manual published by the ITU, Geneva. GMDSS ships shall, while at sea, maintain an automatic Digital Selective Calling (DSC) watch on the appropriate distress and safety calling frequencies in the frequency bands appropriate for the sea area in which they are operating.

LIFE-SAVING ORGANISATION
ON COAST OF THE UNITED KINGDOM

(*a*) **Replies from life-saving stations or maritime rescue units to distress signals made by a ship or person:—**

Signals	Signification
By day.—*Orange* smoke signal or combined light and sound signal (thunder-light) consisting of three single signals which are fired at intervals of approximately one minute. *By night.*—*White* star rocket consisting of three single signals which are fired at intervals of approximately one minute.	"You are seen—assistance will be given as soon as possible". (Repetition of such signals shall have the same meaning.)

If necessary the day signals may be given at night or the night signals by day.

(*b*) **Landing signals for the guidance of small boats with crews or persons in distress:—**

Signals	Signification
By day.—Vertical motion of a *white* flag or the arms or signalling the code letter "K" (— • —) given by light or sound-signal apparatus. *By night.*—Vertical motion of a *white* light or flare or signalling the code letter "K" (— • —) given by light or sound-signal apparatus. A range (indication of direction) may be given by placing a steady white light or flare at a lower level and in line with the observer.	"This is the best place to land".

Signals	*Signification*
By day.—Horizontal motion of a *white* flag or arms extended horizontally or signalling the code letter "S" (- - -) given by light or sound-signal apparatus. *By night.*—Horizontal motion of a *white* light or signalling the code letter "S" (- - -) given by light or sound-signal apparatus.	"Landing here highly dangerous".

Signals	*Signification*
By day.—Horizontal motion of a *white* flag, followed by the placing of the *white* flag in the ground and the carrying of another *white* flag in the direction to be indicated or a *white* star-signal in the direction towards the better landing place or signalling the code letter "S" (- - -) followed by the code letter "R" (- — -) if a better landing place for the craft in distress is located more to the right in the direction of approach or signalling the code letter "L" (- — - -) if a better landing place for the craft in distress is located more to the left in the direction of approach.	"Landing here highly dangerous. A more favourable location for landing is in the direction indicated".
By night.—Horizontal motion of a *white* light or flare, followed by the placing of the *white* light or flare on the ground and the carrying of another *white* light or flare in the direction to be indicated or a *white* star-signal in the direction towards the better landing place or signalling the code letter "S" (- - -) followed by code letter "R" (- — -) if a better landing place for the craft in distress is located more to the right in the direction of approach or signalling the code letter "L" (- — - -) if a better landing place for the craft in distress is located more to the left in the direction of approach.	"Landing here highly dangerous. A more favourable location for landing is in the direction indicated".

ROCKET LIFE-SAVING APPARATUS

(c) **Signals to be employed in connection with the use of shore life-saving apparatus:—**

Signals	Signification
By day.—Vertical motion of a *white* flag or the arms. By night.—Vertical motion of a *white* light or flare.	In general—"Affirmative". Specifically— "Rocket line is held". "Tail block is made fast". "Man is in the breeches buoy". "Haul away".

Signals	Signification
By day.—Horizontal motion of a *white* flag or arms extended horizontally. By night.—Horizontal motion of a *white* light or flare.	In general—"Negative". Specifically— "Slack away". "Avast hauling".

(d) **Signals to be used to warn a ship which is standing into danger:—**

Signals	Signification
The International Code Signals U or NF. The letter U (- - —) flashed by lamp or made by foghorn, or whistle, etc.	"You are running into danger".

If it should prove necessary the attention of the vessel is called to these signals by a *white* flare, a rocket showing *white* stars on bursting, or an explosive sound signal.

Should lives be in danger and your vessel be in a position where rescue by the rocket life-saving apparatus is possible, a rocket with line attached will be fired from the shore across your vessel. Get hold of this line as soon as you can. When you have got hold of it, signal to the shore as indicated in paragraph (c).

Should your vessel carry a line-throwing appliance, it may be preferable to use this and fire a line ashore, but this should not be done without first consulting the rescue company on shore. If this method is used, the rocket line may not be of sufficient strength to haul out the whip and jackstay and those on shore will secure it to a stouter rocket line. When this is done, they will signal as indicated in paragraph (c). On seeing the signal, haul in the line which was fired from the vessel until the stouter line is on board.

Then, when the rocket line is held, make the appropriate signal to the shore (paragraph (c)) and proceed as follows:—

1. When you see the appropriate signal, i.e. "haul away", made

from the shore, haul upon the rocket line until you get a tail block with an endless fall rove through it (called the "whip"), and with a jackstay attached to the becket of the tail block.

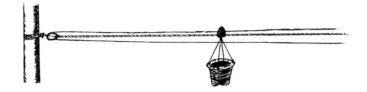

Fig. 1.

2. Cut or cast off the rocket line and make the tail block fast, close up to the mast or other convenient position, bearing in mind that the fall should be kept clear from chafing any part of the vessel. Before cutting or casting off the rocket line, make sure that you have the tail attached to the block well in hand. When the tail block is made fast, signal to the shore again (as in paragraph (c)).

3. The men on shore will then set the jackstay taut, and by means of the Whip will haul off to the ship the breeches buoy into which the person to be hauled ashore is to get. He should sit well down in the breeches buoy and when he is secure, signal again to the shore as indicated in paragraph (c) above, and the men on shore will haul the person in the breeches buoy to the shore. When he is landed the empty breeches buoy will be hauled back to the ship. This operation will be repeated until all persons are landed.

4. During the course of the operations should it be necessary to signal, either from your ship to the shore, or from the shore to your ship, to "Slack away" or "Avast hauling" this should be done as indicated in paragraph (c).

DISTRESS SIGNALS

All ocean going ships are required to carry 12 rocket parachute flares. The rocket is required to reach an altitude of not less than 300 metres when fired vertically and to eject a parachute flare of bright red colour which burns for not less than 40 seconds with an average intensity of not less than 30,000 candelas.

Ship's lifeboats must be provided with:

4 rocket parachute flares (as described above);

6 hand flares of 15,000 candelas which burn with a bright red colour for a period of not less than one minute;

2 buoyant smoke signals which emit smoke of a highly visible colour for a period of not less than 3 minutes.

LINE-THROWING APPLIANCES

All ocean going ships must carry a line throwing appliance capable of throwing a line a minimum distance of 230 m in calm weather. The lateral deflection of the line must not exceed 10 per cent of the length of flight of the rocket. Four rockets and four lines, 4 mm in diameter, of suitable length, having a breaking strain of not less than 2000 Newtons are carried.

The illustrations show the Pains-Wessex Schermuly "Speedline" 250 Line-Throwing Apparatus which has a 275 m of 4 mm polyolefin line in a plastic container. To prepare the apparatus for use the front end cover is removed and the looped end of the line made fast to a holdfast or heavy rope. When the handle is held with the hand close to the arrow the container takes up the correct firing angle (Fig. 3). A squeeze trigger in the handle fires the rocket. The cartridge/firing mechanism is both cocked and released when the trigger is squeezed for firing.

Use of Rockets Dangerous

A vessel which is in distress and carrying highly inflammable liquid which is leaking may use the following signals to show that it is dangerous to fire a line-carrying rocket:

By day	International Code flag "B"
By night	A red light at the masthead
In poor visibility	Sounding "GU" in morse code on the whistle.

Rescue by Helicopter

When a distress message is received from a ship the rescue authorities may request the use of a helicopter to assist in the rescue. The main types of helicopters used for rescue duties in the United Kingdom are the Wessex and Sea King. The Wessex can carry up to 10 survivors at ranges up to about 100 miles from their base. They do not normally take part in operations over the sea at night or when the wind speed exceeds 45 knots. Sea King helicopters can be used out to a distance of 300 miles from the nearest base. They may operate at night and can rescue up to 18 survivors.

It is essential to give the ship's position as accurately as possible if the distress message is sent by radio. The bearing and distance

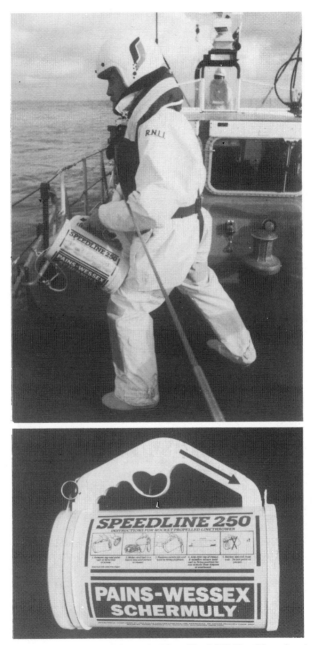

Figs. 2 and 3—Pains-Wessex Schermuly "Speedline" 250 Line-Throwing Apparatus.

from a fixed object should be given if possible. The type of ship and colour of hull should be included in the radio message if time allows. If there is a lot of shipping in the area it will be difficult for the helicopter pilot to pick out the particular ship so a distinctive distress signal such as the orange coloured smoke signal, aldis or, in bright sunlight, the lifeboat heliograph, should be used.

A clear stretch of deck should be prepared and marked with a yellow dot 5 metres in diameter. All loose articles must be tied down or removed from the area and nearby aerials struck, if possible. The ship must be kept on a steady course with the wind 30° on the port bow if the cleared area is aft, 30° on the port bow or abeam if the area is midships and 30° on the starboard quarter if the area is forward. If this is not possible the ship should remain stationary head to wind or follow the instructions of the helicopter crew. An indication of wind direction by flags or other means should be given.

The helicopter will approach heading into the relative wind. The maximum length of winch wire is normally about 300 feet (91 m) but may be only 60 feet (18 m) in some cases. A helicopter can build up a dangerous charge of static electricity so the winch wire should only be handled by personnel wearing rubber gloves. The helicopter crew will normally discharge the static electricity by dropping the wire into the sea or allowing the wire to touch the ship's deck. The wire must not be allowed to foul any part of the ship or rigging. Personnel must obey the instructions given by the helicopter crew.

Aircraft

An aircraft may use the following signals to attract a ship's attention to another aircraft in distress:

(*a*) a succession of white pyrotechnic lights

(*b*) the repeated switching on and off of the aircraft's landing lights

(*c*) irregular switching on and off of navigation lights.

In order to guide a ship to a casualty or survivors it may fly low around the ship or cross close ahead at low altitude opening and closing the throttle before flying off in the direction which the ship should take. British pilots are instructed to rock their aircraft laterally when flying off in the direction of the casualty. The aircraft signals should be acknowledged by a succession of "T's" in Morse code. The aircraft may cancel this instruction by crossing close astern of the ship opening and closing the throttle.

When it is known that an aircraft intends to ditch a ship may indicate her position by transmitting homing bearings and making black smoke by day, or directing a searchlight vertically by night. If practicable, the ship should make a lee of calm water by turning through 360°, and providing an oil "slick". As the captain normally sits on the port side the aircraft will usually ditch on the starboard side of the ship, but a helicopter will normally ditch on the port side. The ship should head into the wind.

At night the ship should illuminate the sea as much as possible on the side upon which the aircraft is expected to ditch. A lifeboat should be prepared for launching.

Abandon Ship

If it seems likely that the ship will have to be abandoned the boats should be prepared for immediate launching. In remote areas where there is little prospect of an early rescue it may be worth taking blankets and extra provisions into the boats but high protein food should not be taken as body water is consumed in its digestion.

It is usually best to wait as long as possible before abandoning ship, especially if a rescue vessel is close at hand. Before giving the order to abandon the engines must be stopped and all watertight doors closed.

Boats should clear the ship's side as quickly as possible but should remain close to the ship. Motor boats can be used to assist other boats and rafts to keep together in a group so as to make detection easier and speed the rescue operation.

When launching an inflatable liferaft check that the painter is secured to a strong point on the ship. Make sure that it is all clear over the side then launch overboard and pull the painter out to its full length giving a further sharp tug to make the raft inflate. The liferaft should preferably be boarded from a ladder or rope but with low freeboard it may be safe to jump on to the canopy. Each liferaft should clear the ship's side before launching the next. It is unlikely that a raft will inflate in the inverted position but if this should happen it can easily be righted by standing on the gas cylinder and pulling on the righting straps.

Persons who are unable to get to a lifeboat or raft should lower themselves into the water, or jump feet first from a low level, on the weather side of the ship. A lifejacket should, of course, be worn but this may cause injury when jumping into the sea so the arms should be crossed tightly across the front and the shoulders of the jacket held down. Clothing should not be discarded as it will give some insulation against the cold.

If, after taking to the boats or rafts, there is no early prospect of rescue, no food or water should be issued for the first 24 hours, except to persons who are injured or ill. After the first day a ration of about half a litre of water per day should be issued together with about 100 gm of each food. Other food, such as fish, should not be eaten unless there is sufficient water to issue at least one litre of water per day. Sea water must not be drunk, even in small quantities.

Rescuing the Crew of a Disabled Ship

When a vessel is in danger of sinking lifeboats and liferafts are not always available for abandoning ship. In such cases passengers and crew should, if possible, remain on the ship until another vessel arrives on the scene and sends boats or rafts across. The rescue should not be attempted in darkness if sea conditions are difficult unless this is the only hope of saving life.

If the sea is rough the assisting ship should launch a motor lifeboat from a position slightly to windward of the disabled vessel. It will usually be advantageous for both vessels to distribute oil to make conditions easier for the boats. A disabled ship tends to lie practically beam on to wind and seas. In some cases it may be best for the rescue vessel to launch her boat or boats from the lee side when lying stopped, beam on to the seas and to windward of the other ship but this may be dangerous if the vessel is "stiff" and liable to roll heavily.

An alternative method is for the rescue vessel to launch the boat when slowly making way through the water with the wind and seas about two points on the bow. This position will give sufficient lee for launching without the dangers of excessive rolling. If this method is used the painter should be taut as the boat is lowered. As the boat reaches the water the engine should be started, the tiller put hard over towards the ship and both falls released simultaneously. The boat should shear away from the ship's side and the painter can then be released. (See Fig. 4).

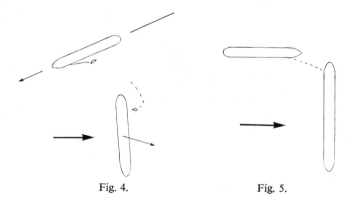

Fig. 4.   Fig. 5.

The rescue vessel should give as much lee as possible to the boat as it makes its way across to the other vessel, then a position should be taken up to leeward so that the boat can make the return journey down wind. The boat should be kept in sight if possible in case it should capsize or get into difficulties.

As the disabled vessel may be drifting fairly rapidly to leeward it could be dangerous for the boat to go alongside amidships on the lee side. In such circumstances the boat should lie off end-on to the ship, on the lee side, and nearer to the end which is lying up wind. The crew can then be taken off, one at a time, using a lifebuoy and lines.

In very bad weather conditions it is dangerous to use lifeboats. The best method of taking the crew off is to haul a liferaft across between the two ships. If both vessels are expected to drift to leeward at about the same rate this operation can be carried out with the two vessels lying parallel to one another but if the rate of drift is appreciably different the rescue vessel should take up a position, stern to wind, off the end of the disabled vessel and to windward of her. This position will enable the rescue vessel to manoeuvre so as to keep at a safe distance from the other ship (Fig. 5).

A rocket line is probably the best method of establishing communication. The liferaft can be hauled from one vessel to the other by a strong fibre rope.

When all the crew have been taken off the disabled ship a TTT message should be sent off reporting a derelict.

The Use of Wave Quelling Oils

Oil can be used, very effectively, to prevent seas from breaking. Vegetable, animal and fish oil are most suitable but if these are not available lubricating oil could be used. Fuel oil and crude oil are not recommended, particularly in cold water, as they tend to congeal and can be harmful to men in the water. Light oils such as kerosene are unlikely to be effective. Large quantities are not required. Tests have shown that about 200 litres (45 gallons) of lubricating oil can be effective over an area of at least 4,500 sq. m, but a larger quantity than this may be necessary.

Oil can be used to advantage in rough seas in such circumstances as when hove to, towing, crossing a bar and to assist in rescue operations. However, it may be best not to use it when men are in the water or when boats are being handled by oars.

The oil should be distributed from both bows when heading into wind and seas and from the weather side when lying stopped or running with the seas on the quarter. It should only be released gradually by such methods as trailing a punctured hose full of oil, or through a punctured canvas bag which has been weighted and filled with oil soaked cotton waste or by flushing through water closets.

Search and Rescue Operations

Detailed guidance concerning search and rescue operations is given in the IMO publication "Merchant Ship Search and Rescue Manual". The following notes are based on the IMO manual.

Co-ordination. It is essential that rescue operations should be properly co-ordinated. Rescue Co-ordination Centres (RCC's) have been set up in some areas. Specialised ships are sometimes used by these authorities. If such a vessel arrives on the scene it can be expected to act as On Scene Commander (OSC), otherwise one vessel with good radio communication facilities must assume the duty of Co-ordinator of Surface Search (CSS). The CSS should display code flags "FR" by day and show a distinctive signal at night.

Action by Assisting Ships. Ships proceeding to the area of distress should plot the position, course and speed of other ships and should attempt to construct an accurate picture of the circumstances attending the casualty. Preparation should be made, depending on the nature of the casualty. The radio direction-finding equipment may be useful to home on the distressed vessel.

Searches. If the casualty has not been located a search should be initiated without delay. A datum should be established, taking into account the reported position and time of the casualty, interval elapsed, drift and subsequent information. The most probable area can be established initially by drawing a circle of radius 10 miles with centre at datum then squaring it with tangents (see Fig. 6).

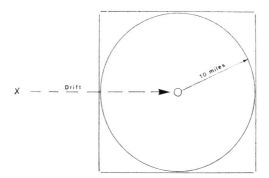

Fig. 6. Most Probable Area.

An expanding square search (Fig. 7), or a sector search (Fig. 8), is recommended when there is only one ship available, the latter being more suitable when the position of the search target is known within close limits as for a man overboard situation. When two or more ships are available a parallel search should be made (Fig. 9).

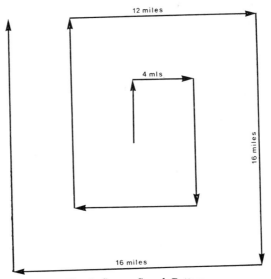

Fig. 7. Square Search Pattern.

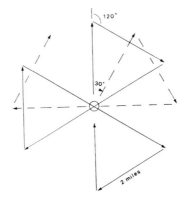

Fig. 8. Sector Search—1 Ship.

When the casualty, or survivor, is sighted the CSS should assess the best method of rescue and direct the most suitably equipped ship or ships to the scene.

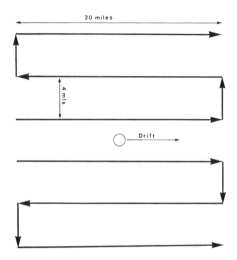

Fig. 9. Parallel Track Search—2 Ships.

Man Overboard

If a person is seen to fall overboard when the ship is making way through the water a lifebuoy should be released and the helm should be put hard over to the side from which the man has fallen. The signal "O" can be made by whistle and flag to warn any vessels which are in the vicinity. There is little point in stopping the engines, unless they are on stand-by and the person falls from the fore part. As many people as possible should be told to try to keep the man, or the lifebuoy, in sight, and it may be worth releasing a second lifebuoy, or a conspicuous object which will float, to give a transit. The first lifebuoy to be released should be fitted with a self-igniting light and self-activating smoke signal.

Turning under full helm through 360° will not bring the vessel back to the position at which the man fell (see p. 181). One method of returning to this position is turn through 180° under full helm then steady up on the reciprocal of the course for a few minutes to regain speed before putting the helm hard over in the same direction to come back to the original track (Fig. 10).

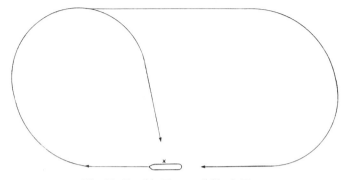

Fig. 10. Double Turn and Single Turn.

An alternative method of automatically returning to the same position is to make a Williamson turn. After turning under full helm through approximately 60° the rudder is put hard over in the opposite direction to bring the vessel round to the reciprocal of the original course (see Fig. 11). This manoeuvre should be executed at sea trials to determine the exact change of heading before applying opposite helm.

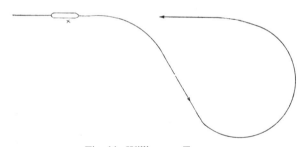

Fig. 11. Williamson Turn.

If the man can be kept in sight the vessel can be turned under full helm until the man is directly ahead (Fig. 10). Speed is reduced during the turn. If the vessel is not proceeding at full speed when the man falls overboard the engines could be used to manoeuvre into position.

The ship should preferably be stopped to windward of the man and allowed to drift down to him. Ladders and nets should be put out and a boat prepared for launching.

CHAPTER VIII

FIRE FIGHTING

Combustion is a chemical reaction, giving off heat and light, which is the result of a rapid union of oxygen with other substances. Three elements must be present to enable combustion to occur; there must be inflammable material, a supply of oxygen, and heat to cause the material to give off sufficient vapours. These three elements may be represented by the "fire triangle" (Fig. 1). If one side is removed the triangle will collapse, if one element is removed a fire will go out.

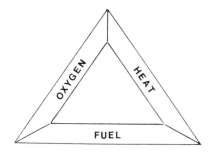

Fig. 1. The fire triangle.

The three basic methods of fire fighting are STARVING, SMOTHERING and COOLING. If the fire is starved of inflammable material it will soon burn itself out. Oxygen is present in the air but if the oxygen content is reduced to below 15 per cent by volume by adding other gases, or if the air is excluded by blanketing off, the fire will be put out by smothering. Finally, if the substance is cooled until it does not give off sufficient vapours to support combustion the fire will be extinguished.

Flash Point is the lowest temperature at which a substance gives off sufficient vapours to flash across the surface when a flame is applied. Substances with flash points below 23°C are classed as highly flammable. The flash point of petrol is below −18°C.

Fire Point is the lowest temperature at which a substance will give off sufficient vapour to continue to burn when ignited.

Ignition Temperature is the lowest temperature at which a substance will spontaneously ignite. Examples of ignition temperatures are petroleum oils 250°—400°C, coal 200°—400°C, wood and paper 230°—270°C and wool 200°C.

Spontaneous Combustion. Heat may be generated by chemical action (oxidation) in some substances. As the heat increases the oxidation takes place at an increasing rate until the ignition temperature is reached. Spontaneous combustion is likely to occur in cargoes such as oil cake, fish meal and seed expellers, especially when loaded wet, and in some types of coal. Copra and jute also generate heat when wet but are less liable to spontaneous combustion. Cargoes of this type must be kept cool, dry and well ventilated. In store rooms, and elsewhere, rags soaked in oil or paint are a source of danger.

Flammable Mixture. If the ratio of air to vapour is too high or too low the mixture cannot be ignited. With petroleum vapours a flammable mixture consists of over 90 per cent air and between 1 per cent and 10 per cent vapour depending on the grade.

PREVENTION OF FIRE

As oxygen, one of the three essential elements of fire, is normally present in the air it is important to avoid a combination of the other two. Inflammable material should not be placed near sources of heat, smoking should not be permitted in the vicinity of highly inflammable substances and the possibility of sparks falling on combustible material must be considered.

In the engine room, where there are numerous installations generating heat, cleanliness is essential. Accumulations of oil should be avoided, settling tanks and other oil tanks must not be allowed to overflow and oil leaks must receive immediate attention. Discarded cotton waste and cleaning rags should be put into metal containers which are emptied regularly.

The risk of fire is greater when the ship is in port, especially when repairs are being carried out or when inflammable material is being loaded or discharged. Before burning or welding operations are commenced inflammable material must be removed from around and behind the part to be worked on and fire appliances should be close at hand. Precautions must be taken against sparks falling into open holds and ventilators. When workmen leave the ship a check should be made to see that no material has been left smouldering and that there are no other fire hazards.

Personal portable electric space heating appliances and unauthorised electrical apparatus should not be used and amateur repairs to electrical fittings must not be allowed. Clothing should not be left to dry around electrical lamps or heaters. Care must be taken when using aerosol sprays as the contents are sometimes highly inflammable. Smoking in bed, and failure to stub-out cigarettes properly has caused many fires.

Extinguishing Agents

Water is an excellent cooling agent and is normally available in large quantities aboard ship in the form, of sea water. It has a high thermal capacity which means that it absorbs more heat for a given increase of temperature than the same mass of almost any other substance. A more important reason for its value as a cooling agent is that when water is applied to a fire and converted to steam a great deal of heat is extracted. If water at near freezing temperature is used in fire fighting over five times as much heat is extracted in converting the water into steam than is absorbed in the process of raising the temperature of water from freezing point to boiling point. The smothering effect of the steam produced at the seat of the fire may also assist in the extinguishing process.

If water is to have its maximum cooling effect it is essential that it should be absorbed in the fire and converted to steam so a large proportion should not be allowed to escape in liquid form. In some cases water is more effective when applied in the form of a spray or fog. The greatly increased total surface for absorption makes the cooling action more efficient and fog or spray is less likely to cause damage than a solid jet of water.

The disadvantages of water are that it may have an adverse effect on the vessel's stability, that it may react dangerously with some substances such as acids and carbides and that if poured on to burning oil it will sink beneath the surface causing the fire to erupt. Sea water must not be used on electrical fires as it is a good conductor. It may cause considerable damage to cargo and produce corrosion.

Carbon Dioxide (CO_2) is an excellent smothering agent. It is heavier than air which makes it effective against fires which are low in the compartment. It is usually stored at high pressure in heavy steel cylinders which enables it to be rapidly directed into a compartment. It is not likely to damage cargo.

The principal disadvantage is that it is not available in continuous supply. When the gas has been used up the supply cannot be renewed until the vessel reaches a port with facilities for recharging cylinders. A further disadvantage is that, although it is not toxic, it will cause suffocation if inhaled in heavy concentrations. It has no appreciable cooling effect.

Halon. Halogenated hydrocarbon vapourising liquids are still accepted for certain uses on ships but are being phased out for environmental protection reasons. No new Halon systems will be permitted. Halon 1211, bromochlorodifluoromethane (BCF), and Halon 1301, bromotrifluoromethane (BTM), are stored as liquids under pressure but will vapourise rapidly when released to form a dense cloud of gas which smothers the fire and also interferes with the chemical reaction of combustion. These vapourising liquids are excellent for electrical fires and may also be used for fires involving inflammable liquids and Class A fires. They are not suitable for fires in materials containing their own oxygen.

Halon 1211 and Halon 1301 may cause dizziness but are not very toxic at temperatures up to nearly 500° C. At higher temperatures they will decompose and may become very hazardous.

Inert Gas. When used in connection with fire extinguishing for ships this term is generally taken to mean a gas, which will not support combustion, produced by burning oil in air. It consists mainly of nitrogen (about 85 per cent) and carbon dioxide (over 14 per cent). The gas may be produced by an inert gas generator or by drawing off boiler flue gases from the funnel. Inert Gas Systems for oil tankers use gas from the boiler uptake to reduce the oxygen content of the cargo tanks as a preventative measure rather than for fire fighting. In both systems the gas is washed and cooled before being pumped through ducts into the compartments. The advantages are that it can be continuously produced, it is not likely to damage or react dangerously with the cargo and it does not depend for its efficiency on rigorous battening down of holds. The main disadvantage is that it cannot be produced at a very high rate compared with the release of carbon dioxide. It is not acceptable for use in engine rooms.

Foam is a very effective smothering agent for oil fires. Bubbles containing air are produced by agitating a single solution of water mixed with a foam compound. A disadvantage is that it may take a long time to get rid of the foam.

There are three basic classifications for fire fighting air foams:
1. High expansion foam with an expansion ratio of up to 1200:1
2. Medium expansion foam with an expansion ratio of up to 300:1
3. Low expansion foam with an expansion ratio of up to 20:1

High expansion foam is particularly suitable for large deep seated three-dimensional fires and for those involving large quantities of flammable liquids. Medium and low expansion foam is most suitable for two-dimensional fires or in circumstances where a heavier foam is required.

Dry Powder consists mainly of bicarbonate of soda with other substances added. It is particularly suitable for extinguishing running fires in highly inflammable liquids and can be used on electrical fires. The extinguishing effect is based on the ability of the powder to interrupt the chain reaction of combustion by preventing the combination of oxygen with the burning material.

TYPES OF FIRE

In 1970 agreement was reached between European countries on the following classification:

Class A. Fires involving solid materials normally of an organic nature such as wood, paper, textiles, fabrics and plastics. The most effective extinguishing agent is water.

Class B. Fires involving liquids or liquefiable solids. Extinguishing agents include water spray, foam, vapourising liquids, carbon dioxide and dry powder.

Class C. Fires involving gases or liquified gases in the form of a jet or spray, e.g. methane, propane and butane.

Class D. Fires involving metals. Carbon dioxide and dry powder are normally suitable.

Fires involving live electrical equipment are sometimes referred to as Class E.

Fire Appliances for Merchant Ships

Fire appliances for merchant ships should be in accordance with the IMO Safety of Life at Sea. (SOLAS) Convention, Chapter 11-2, and with any additional requirements of the national administratation. Ships registered in the United Kingdom must be fitted with fire appliances in accordance with the Merchant Shipping (Fire Appliances) Regulations.

Requirements for cargo ships of over 1000 gross tons:

(a) At least two independently operated fire pumps, and if a fire in any one compartment could put all the fire pumps out of action an emergency fire pump, must be provided outside the machinery space and be independently driven. Water service pipes and hydrants must be placed so that two jets of water may be directed into any part of the ship. One fire hose must be provided for each 30 m of length of ship and one spare, in no case less than 5 in all, in addition to hoses required in the engine or boiler room.

In each space fitted with boilers or propelling machinery there must be at least one hydrant with a fire hose and dual purpose nozzle on each side.

At least one international shore connection, together with its gasket, bolts and washers, must be kept on board.

(b) At least five portable fire extinguishers of approved type and design must be provided in the accommodation spaces, service stations and control stations.

(c) A fixed fire extinguishing system must be provided to protect every cargo space. Ships may be exempt from this requirement if steel hatch covers are provided and the ship is employed solely in the carriage of ore, coal, grain or other non-dangerous cargo. Tankers must have a fixed deck foam system. Tankers of 20,000 tonnes deadweight and upwards must also have a fixed inert gas system.

(d) Machinery spaces containing oil-fired boilers or internal combustion machinery must be protected by one of the following fixed fire extinguishing installations:

A pressure water-spraying system; or, a fire smothering gas system; or, a high expansion foam system.

In addition, in each boiler room one or more foam-type fire extinguishers of at least 135 litres capacity and a portable foam applicator, two portable extinguishers suitable for oil fires in each firing space and a receptacle containing sand or other dry material for quenching oil fires with a scoop in each firing space. In addition, in each space containing internal combustion machinery, one foam extinguisher of at least 45 litres capacity or equivalent extinguisher, at least one portable foam applicator and portable extinguishers at no more than 10 metres from any position within the space (not less than two).

(e) A fire detection and alarm system must be installed in periodically unattended machinery spaces, in ro-ro cargo spaces and in other cargo spaces containing motor vehicles with fuel in their tanks.

(f) At least two fireman's outfits, at least four on tankers, must be provided. They must be stored in easily accessible, widely separated, positions and kept ready for use.

Fixed Installation

A **Water Spraying System** may be provided in machinery spaces but relatively few ships use this type of installation. Spray nozzles are placed in such a way as to cover the entire tank top and places of special fire risk. An air vessel and pump keep the system pressurised.

A **Carbon Dioxide Installation** may be fitted for use in cargo spaces and/or machinery spaces and many ships use this method. For the engine room rapid injection is necessary if the gas is to be effective so the requirement is that 85 per cent of the full quantity must be released within 2 minutes. A gang release arrangement is used to ensure a quick discharge. For cargo spaces the gas is released, cylinder by cylinder, by a planned sequence over a longer period of time. The quantity of gas available must be 30 per cent of the gross volume of the largest cargo compartment and 35 per cent of the gross volume of the largest space containing boilers and machinery, including the casing. If a combined system is provided the quantity of gas is not required to be more than the maximum required for either the machinery space or the largest cargo space.

An alarm system must be fitted to give audible warning before the gas is released into any working space. In some systems the alarm is operated when the door of the cabinet containing the control valves is opened; in others it is operated when the valve is turned.

A **Halon Installation** may be provided for use in machinery spaces and pump rooms of some existing ships, but is not permitted for new ships. Halon 1301 (BTM) is mainly used. Where the medium is BTM the vapour concentration must be not less than 4·25% of the gross volume and not more than 7% of the net volume of the machinery space, including the casing. It should be possible for the liquid phase of the minimum quantity required to be discharged into the space within 20 seconds or less.

A **High Expansion Foam System** is permitted for use in machinery spaces but is unlikely to be provided on ships. If fitted, it must be capable of rapidly discharging through fixed outlets a quantity of foam sufficient to fill the greatest space to be protected at a rate of at least 1 m in depth per minute. The quantity of foam-forming liquid available shall be sufficient to produce a volume of foam equal to five times the volume of the largest space to be protected. The expansion ratio of the foam must not exceed 1000 to 1.

A **Low Expansion Foam System** may be fitted to machinery spaces in addition to the fixed fire extinguishing installation required by the SOLAS Convention. Such a system must be capable of discharging through fixed outlets in not more than five minutes a quantity of foam sufficient to cover to a depth of 150 mm the largest single area over which oil fuel is liable to spread. The expansion ratio of the foam must not exceed 12 to 1.

A **Fixed Deck Foam System** must be provided for tankers. Such a system must be capable of delivering foam to the entire cargo tank area as well as into any tank, the deck of which has been ruptured. It must be capable of simple and rapid operation. The rate of the supply must be not less than the greatest of the following:
   (i) 0·6 litres per min. per sq. m of cargo deck area.
   (ii) 6 litres per min. per sq. m of area of largest tank.
   (iii) 3 litres per min. per sq. m of area protected by largest monitor, not less than 1·25 litres per min.
Sufficient foam concentrate must be supplied to ensure at least 20

minutes of foam generation in tankers with an inert gas installation, or 30 minutes of foam generation in tankers not fitted with an inert gas installation.

An Inert Gas System must be fitted to certain tankers, depending on size and age of ship. It must be capable of inerting empty cargo tanks by reducing the oxygen content in each tank to a level at which combustion cannot be supported and of keeping the oxygen content below 8% by volume. The system must be capable of delivering inert gas to the cargo tanks at a rate of at least 125% of the maximum rate of discharge capacity, expressed as a volume, and with an oxygen content of not more than 5% by volume in the inert gas supply main to the cargo tanks at any required rate of flow.

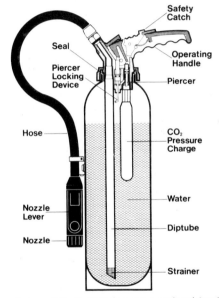

Fig. 2. Sectional view of Nu-Swift 9 litre water extinguisher Model 1321

Portable Extinguishers

Water type extinguishers are most suitable for class A fires. The water is expelled by release of gas from a cartridge. The extinguisher is filled with water and has an internal tube from the nozzle at the top to the bottom of the liquid. The Nu-Swift 9 litre water extinguisher, Model 1321, is shown in cross section in Fig. 2. This type is operated by pulling up the ring on the safety catch and depressing the handle fully then squeezing the nozzle lever. Other types may be operated by depressing a strike-knob.

Foam type extinguishers are particularly suitable for fires involving inflammable liquids (class B) and may also be used on class A fires. The Nu-Swift 9 litre foam extinguisher, Model 7077, is shown in cross section in Fig. 3. The extinguisher has a container of foam concentrate with a pressure charge of carbon dioxide in an outer container of water. It is operated by pulling off the safety clip on the nozzle, depressing the strike-knob and squeezing the control lever of the nozzle.

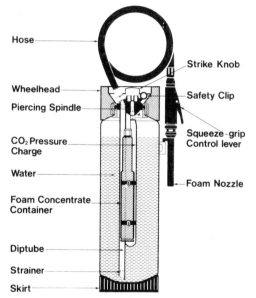

Fig. 3. Sectional view of Nu-Swift 9 litre foam extinguisher Model 7077

Foam extinguishers should not be used on electrical fires. When being used on oil fires the jet should preferably be directed on to a bulkhead above the burning surface so as to permit the foam to flow over the oil. Directing the stream on to the burning liquid may increase the spread of fire.

Carbon dioxide portable extinguishers are suitable for fires involving inflammable liquid (class B) and live electrical appliances. The carbon dioxide is kept under pressure in the extinguisher which causes it to be mainly in liquid form. A cross section of the Nu-Swift carbon dioxide extinguisher, Model 1502, is shown in Fig. 4. Operation of the squeeze grip control allows the carbon dioxide to expand and a fire smothering cloud of gaseous and solid carbon dioxide is directed through the non-conducting discharge horn.

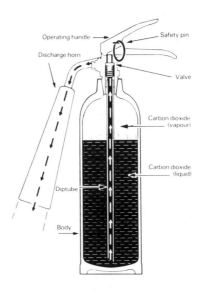

Fig. 4. Sectional view of Nu-Swift carbon dioxide extinguisher Model 1502

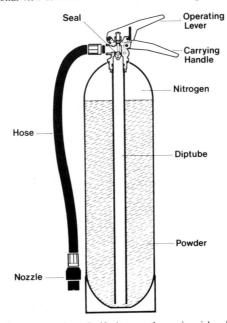

Fig. 5. Sectional view of Nu-Swift dry powder extinguisher Model HS10

Dry powder extinguishers are suitable for fighting class B fires involving inflammable liquids and for electrical fires. They are also effective on Class C and D fires and small class A fires but they are not suitable for deep-seated class A fires as there is no cooling effect. The United Kingdom Fire Appliances Regulations specify that if portable dry powder extinguishers are provided in accommodation and service spaces or in machinery spaces at least half the extinguishers must be of another type.

The powder is hermetically sealed under pressure with nitrogen in the extinguisher. The Nu-Swift dry powder extinguisher, Model HS10, is shown in cross section in Fig. 5. The extinguisher is operated by pulling out the safety clip and squeezing the operating lever.

Halon extinguishers are suitable for fighting class B fires involving inflammable liquids and class C fires involving inflammable gases if there is no explosion risk. They are also suitable for use on fires involving electrical appliances.

Halon extinguishers must not be located in the accommodation spaces and their number must not exceed half the total number of extinguishers in machinery spaces.

The halon, usually 1211 (BCF), is stored in the extinguisher in liquid form, which on discharge from the nozzle produces a non-flammable heavier-than-air vapour.

Fire Detection Systems

In ro-ro spaces, in other cargo spaces containing motor vehicles with fuel in their tanks and in periodically unattended machinery spaces of cargo and passenger ships an automatic fire detection and alarm system must be fitted. Such a system must also be fitted to passenger ships in parts of the vessel not accessible to the fire patrol.

The detection and alarm system must be capable of immediate automatic operation at all times and include facilities for periodic testing. The system may be operated by heat, smoke or other product of combustion, or any combination of these factors. Each section of detectors must include means for giving both visual and audible alarm automatically at the control panel and indicating units. There must be at least two sources of power, including an emergency source.

Fire Drills

Fire Drill is required to be held at intervals of not more than 7 days in passenger ships and not more than 14 days in cargo ships. Recommendations concerning fire drill and lifeboat drill are given in Merchant Shipping Notice M1217. For the purpose of a fire drill an outbreak of fire should be assumed to have occurred in some part of the ship and a mock attack should be made. The type and position of the fire drill should be varied.

When the fire signal is given members of the crew should assemble at their appointed stations. The fire pump should be started to give full pressure on the fire main and the emergency fire pump should also be started. Hoses should be laid out at the scene of the assumed fire and water played through them.

The crew should be instructed in the use of extinguishers appropriate to the mock fire and at each drill a different person should discharge an extinguisher. The crew should be exercised in the closing of doors and other openings including the annular space around the funnel. As many of the crew as possible should be made familiar with the remote controls for fans, fuel pumps and oil tank valves.

Fuel installations and alarm systems should be tested with as much realism as is reasonable and practicable. The fire party should be exercised in the use of breathing apparatus.

Following the loss of a cargo vessel due to fire a Court of Formal Investigation commented on the need for deck department staff to have knowledge of the means of operating the emergency fire pump. In Merchant Shipping Notice M443 it is recommended that the emergency fire pump should be used for regular wash down service.

Fire Fighting

The person who discovers a fire aboard ship must immediately raise the alarm and attempt to extinguish the fire shutting off the air supply as much as possible. He must not try to tackle the fire without raising the alarm unless it is very small. If it is necessary to leave the scene of the fire to get help the door of the compartment must be closed. Speed is essential as the fire may rapidly become impossible to control.

When a fire on a ship at sea is reported to the bridge the fire alarm must be operated. Mechanical ventilation should be closed down and the vessel either stopped or manoeuvred so as to get the fire on the lee side. Water must be supplied at full pressure to the fire main and the emergency fire pump started. Boats should be swung out if considered necessary.

An XXX or PAN PAN PAN urgency signal should be sent off with the vessel's position given as accurately as possible. This does not require other vessels to come to give assistance but some ships may be prepared to make a diversion. It serves to warn the authorities of the situation and if the urgency signal is not cancelled aircraft will probably be sent to find out what is wrong. A distress message may have to be sent at a later stage, or possibly immediately if there is serious fire or explosion. It is important to cancel the urgency or distress signal when the emergency is over.

Fire in the accommodation must be tackled rapidly as there is likely to be a considerable amount of flammable material present and it is difficult to exclude oxygen. Doors and ports should be closed and the ventilation system shut off. Portable extinguishers will be available to tackle the fire in the initial stages but if the fire is not quickly extinguished water will be the only effective medium.

Breathing apparatus should be used as there is likely to be a great deal of smoke. Burning mattresses are a particular hazard. Electricity may have to be cut off. The door of a burning compartment should be kept closed until sufficient men are available and the equipment is ready then the fire should be tackled from low down, preferably by breaking in a bottom panel, with the man using the hose crouching or lying near the deck. The jet of water should be first directed to the top of the compartment to cool the atmosphere. There is great danger of the fire spreading so attention must be paid to all surrounding compartments.

Fires in the engine room are likely to involve oil fuel. If a small fire cannot be quickly put out with the extinguishers provided the fuel supply and ventilation should be cut off and sky lights closed. Water spray or water fog may be particularly effective. For a serious fire the fixed installations should be used. Carbon dioxide should preferably not be admitted until all men are out of the compartment but the gas is unlikely to be effective if there is much delay and the heat builds up.

After flooding with carbon dioxide the space should not be opened up for at least 10 minutes to allow the burning substances to cool down below ignition temperature. Entrance to the engine room should preferably be made from the tunnel as the smoke and gases rise to the top of the compartment. Water fog or spray from the hydrant at the tunnel entrance can be used to cool the hot surfaces and to protect the fire-fighters.

Fires in cargo spaces. When a fire is detected in a ship's hold at sea it will usually be best not to open the hatches but to use smothering gas keeping the compartment tightly battened down. Precautions should be taken against the fire spreading to adjacent compartments and boundary cooling may be necessary. After using smothering gas the compartment should not be opened up until the vessel reaches port and the fire brigade have arrived. Smothering gas has a negligible cooling effect so the fire is likely to break out again with renewed vigour as soon as air is admitted to the smouldering material.

In certain circumstances, with limited fires, it may be appropriate to tackle the fire directly with hoses. If this is to be done the compartment should not be opened until all the necessary gear has been assembled. With a cargo of nitrates or sulphates smothering gas is unlikely to be effective so water should be applied as rapidly as possible.

Smothering gas is unsuitable for coal, and water in limited quantity may cause dangerous gases to be given off. The safest procedure in the event of a coal fire at sea would probably be to proceed to the nearest port where discharge facilities are available shutting off the ventilation, spraying heated decks and cooling bulkheads.

Oil Fires in tanks should be tackled by closing the tank lids and other openings to completely shut off the air supply then applying smothering gas or foam. Water in the form of a solid jet should be used to cool the surrounding decks and all inflammable material moved clear of the area. Water fog is a good extinguishing agent as it is effective in cooling the oil. Carbon dioxide, foam and dry powder extinguishers are suitable for small oil fires.

Galley Fires are likely to involve burning fat or fuel for stove burners. Foam and carbon dioxide extinguishers are likely to be most effective. Water must not be used on burning fat. A fire blanket must be provided in the galley of a passenger ship.

Electrical Fires. Salt water and foam should not be used as they are good conductors and fresh water should not be used where there are high voltages. Carbon dioxide and dry powder are most suitable but the latter leaves a residue. The power should be cut off if possible.

Fires in Port. Whenever a fire occurs on a ship in port the fire brigade should be called, even if the fire is small. At least one international shore connection is required to be provided to enable water to be supplied from the shore. This should be readily available when the ship is in port. When a vessel goes into dry dock it is essential to ensure that water is continuously available for fire fighting purposes.

CHAPTER IX

SHIP HANDLING

General Principles. Several factors must be taken into account in ship handling. The ability to manoeuvre will depend upon the characteristics of the vessel including the type of machinery, the number and type of propellers, the type of rudder, the manoeuvring devices fitted, the displacement, the trim and the shape and condition of the hull. It will also depend on external factors such as the depth and extent of surrounding water, the strength of tide or current and on the wind.

Type of Machinery. Diesel engines are fitted to the majority of merchant ships. Compared with steam turbines they have the advantage of giving almost as much (85 per cent) astern power as ahead power. However the time taken to reverse the shaft and develop astern thrust after going ahead at full speed is likely to be longer than for a steam turbine. The number of stops and starts which can be made in a certain time may be restricted as compressed air has to be used.

A vessel fitted with geared steam turbines must have separate turbines for going astern which usually give astern power of between 40 per cent and 60 per cent of the full ahead power. There is a risk of distorting or stripping the blades if full astern steam pressure is applied too soon after going full ahead but reversing can normally be achieved more rapidly than with Diesel engines.

Propellers. Most vessels have a single right-handed propeller, i.e. one which turns clockwise, viewed from astern, when the engines are going ahead. Twin screw vessels usually have outward turning propellers, which means that the starboard propeller is right-handed and the port propeller left-handed. Controllable pitch propellers are now available for ships of all sizes. With this type the shaft and propeller rotate in a constant direction and astern power is achieved by reversing the pitch of the blades.

Rudders may be of various types. The majority of modern vessels are fitted with a single balanced, or semi-balanced, rudder which has up to 30 per cent of the area forward of the turning axis to reduce the power required to turn the rudder when moving ahead.

The turning effect of the rudder depends upon the direction and strength of the force produced on it by the flow of water. The turning effect increases as the angle which the rudder makes with the fore

175

and aft line is increased for rudder angles up to about 45°. If the rudder angle is increased beyond this value the rudder may stall giving reduced turning effect, and resistance to forward motion will increase. Stops are fitted to prevent the rudder being turned beyond an angle of about 35° which is considered to give maximum efficiency. The transverse component acting on the rudder causes the vessel to be displaced bodily away from the side to which the rudder is turned.

Active Rudder. Some vessels are fitted with an active rudder which has a submerged motor, driving a fixed or controllable pitch propeller installed at the trailing edge. The rudder can be turned through 90° with the engines stopped and the propeller will spin the ship about a vertical axis. An active rudder is of particular value when manoeuvring at very low speeds.

Tunnel Side Thrusters are fitted to some ships to assist in manoeuvring. They are commonly known as bow thrusters as they are usually fitted near the bow but it is possible to fit them elsewhere. The unit consists of a straight tunnel through the ship with an axial propeller-type pump. Thruster units can be used to advantage in turning short round but their main value is for berthing and leaving the berth.

The effect of the propeller upon steering will now be considered for a single screw vessel.

Transverse Thrust

When the engines are going either ahead or astern the rotation of the propeller tends to turn the ship, even when the rudder is amidships. If the ship is in light condition the upper blades of the propeller are likely to churn and break up the water near the surface with the result that the lower blades have to overcome greater resistance than the upper ones. As most vessels have a single right-handed propeller the lower blades turn to port when going ahead causing the stern to swing to starboard. On going astern the lower blades turn to starboard and the stern swings to port.

The transverse thrust effect may still be present when the propeller is immersed well below the surface, in which case it cannot be attributed to the greater resistance encountered by the lower blades. The influx of water to the propeller is not parallel to the axis and the thrust of the rotating propeller is consequently distorted. The amount of transverse thrust is related to the shape of the hull in the vicinity of the propeller. A bluff stern vessel will have more bias due to this effect than a fine lined vessel.

When a controllable pitch propeller is fitted the bias will always be towards the same side, as the direction of rotation is not changed when going astern.

The Wake Current

As a ship moves forward through the water there is a tendency to form a cavity or hollow at the stern. Water swirls round the sides to fill the cavity. This follow up is called the wake current.

The current is strongest at the surface and decreases as the depth increases towards the keel. The wake current is more pronounced in vessels of full form than in those of fine line. Flat-bottomed, square-sterned barges are difficult to steer as the strong wake current tends to neutralise the effect of the flow of water aft towards the rudder due to the vessel's headway. The wake current reduces the steering power of the rudder when going ahead.

SUMMARY OF RUDDER AND PROPELLER EFFECTS

Starting from rest when going ahead. The transverse thrust effect will tend to swing the stern to starboard and the bow to port. The engines working ahead cause the propeller to drive a spiral flow of water towards the rudder (screw race) so the helm can be used to counteract the effect of transverse thrust.

Moving at steady speed ahead. The transverse thrust of the propeller will tend to swing the ship's head to port. The wake current reduces steering power but the helm can be used very effectively to counteract the effect of transverse thrust as there is a strong flow of water against the rudder due to the screw race and the vessel's headway.

Moving ahead with engines stopped. There is no transverse thrust effect from the propeller. The helm is less effective when the engines are stopped as there is no flow of water from the propeller against the rudder. If the vessel has good headway the rudder will have some effect but this is reduced by the wake current.

Starting from rest when going astern. The transverse thrust effect of the propeller and the effect of the propeller slipstream on the hull causes the stern to swing to port. The helm cannot be used effectively to counteract the swing as there is no flow of water against the rudder from the propeller, or from the movement of the ship.

Moving at steady speed astern. The transverse thrust effect is reduced as the ship gathers sternway so the tendency to turn is less than when starting from rest. The rudder may become effective if the vessel moves astern rapidly but, for many ships, the steering effect is unpredictable.

Twin Screws

The effects of twin-screw propellers are not so complicated as those of single screws. It is only necessary to take into account

(1st) the current caused by the screw, and to consider whether it is a discharge current acting against the fore side of the rudder, or whether it is a suction current drawn in against its after-side; (2nd) the transverse thrust of the screws; (3rd) the athwartships distance between the propellers which results in a couple being set up when going ahead on one engine and astern on the other.

As the screws revolve in opposite directions when both are going ahead at the same speed, there should not be any turning effect from the transverse thrust of the screws, and if the helm is ported or starboarded they will assist the action of the rudder.

TURNING SHORT ROUND

To turn a single screw vessel short round.—A consideration of what has already been stated will show that a ship with a right-handed propeller can be turned more easily with her head going to starboard than in the other direction. When necessary to turn short round put the rudder to starboard, and the engines full speed ahead. The screw race will press against the rudder, even if the vessel has no headway, and she will cant to starboard. Before she gathers too much headway the engines should be reversed to full speed astern, the helm being shifted accordingly so as to obtain the benefit of the suction current. Before she gathers too much sternway go full speed ahead again with rudder to starboard and so on, alternately until round.

It is advisable to have an anchor ready for dropping when turning short round in narrow channels and to know that there is sufficient depth of water when manoeuvring close to the banks.

To turn a twin-screw vessel short round.—This is done by going ahead on one and astern on the other; the bow of the ship then turns towards that side on which the screw is going astern. By regulating the speeds of the propellers so as to prevent the vessel gathering headway, the ship can be made to turn round in her own length, but this is a slow process. A more rapid swing can be achieved by adjusting propeller speeds to cause the ship to move ahead and astern alternately, if there is sufficient space available. The rudder should be kept hard over in the direction of the turn.

If the starboard screw is right-handed and the port one left-handed, the transverse thrust of both screws will assist in turning the ship short round in either direction.

STOPPING DISTANCES

Inertia Stop. When the engines are stopped with the vessel moving ahead and the way is run off without putting the engines astern the manoeuvre is described as an inertia stop. The total distance run will depend upon the type of ship, the initial speed, the displacement, the trim, the condition of underwater plating and other factors. The distance in miles may be only one-tenth of the initial speed in knots for cross channel ships and warships but more than half the speed for fully loaded tankers.

Crash Stops. When the engines are put astern to stop the ship as rapidly as possible after going full ahead the manoeuvre is known as a crash stop. The total distance travelled along the ship's actual path is known as the track reach and the total distance travelled in the direction of the ship's initial course is the head reach. In addition to the factors which govern the distance travelled for an inertia stop the head reach for a crash stop will depend upon the type of machinery and it will also be affected by the use of the rudder.

The conventional way of carrying out a crash stop is to stop the engines then put them full astern as soon as possible leaving the rudder amidships. The time taken to reverse the shaft and develop astern thrust depends upon the type of machinery. Under trial conditions the delay is usually about one minute for steam turbines and nearer two minutes for Diesel engines. The stern of a right-handed single screw vessel will probably be swung to port when the engines are put astern causing the ship to turn to starboard by as much as 90° or more before coming to rest (see Fig. 1). Wind may also have an important effect on the heading after steerageway is lost so the vessel will not necessarily turn to starboard.

Fig. 1. Crash Stop.

The track reach may be conveniently expressed in terms of ship lengths when considering the crash stop. It may be less than 5 ship lengths for cross channel ships and warships but a large fully laden tanker or bulk carrier may have a track reach of more than 15 ship lengths. The head reach may be appreciably less than the track reach due to the turning effect. The time taken to bring the vessel to rest will obviously vary considerably. It may be possible to stop a cargo vessel of 3000 tonnes displacement going at a speed of 16 knots in less than two minutes, but it may take 25 minutes or more to stop a loaded tanker of over 200,000 tonnes moving at the same initial speed.

Use of the rudder. The rudder can be used to advantage to give additional retarding effect when stopping in an emergency. If the engines are put full astern at the earliest possible moment the rudder will soon become ineffective but it is possible to achieve an equivalent braking effect for some ships by initially putting the engines to slow ahead to use the negative thrust given by a slowly rotating propeller when a vessel is still moving at high speed.

In the manoeuvring trials of the 193,000 tonne tanker *Esso Bernicia* the British Ship Research Association carried out a stopping test using what is described as rudder cycling. With the vessel going at full speed of approximately 16 knots the wheel was put hard over to port and the engine revolutions reduced to 60 r.p.m. After turning 40° to port the wheel was put hard over to starboard and the engine speed reduced to 48 r.p.m. As the ship's head came past the original course the rudder was put hard over to port and speed reduced to 30 r.p.m. Finally as the vessel came back to the original heading the rudder was put hard-a-starboard and engines full astern. By this technique the head reach was reduced to less than half the crash stop head reach for the same displacement and speed. (See Fig. 2).

Fig. 2. Rudder Cycling.

It is not suggested that rudder cycling as described above should be used for an emergency stop. It would probably be difficult to carry out such an elaborate procedure in an emergency and the long delay before putting the engines astern may have to be justified in a Court of Inquiry. The action to be taken must depend upon the particular circumstances. Putting the engines full astern at the earliest possible moment may be the most effective way of stopping some ships but there is a risk of damaging the machinery if astern power is applied too rapidly.

If a sudden stop is necessary it will probably be best to shut off the ahead power immediately and to put the rudder hard over to port or to starboard. Subsequent use of the rudder will depend upon the nature of the emergency and the direction of the danger. The engines should be put full astern after a delay of not more than about three minutes.

TURNING CIRCLES

If the rudder is put hard over when the vessel is going ahead, and kept in this position, the ship will describe a turning circle similar to that shown in Fig. 3. The curvature of the path increases as the vessel turns through the first 90° then remains fairly constant. There is a slight lateral displacement away from the side to which the rudder is turned.

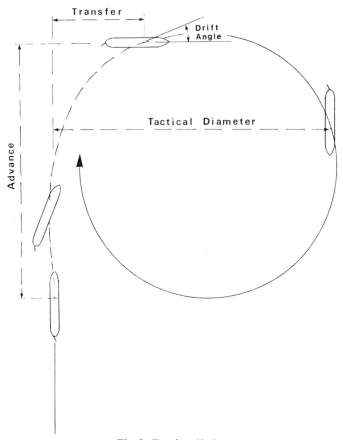

Fig. 3. Turning Circle.

The following terms are used in connection with turning circles:

Advance. The distance travelled in the direction of the original heading measured from the point at which helm was first applied.

The maximum advance is usually between 3 and 5 ship lengths for a merchant ship of any size going at full ahead and using full helm.

Transfer. The distance of the centre of gravity of the ship from the original track line measured in the direction 90° to the original heading. The transfer for a turn of 90° is about 2 ship lengths.

Tactical Diameter is the transfer for a turn of 180° which is almost equal to the maximum transfer. It is usually about the same distance as the maximum advance.

Drift Angle is the angle between the tangent to the turning circle at any point and the fore and aft line of the ship.

Pivot Point is the point about which the vessel pivots with the bow swinging inwards and the stern swinging outwards. It is about one third of the vessel's length from forward when going ahead. When going astern the vessel pivots about a point approximately one quarter of the length from the stern.

The time taken to turn through the first 90° is between 2 and 3 minutes for most vessels and a turn of 360° will usually take between 5 and 12 minutes. The speed is reduced by about one-quarter in turning through the first 90° and by between one-third and one-half after turning through the first 180°, after this the speed remains almost constant.

The turning circle may be slightly less when turning to port than when turning to starboard due to transverse thrust, but other factors such as wind are likely to have a greater effect. A listed vessel will normally have a smaller turning circle towards the high side.

WIND EFFECT

Wind can have a considerable effect on manoeuvring, especially when the vessel is in light condition. The effect will depend on the trim and disposition of the superstructure. A vessel which is stopped will tend to lie with the wind approximately abeam. When moving ahead with the wind on the bow a vessel with the bridge forward of amidships trimmed by the stern will probably tend to pay off the wind, but the bow of a vessel with superstructure aft may tend to come into the direction of wind.

When going astern the pivot point usually comes well aft of amidships so the stern will tend to fly into the wind. This is less likely to apply to vessels with all superstructure aft. If the wind is on the starboard quarter the tendency for the stern to fly into the wind is opposed by the transverse thrust effect. The stern will probably swing to port at first but may swing to starboard due to wind effect as the vessel gathers sternway.

HYDRODYNAMIC EFFECTS

When a ship moves through the water hydrodynamic forces affect ship handling in several ways. The effects become greater in shallow water, especially when the depth of water is less than 1·5 times the draught of the ship.

Squat. The changes of pressure which occur as a ship moves through the water are likely to cause both a bodily sinkage and a change of trim, especially in shallow water. An increase of mean draught in excess of 2 m may be experienced by a large vessel moving at a fairly high speed. At moderate speeds most vessels will tend to trim by the head but an increase to a high speed may cause a rapid change to a trim by the stern. This effect will obviously increase the risk of grounding when moving through relatively shallow water so the speed should be moderate.

Steering. In shallow water the rate of turning for a given rudder angle is likely to be decreased and a vessel will have a larger turning circle. The increase in the radius of turning circle is due partly to the fact that the loss of speed due to turning is less in shallow water.

Bow Cushion and Bank Suction. In a restricted channel there is a tendency for the bow of a ship to be pushed away from the bank and for the vessel to be attracted bodily towards the bank. The first effect is known as bow cushion, it is caused by the pressure field of the bow, forcing the bow away from the bank. The second effect—bank suction—is caused by the loss of pressure associated with the increased velocity of water in the restricted space between the vessel and the bank. A vessel approaching a bank will probably have to apply helm in the direction of the bank in order to prevent a sheer from developing.

Interaction. When two vessels moving at high speed pass close to each other the pressure fields may combine to cause one or both vessels to be swung off course and to cause a lateral displacement towards or away from each other. The effect is of greater importance when both vessels are moving in the same direction as the forces will be acting over a much longer period than for vessels passing close on opposite courses. It is also greater in shallow water.

In the case of a large vessel overtaking a smaller one at close distance there will be two dangerous stages. When the bow of the overtaking vessel approaches the stern of the other vessel the smaller ship will tend to swing across the path of the overtaking ship (Fig. 4). When the sterns of the two vessels are opposite one another the smaller ship will tend to turn into the side of the larger ship (Fig. 5).

Interaction between ships can also occur in deep water and vessels engaged in replenishment at sea have to make allowances for it. However, the effect is much less than in shallow water and should not be appreciable at distances of over 300 m. There can be little justification for overtaking at distances which would cause the forces of interaction to be effective except in narrow channels.

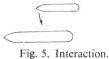

Fig. 4. Interaction.
First dangerous position.

Fig. 5. Interaction.
Second dangerous position.

ANCHOR WORK

Coming to a single anchor. On approaching an anchorage from the sea both anchors should be prepared for use in good time by clearing the hawse pipes and spurling pipes and taking off the bow stoppers. When the speed has been reduced the anchor should be lowered clear of the hawse pipe by putting the windlass in gear, releasing the brake and walking out the cable. The brake is then screwed up and the windlass taken out of gear ready for letting go. The anchor ball or light must be prepared so that the anchor signal can be displayed as soon as the anchor is dropped.

If there is a tide running the vessel should, preferably, stem the tide on approaching the anchorage and reduce speed so as to make slow headway over the ground. On reaching the required position the engines are stopped, and if necessary put astern, then as the vessel begins to make sternway the anchor is let go. At first the cable is allowed to run out until the amount released is approximately twice the depth of water then the brake should be applied and the cable paid out gradually. As the cable goes out the bell should be rung to indicate the amount rendered. The number of strokes on the bell indicates the number of shackles run out. In a tideway the vessel can be allowed to drop back with the tide keeping the engines stopped but if there is no tide running it will be necessary to use astern power. The vessel should be headed into the wind if there is no tide or current.

When the anchor is let go the ship should be making way over the ground otherwise the cable may pile up on top of the anchor and foul it. An alternative method of anchoring is to let go when making slight headway paying out cable as the vessel moves slowly ahead. In a strong wind or tide it may be best to approach the anchorage with the wind or stream broad on the bow and to drop the weather or upstream anchor whilst making headway. The vessel then falls back with the wind or tide dragging a bight of cable over the ground so that she will be brought up with less strain on the cable.

Anchoring in Deep Water. When anchoring in depths of over 30 m the cable should be walked back until the anchor is within 10 m from the bottom before being allowed to run so that the anchor will not gain too much momentum making it difficult to check with the brake. In depths of over 60 m the windlass should be kept in gear and the cable walked out to the length required without being allowed to run at any stage of the operation.

Amount of Cable to use. The scope of cable is the ratio of the amount of the cable outside the hawse pipe to the depth of water. The scope required will depend upon the depth of water, the nature of the holding ground, the duration of stay and the strength of tide or wind expected. Sand or shingle provides good holding ground, soft mud is poor and on rock the flukes cannot bite into the ground.

Sufficient cable should be paid out to ensure that the chain is not lifted off the ground close to the anchor. Tests have shown that if the pull on the cable leads 5° above the horizontal the holding power is reduced by one quarter and if the direction of pull is 15° above the horizontal half the holding power is lost. The principal advantage of paying out more cable is that it enables the anchor to be used to its full effect, the extra weight of cable makes little difference.

The minimum scope of mild steel cable to use according to depth of water is given by the following rough guide:

Below 20 m	6 to 8
20 m to 40 m	4 to 6
Over 40 m	less than 4

The length of mild steel cable to use in metres may be taken as approximately 25 times the square root of the depth of water in metres.

If the cable is made of special quality steel a greater scope should be used than for mild steel cable.

Anchor Watch. When the vessel is at anchor the officer of the watch should check that the vessel is not dragging the anchor by taking cross bearings of fixed objects ashore or by observing transit marks near the beam. If it is suspected that the vessel is dragging the cable should be inspected to see whether it tightens and slackens alternately and whether vibration can be felt. In poor visibility the hand lead could be used to detect dragging by lowering it to the bottom and seeing whether the line leads ahead. Radar can also be used to check the vessel's position.

In rough weather the engines should be kept on stand-by and used if necessary to ease the strain on the cable. If the vessel yaws about, i.e. swings across from one side to the other of the resultant of wind or tide, there is increased risk of dragging the anchor. The second anchor should either be lowered to the bottom at the centre of the yaw, or dropped at the extremity of the yaw when the vessel swings the right way so that the cable will lead out on the opposite bow. Both cables should be veered if the second method is used.

Weighing Anchor. The cable should be hosed down and stowed as it comes in and the bell rung to denote the number of each shackle as it appears. The officer in charge should occasionally indicate to the bridge how the cable is leading and if it is badly nipped, leading astern, the windlass must be stopped as there will be considerable strain imposed on it. When the cable is 'up and down' indicating that the anchor is aweigh the bell is rung rapidly and the anchor signal removed. The brake is applied when the anchor is finally hove up into the hawse pipe, the windlass is then taken out of gear and the bow stopper secured.

Foul Anchor. When the anchor is hove to the surface it may be found to be foul of its own cable or to have picked up some wire, chain or other object from the sea bed. It may be possible to clear it by letting it go again but if this does not prove successful a wire should be passed round the obstruction and brought back on board again with a suitable lead then the cable walked back. Fibre rope must be used for clearing a submarine cable (see page 144).

Dredging Anchor. A cable is said to be at short stay when only a small amount has been paid out so that it leads down to the anchor at a steep angle. As the pull is almost vertical the flukes cannot dig into the ground so the anchor only acts as a drag. Dredging is the term used to describe the towing of an anchor at short stay. This gives a braking effect enabling the vessel to use helm and engines to move forward with good control whilst only making low speed over the ground.

A vessel is said to be dredging down when she drags the anchor astern, with the cable at short stay, as she falls back with the tide. The anchor causes the vessel to have headway with reference to the tidal stream so the rudder can be used, assisted if necessary by short bursts of ahead power, to give the vessel a sheer. The ship will move diagonally across the tide in the direction towards which the rudder is turned (see Fig. 6). A vessel is said to drop down when she drifts back with the tide without having the anchor on the bottom.

Fig. 6. Dredging down.

Turning on an anchor. In a narrow channel or restricted space an anchor can be used to assist in making a tight turn. This is particularly useful for a vessel with the stream astern which has to stem the tide in order to approach the berth or anchorage.

With the minimum of headway starboard helm is applied and as the vessel cants to starboard the engines are put astern and the starboard anchor let go. As the pull on the cable and the effect of transverse thrust moves the stern to port the engines are stopped and the vessel will swing round to stem the tide.

In a narrow river the stream is likely to be stronger in the centre of the channel then at the sides. A vessel turning to stem the stream should therefore manoeuvre the bow into the relatively slack water near the bank to allow the after end to be pushed downstream.

Riding to two anchors. If, as in rough weather, a ship lets go a second anchor and slacks back on both cables so that both are leading ahead, or well forward of the beam, and taking the strain she is said to be riding to two anchors. When the vessel swings at the turn of the tide the amounts of cable may have to be adjusted if both anchors are to take some of the strain but a vessel is unlikely to be riding to two anchors for long periods.

Mooring to two anchors. In order to occupy less space in an anchorage a vessel may moor to two anchors with one cable leading ahead taking the strain and the other leading astern. At the change of tide the ship swings tightly round and lies to the other anchor. The cable taking the strain is known as the riding cable, the other cable is known as the sleeping cable. The two cables should lie at 180° to each other to give a tight span.

The disadvantages of mooring to two anchors are:

(1) The second anchor is not available to back up the one to which the vessel is riding in the event of bad weather.

(2) If a strong wind blows across the line of the cables near the time of slack water the stern will fall down-wind but the cables will lead out almost abeam. The cables must be veered or the anchors will be dragged inwards.

(3) If the vessel swings the wrong way at the change of tide the cables will be crossed. The foul hawse must be cleared before weighing anchor.

Dropping Moor. This method of mooring to two anchors is also known as the standing or ordinary moor. The vessel stems the tide and moves slowly ahead until she is about a ship's length upstream of the desired final position then the engines are stopped and the anchor is let go as she begins to drop back with the tide. Cable is rendered until the amount paid out is equal to the sum of the lengths required for both anchors. After putting the windlass in gear the cable is then hove in and the second anchor is let go as the vessel begins to move ahead. The ship is middled between the two anchors by heaving on the cable from the first anchor and rendering the cable for the second anchor.

If the wind is blowing across the line of the tide the lee anchor should be dropped first so that the cables will not be crossed when the vessel is brought up.

Running Moor. As in the case of the dropping moor the vessel stems the tide but the first anchor is let go when about a ship's length downstream of the desired position and still moving ahead. Cable is rendered as the vessel moves forward against the stream and helm is used to keep in line with the direction of tide. When the amount of cable paid out is equal to the sum of the required amounts for both anchors the engines are stopped, the brake applied to the first cable and the second anchor is let go. The cable leading astern is then hove in and the cable leading ahead rendered until the vessel is middled between the two anchors.

The weather anchor is dropped first when making a running moor with a cross wind. The amount of cable to use on each anchor will depend on the depth of water, the holding ground and the total length of each cable which can be rendered when mooring. When moored in a river more cable should be paid out on the upstream anchor as the ebb tide will flow faster than the flood.

The running moor is generally used in preference to the dropping moor, especially when the stream is weak, as it can be carried out under greater control and takes less time to complete. The dropping moor may be preferable if the tide is strong but in a weak stream it will probably be necessary to put the engines astern to drop back after letting go the first anchor, which will cause the vessel to swing out of the direction of the tide due to transverse thrust effect.

Foul Hawse. One of the disadvantages of mooring to two anchors is that the vessel may swing the wrong way when the tide turns causing crossed cables. If this happens once the sleeping cables comes over the top of the riding cable to form a cross. At the next change of tide the vessel may swing the correct way to clear the cables but another swing in the wrong direction would result in the sleeping cable crossing over the riding cable then leading into the hawse pipe from beneath to form an elbow. A further swing in the wrong direction gives a cross and elbow with the sleeping cable crossing over and under the riding cable then leading into the hawse pipe from over the other cable. In each case the riding cable for the new tide will straighten out as the strain comes on it and the other cable wraps itself around the riding cable. Several turns may be formed if a vessel stays moored to two anchors for a long time.

Everything possible should be done to prevent a foul hawse

developing. An attempt can be made to give the vessel a sheer just before slack water by putting the rudder over towards the sleeping cable side and using the engines if necessary. A small tug could be used for this purpose if available.

If a foul hawse develops a tug can be used to swing the vessel round to clear the turns. With a cross it should be possible to slack back the riding cable and heave in the sleeping cable which is the normal method of unmooring. It may, however, be necessary to clear a foul hawse by disconnecting the sleeping cable and passing the outboard end around the riding cable then bringing it back through the hawse pipe. For this operation it would be an advantage to have a barge or other suitable craft close up to the cables to work from.

There will usually be a period of about 6 hours between slack waters but everything should be ready to start the operation just after the change of tide. If the turns are below the surface the riding cable must be hove in to bring them out of the water. A mooring wire is shackled to the sleeping cable below the turns, hauled tight, then made fast on board. This acts as a preventer and takes some of the weight. The two cables are either lashed together immediately below the turns with fibre rope or nipped together by passing a light wire rope through adjoining links then bringing the end back on board and making fast. The sleeping cable is walked back until a joining shackle is just forward of the windlass.

A mooring wire is shackled to the sleeping cable just forward of the joining shackle and made fast on the bitts. The end of another mooring wire is lowered down the hawse pipe and passed round the riding cable, following the run of the sleeping cable, then brought back through the hawse pipe and shackled to the sleeping cable just forward of the joining shackle. The sleeping cable is walked back until the strain is taken on the wire to the bitts then the joining shackle is disconnected. The wire through the hawse pipe is now taken to the windlass and used to haul the end of the sleeping cable round the riding cable and back into the hawse pipe as the other wire is slackened back. The sleeping cable is re-connected, the wires taken off and the lashing cut.

BERTHING

It is not possible to give definite instructions for bringing a vessel alongside a wharf, dock or pier, which will apply to all cases. Much will depend upon local conditions, strength and direction of wind and/or tide, type of ship, use of tugs, etc. Some general principles and basic procedures will be outlined for a single screw vessel with a right-handed propeller manoeuvring without the assistance of tugs.

If there is any tide or current running the vessel should, whenever possible, head into the stream as she approaches the berth. This will make it possible to manoeuvre under full control using helm and engines with minimum headway relative to the ground. If the tide is initially astern the vessel should be turned short round, using an anchor if necessary, in order to stem the tide.

Berthing with tide ahead. In a strong stream the vessel should move forward against the tide parallel to the berth and let go the offshore anchor when close to the berth and about a ship's length ahead of the required position. The rudder is then put over towards the berth and cable veered so that the vessel falls back and sheers in. Alternatively the vessel may be brought round on a circular path to which the berth forms a tangent. The engines are stopped so that headway is checked by the tidal stream as the berth is approached.

Berthing with no wind or tide. When berthing without tugs it is best to berth port side alongside in a right handed single screw vessel to take advantage of transverse thrust effect. The berth is approached slowly at an angle of about 20° then the engines are stopped and worked astern as the vessel nears the berth. The astern movement checks the headway and causes the stern to swing in.

When berthing starboard side to the stern will swing out if the engines are put astern to check the headway. To allow for this the vessel could approach the berth at a fine angle and put the rudder to port to cause the stern to swing inwards before putting the engines astern but it would be preferable to approach the berth with the anchor at short stay so that an astern movement is not required.

Berthing with wind onshore or offshore. With an onshore wind the berth should be approached at a broad angle and the anchor dropped when about a ship's length away. The rudder can then be put over towards the quay, as the engines are worked ahead, to prevent the stern falling too rapidly on to the berth.

One method of berthing with an offshore wind is to approach at a very broad angle and to have a messenger, secured to a good stern line, brought forward outside of everything and sent away when the bow is close in. A second stern line must be sent off as soon as possible to assist in heaving the stern in.

Mediterranean Moor. This is a method of securing the vessel stern on to the berth with both anchors leading ahead to hold the bow in position. The approach should preferably be made with the berth on the port side. The starboard anchor is let go about two ship lengths off the berth as the vessel continues to move ahead. Starboard helm is applied as the cable is veered. The engines are then put astern and the port anchor is let go. As the vessel comes astern transverse thrust will swing the stern to port towards the berth (See Fig. 7). Stern lines can then be sent away.

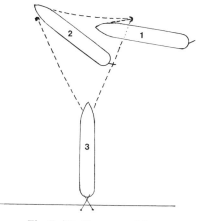

Fig. 7. Mediterranean Moor.

Mooring Lines. Breastlines are used from forward and aft to keep the vessel alongside. Headlines leading forward and forward backsprings leading aft keep the bow in position, sternlines leading aft and after backsprings leading forward keep the stern in position. (Fig. 8).

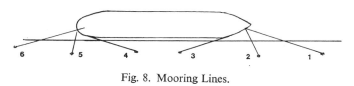

Fig. 8. Mooring Lines.

1.	Headline	4.	After Backspring
2.	For'd Breastline	5.	After Breastline
3.	For'd Backspring	6.	Sternline

LEAVING THE BERTH

Before using the engines make sure the propeller is clear. The vessel is singled up by taking in all mooring lines except those to be used for manoeuvring clear of the berth.

Unberthing with no wind or tide. Single up to an offshore headline forward backspring and after breastline. Heave on the offshore, headline to nip the stem in then let go the headline and breastline, put the rudder hard over towards the quay and the engines to slow ahead. The stern swings out as the engines are worked ahead against the backspring. When the stern has swung out sufficiently stop the engines then put the engines astern with the rudder amidships and let go the backspring. (Fig. 9).

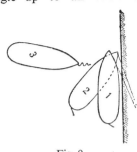

Fig. 9.

When berthed starboard side to the breastline can be held until the engines are put astern to prevent the bow scraping along the quay by checking the initial swing of the stern to port.

Unberthing with wind onshore or offshore. With an onshore wind the method is the same as for calm conditions but the backspring should be doubled up as greater ahead power will be required. Tugs must be used if the wind is strong.

With an offshore wind the vessel is singled up to a headline forward and sternline aft which are eased off until the ship is clear of the berth.

Unberthing in a stream. Single up to a backspring leading upstream and a breastline at the downstream end of the ship. Slack away on the breastline with the rudder away from the quay allowing the upstream end to cant clear then let go fore and aft. (Figs. 10 and 11).

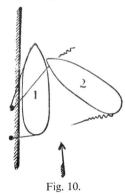

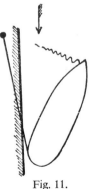

Fig. 10.   Fig. 11.

CHAPTER X

EXCEPTIONAL CIRCUMSTANCES

Heavy Weather

Preparing for heavy weather. If rough seas are expected all hatches must be securely battened down. Weather deck ventilators should be unshipped in good time and the flanges covered. Derricks, lifeboats and deck cargo should be well secured. Lifelines may have to be rigged on exposed parts of the deck. Any loose weights must be secured and, if necessary to ensure adequate stability, slack tanks either pressed up or emptied to avoid free surface effect (see page 310). A check should be made on port holes in store rooms, and other infrequently attended spaces, to see that they are closed with deadlights screwed down.

Beam to sea. In a rough sea the ship is likely to roll heavily if the direction of the wind and sea is on or near the beam and if the vessel is relatively "stiff" (see page 300). If the natural period of roll of the ship is the same as the period of encounter with the waves synchronous rolling may be set up. An alteration of course should be made to escape from this dangerous condition either turning into the wind to reduce the period of encounter with the waves or turning away to increase the period of encounter.

Head to sea. When heading into the sea the vessel may be subject to stresses arising from pitching, panting, pounding, hogging, sagging and racing of the propeller (see pages 245–249). The impact of the waves will be greatest as a result of moving into a head sea. Panting and racing of the propeller are more likely to occur when the vessel is light. Decreasing speed will lessen the impact of the waves and reduce the strain due to racing.

Running before the sea. If the vessel has the sea abaft the beam it will take longer for the crests of the waves to pass. When a large wave sweeps over the upper deck from aft the vessel is said to be pooped. A small vessel running with the sea on the quarter may be suddenly swung round broadside-on to the waves causing her to heel over and possibly capsize. This is known as "broaching-to". Difficulty is likely to be experienced with the steering.

Heaving to. In very rough seas it may be necessary to manoeuvre the ship into the position which is likely to give least risk of damage, temporarily discontinuing the voyage. This is known as heaving to. The conventional method is to bring the wind and sea fine on the bow and to reduce speed to the minimum which will enable the vessel to stay on that heading. Some vessels will find it difficult to maintain this attitude as the bow may tend to pay off the wind. There is also danger of excessive stresses due to panting, pounding and racing, particularly with a light ship.

An alternative method is to lie beam on to the sea with the engine stopped. The stresses associated with heading into the sea will be avoided but the vessel may roll heavily causing racking stresses and greater risk of cargo shifting. This method is therefore not suitable for a vessel which is stiff. When lying beam on to the sea a ship is likely to drift rapidly to leeward so there needs to be plenty of sea room in that direction.

A third method is to run with the sea on the quarter at the minimum speed to keep steerage way. The stresses associated with the other two methods will all be present, but will be less severe in this attitude. Steering will be difficult, especially at low speed; there is danger of pooping and plenty of sea room is required to leeward.

The best method will depend upon the type of vessel, the displacement, trim, metacentric height, nature of cargo, amount of sea room and other circumstances. Oil may be used to advantage when hove to in rough seas (see page 156).

Turning in Rough Seas. Large waves tend to come in cycles so if it is necessary to turn through a large angle in a heavy sea an attempt should be made to take advantage of a relatively calm period. Warning should be given to engine-room and catering staff before commencing the turn. The ship should be brought round gradually, using short bursts of ahead power against full rudder at appropriate times.

Disabled Ship. A vessel which is disabled and stopped will tend to lie beam-on to wind and sea. In this position she may roll heavily, making it more difficult to effect repairs, and there may be danger of cargo shifting. It may be possible to bring the vessel round to a safer and more comfortable attitude by streaming some form of drag, or sea anchor, from the end of the ship which tends to lie up-wind.

In relatively shallow water many vessels have been able to bring the bow into the wind by lashing the anchor(s) in the pipe(s) and paying out cable through a fairlead to drag along the sea bed. In deep water some ships have lowered one or both anchors into the water to act as a drag. Bights of mooring ropes may prove effective in bringing either bow or stern up to wind. Several oil drums or cargo baskets, streamed out from forward or aft may be sufficient for this purpose on a small ship.

If the wind is not too strong it may be worth rigging a spread of canvas near the bow or stern to give a steadying effect, and to assist in turning the vessel by increasing the windage area so that the end which is down-wind may pay off the wind. A tarpaulin could, perhaps, be suspended from a wire stretched fore and aft between samson posts, or from the span of a derrick.

The larger the ship the less likely it is that these measures will prove effective, but in such a dangerous situation it is worth attempting to bring about an improvement.

Lee Shore. In a strong wind some low-powered vessels find it impossible to keep head up to wind and may therefore drift rapidly to leeward if in light condition. If the wind has been blowing strongly in the same direction for a considerable time there may be a strong surface drift current. The situation becomes dangerous when the vessel is being blown towards a lee shore.

It may be possible to make helm and engines more effective by increasing the draught. Assuming that all available tanks have been filled a cargo vessel in light condition could flood a hold towards the after end, but preferably not the one furthest aft as an increase of trim by the stern will make it more difficult to bring the ship's head up into the wind. A vessel with the engine room amidships should flood the hold immediately abaft the engine room until the level of water is just beneath the top of the tunnel. The tunnel will considerably reduce the free surface effect (see page 311).

Sea water can be taken in through the bilge lines, after dismantling the non-return valves, and by use of hoses from the hatchway. Another possibility is to remove the manhole cover and flood through the double bottom tank.

If there is still plenty of room to leeward it may be worth attempting to turn through nearly 270° to bring the wind fine on the bow on the other side. This is known as a wearing turn. However, it is dangerous to turn the vessel too rapidly in a heavy sea and a gradual turn is unlikely to be successful.

When the vessel comes into shallow water the anchors can be used to prevent the vessel drifting on to the shore. The weather anchor is dropped when still making some headway then the engines are stopped and the lee anchor let go. Both cables should be veered to give a good scope.

An alternative method is to put the engines astern, as the type of vessel which pays off the wind when making headway is likely to bring the stern rapidly into the wind when making sternway. This is a hazardous manoeuvre which should only be used as a last resort to avoid being driven aground, but it may buy valuable time to complete the operation of flooding compartments.

STEERING DIFFICULTIES

Defective Steering Gear. If the transmission system connecting the wheel on the bridge to the controls of the steering engine becomes defective the auxiliary arrangement usually consists of a wheel on the poop which is made to control the operation of the steering engine by rods or by hydraulic pressure.

In the event of a failure in the steering engine the emergency steering gear must be used. For the majority of ships fitted with electric-hydraulic steering gear this is normally a completely independent system consisting of spare motor, spare pump and duplicate wiring. For some vessels, fitted with quadrants, wire tackles are supplied by the builders and appropriate leads are fitted so that the hauling parts can be taken to the winch or capstan.

Damaged Rudder. If the rudder fails to operate and the steering gear is found to be satisfactory the rudder stock may be fractured. An attempt must be made to secure the rudder hard over to one side by lowering knotted chain, or a small kedge anchor if available, to catch against the trailing edge. Wires leading forward on each side are then used to secure the rudder in position.

It might be possible on some ships to cut into the rudder trunk and effect a repair to the fractured stock, depending on circumstances and on the materials and equipment available. Another possibility is that wires could be attached to the rudder and taken forward through suitable leads to a winch on the main deck to form a jury steering arrangement, but this would not be practical on the majority of ships.

Jury Rudders. In the event of the rudder being lost or damaged a vessel will probably have to be taken in tow but it may be possible to devise a jury rudder or alternative steering arrangement to enable the vessel to reach the nearest repair port or, at least, to reduce the distance to be towed. This would apply particularly to smaller vessels. Twin screw ships should be able to keep reasonably on course by keeping the revolutions constant on one propeller and increasing or decreasing speed as necessary on the other.

The general principle of a jury rudder is to provide some kind of drag, either one at each side of the ship or one at the stern which is moved from one side to the other, to cause the vessel to turn towards the side where there is increased resistance. Some ships have been able to rig a jury rudder consisting of a derrick with steel doors attached secured to the top gudgeon of the rudder post, or a similar device or gangway secured at the edge of the poop deck. The main difficulty with such an arrangement is to find a satisfactory method of securing the inboard end.

A more practical form of jury steering is to suspend drags from derricks swung over the side. The drags may be coils of wire, steel plates or other large heavy objects which will dip beneath the water surface and give appreciable resistance. Ropes from the drags must be led well forward and secured. The appropriate drag is lowered into the water in order to turn the vessel in the correct direction, or to counter the tendency to veer to one side. (See Fig. 1).

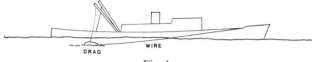

Fig. 1.

COLLISION

Action to avoid collision. Every vessel which is directed to keep out of the way of another vessel is required to take early and substantial action to keep well clear (Rule 16). The other vessel is initially required to keep her course and speed but may take action to avoid collision if it becomes apparent that the other vessel is failing to keep out of the way. The stand-on vessel must take such action as will best aid to avert collision when collision cannot be avoided by the give-way vessel alone. The "wake-up" signal of at least five short blasts on the whistle must be used in such circumstances and this may be supplemented by a light signal of at least five short and rapid flashes.

Collision inevitable. If the vessels get so close that collision appears inevitable each ship should use helm and engines in such a way as to minimise the damage by endeavouring to achieve a glancing blow rather than direct impact. Loss of lives and serious damage are more likely to occur if one vessel strikes the other in the amidships section where compartments are largest, especially if the collision is at a broad angle.

Master's Duties. In the event of a collision the master, or person in charge, of a British vessel is required by the Merchant Shipping Act:

(*a*) to render to the other vessel and persons aboard such assistance as may be practicable and necessary to save them from danger, and to stay by the other vessel until he has ascertained that further assistance is not required, and

(*b*) to give to the master or person in charge of the other vessel the name and port of registry of his own vessel, also the ports of departure and destination, and

(*c*) to make a statement in the Official Log Book.

Reports of Shipping Casualties. Loss, or damage to the ship, loss of life due to accident, or damage caused by the ship, must be reported by the master or owner of a ship registered in the United Kingdom. to the Department of Transport, as soon as practicable and in any case not less than twenty-four hours after the ship's arrival at the next port.

Action following collision. At the moment of impact the compass heading should be noted, if possible, and the approximate angle between the two ships. This information will be useful for a subsequent inquiry.

Unless the collision is a minor one the general alarm should be sounded and watertight doors closed. The engine telegraph will normally have been put to "stop" or full astern to check the vessel's way before the collision, but if the bow has penetrated the side of the other ship it may be important not to come astern, and even necessary to work the engines ahead, in order to plug the gash in the other vessel. An urgency or distress signal should be sent if the ship is in any danger. The not under command signals should be exhibited if the vessel's ability to keep out of the way of other ships has been seriously affected.

Assistance to the other ship. If either vessel is in serious danger of sinking the lifeboats should be swung out and launched if necessary. If the stem overhangs the side of the other ship, ladders and nets should be put over the bow to enable the crew to be transferred. A small vessel struck amidships may sink rapidly without sufficient time for boats to be launched.

Damage to own ship. The extent of the damage should be assessed as soon as possible by visual inspection and by sounding all compartments below the waterline. If the damage is at the stem it may be necessary to shore up the collision bulkhead before moving ahead. Shoring should be concentrated about the centre of pressure which is halfway down from the waterline in the case of a triangular bulkhead (apex down) and two-thirds of the vertical distance down from the waterline for a rectangular bulkhead.

Whenever possible the vessel should be trimmed or listed to bring the damaged part out of the water. Pumps would probably be unable to cope with the entry of water into a breached compartment and may be more effectively used to deal with leakage in adjacent spaces.

If the damage is confined to a small area of the ship's side which is mainly above the waterline it may be possible to make a temporary repair by fitting a patch. This could be made up of several thick boards backed by canvas and stiffened by securing them to vertical timbers or pieces of angle iron. To make it reasonably watertight the canvas is doubled over around the inside edge and filled with soft material to form a "pudding" which is squeezed up against the ship's side. The patch could be fastened internally by hook bolts or by securing it to a piece of angle iron or to a strong timber placed against the damaged part on the inside. (see Fig. 2).

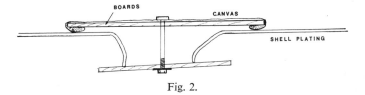

Fig. 2.

When the damage extends well below the waterline it will not usually be possible to fit a patch outside the hull and the rapid entry of water will make it difficult to work from the inside. A method of restricting the flow of water to enable the pumps to lower the level of water inside the compartment is to fit a collision mat. This can be made from two or more layers of canvas or tarpaulin edged with rope and preferably stiffened with spars to prevent it from being drawn into the gash in the ship's side.

Two long wires are taken forward to be passed beneath the ship by lowering bights under the forefoot. The wires are dragged aft, until they are on either side of the damaged part, then the ends are secured to the bottom edge of the collision mat. The mat is lowered over the side by means of two more wires attached to the upper corners, then it is unrolled over the damaged area by hauling on the wires passing beneath the ship. All four wires are pulled tight and secured. (see Fig. 3).

Fig. 3.

When the collision mat is in place and most of the water pumped out of the compartment it should be possible to fit some form of patch to the inside of the damaged part. Mattresses may be suitable to use as a pad.

Cement boxes can be used for some repairs. A wooden box must first be constructed and secured to the frames or other adjacent parts of the structure. All leaks must be plugged, or the water must be directed through condenser tubes or similar piping, as cement will not set in running water. Any oil or grease should be removed from surfaces. The cement must be mixed with sand or gravel in the ratio of one part cement to not more than three parts sand or gravel. Sea water can be used if necessary. If water is seeping through, the mixture should be put in fairly dry. The cement will set more rapidly if a small quantity of washing soda is added.

BEACHING

If, after a collision or other accident, or as a result of heavy weather damage, water is being taken in so rapidly that the pumps are unable to cope it will normally be preferable to run the ship on to a beach rather than allow her to become a total loss in deep water. If the vessel can be placed on a gently sloping beach it may be possible to effect repairs so that she may be refloated to enable her to reach a repair port.

The beach should, preferably, be of sand or gravel and free from rocks. A sheltered position is also desirable but there is unlikely to be much choice of location when such a situation develops. If there is an appreciable range of tide it will be best to beach the ship on the falling tide, just after high water, to give as much time as possible to secure the vessel before the tide rises to the same level again, and to give more opportunity to effect repairs.

It is usual to beach heading towards the shore but in some cases vessels are beached stern-on or even broadside-on. If possible the trim should be adjusted according to the method of approach and the slope of the beach. Ballast should be taken in during the beaching operation to cause the ship to settle securely on the bottom. The approach should, preferably, be made at slow speed at right angles to the line of the beach and the engines stopped in good time to allow the vessel to touch down gently.

When the ship has been beached the outer end must be secured by means of ground tackle. In order to avoid carrying the anchor out by boats it may be possible to drop an anchor on the way in, when beaching bow-on, with a wire attached from aft to secure the stern. This method is not recommended as it calls for extremely good judgement. There is a risk that the anchor will be dropped too soon, which would impede the beaching operation, or too late, so that the anchor would be close under the stern and of no value for securing the after end of the ship. There have been instances of vessels being damaged due to sitting on their own anchors.

It will usually be preferable to have the ground tackle carried out by a tug or salvage vessel after the ship has been beached so that the anchor can be taken out as far as possible in the best direction for holding the stern in position. If such craft are not available it will be necessary to carry the anchor out using the ship's boats (see page 202).

When temporary repairs have been completed the ship can be refloated by pumping out the ballast on the rising tide and taking the strain on the ground tackle. By putting the engines astern, when the propeller is clear, it should be possible to manoeuvre the vessel clear of the beach. The ground tackle can then be recovered.

STRANDING

The term "stranding" is normally used when referring to accidental grounding, as distinct from "beaching" which is intentional. When a ship goes aground the engines should be stopped immediately. If the vessel is likely to be in any danger, as in the case of striking rocks at high speed or in rough weather, the alarm should be sounded, watertight doors closed, boats prepared and a distress or urgency signal transmitted.

It may be worth making an immediate attempt to refloat the ship. The engineers should be informed before the engines are used as it may be necessary to change over to a high injection valve for circulating cooling water in order to avoid the risk of drawing sand or silt into the condenser tubes. If putting the engines astern has no effect it is possible that going ahead with the rudder hard over to one side will slew the stem round so that the ship may come off with a subsequent astern movement.

The engines must not be used excessively as there is a risk that sand or silt will bank up against the side of the ship due to the action of the propeller. All compartments should be sounded to determine the extent of the damage. Soundings should also be taken with the hand lead at various positions around the ship and the draught forward and aft carefully read to ascertain over what portion of the length the ship is aground.

A common mistake is to immediately begin to lighten the vessel by discharging or jettisoning fuel, water cargo and even stores. This could result in the vessel pounding upon the bottom, slewing round broadside to the beach or being driven further ashore. If there is any movement the best action would probably be to flood tanks in order to settle the vessel firmly on the bottom, and to carry out ground tackle.

The loss of buoyancy due to grounding may be found by multiplying the mean loss in draught by the T.P.C. (see page 342). The pull required to refloat a ship has been estimated by salvage experts to be about 30% of the lost buoyancy on smooth sand, 50% on hard gravel, 60–80% on coral and 80–150% on rock. The high figure quoted for rock is due to the possibility of pinnacles piercing the ship's hull. These figures can be used to estimate the approximate pull required and to decide whether it is worth lightening the ship.

A ground tackle is likely to be of considerable value and is often used by salvage experts. By using two anchors in tandem connected by a wire strop, a heavy wire between the nearer anchor and the ship and a threefold purchase to give a good mechanical advantage it should be possible to develop a pull of the order of 20–30 tonnes, assuming good holding ground. A harbour tug can only exert a stress of about 15 tonnes. Salvage tugs are capable of developing pulls of 50–80 tonnes but the ground tackle has the advantage of exerting a steady strain.

Tugs and ground tackle should not be considered as separate alternatives. They can be used together as each have particular advantages. A tug can be used to swing the vessel's stern from one side to the other or to scour sand away from the ship's side.

Lightening ship by discharging or jettisoning cargo, etc., may be the only effective method of refloating the vessel but it should generally be used as a last resort, and not before ground tackle has been laid out. It may be worth lowering the boats into the water to assist in the process. When aground forward on rock, or coral, the ship should be lightened forward. Cargo could be transferred aft in order to trim by the stern. In some circumstances, however, particularly when aground forward in sand, it may be best to discharge from aft. Although the stem will be pushed deeper into the sand a greater area of the ship's bottom may thus be exposed to water pressure acting upwards so that buoyancy is increased.

A vessel aground must display three black balls in vertical line by day and two red lights in vertical line, in addition to the lights required for a vessel at anchor, by night, as prescribed in Rule 30 of the International Regulations for Preventing Collisions at Sea.

Laying out ground tackle. The gear used in salvage operations to secure a vessel firmly in position, following upon beaching or stranding, or to assist in hauling the ship off, is generally referred to as ground tackle. This consists of one or more anchors attached to a heavy wire or cable and possibly used with a good purchase to give increased hauling power. The task of carrying out and setting up the gear is likely to be difficult unless specialist help is available but a ground tackle is likely to be of considerably advantage in such circumstances.

One or both bower anchors will generally have to be taken out together with a heavy wire (35–50 mm). The most difficult part of the operation is likely to be the transporting of the gear away from the ship if the lifeboats have to be used. It would be preferable to have the anchor carried out by a tug or similar vessel or to first take out a small kedge anchor or stream anchor, if available, attached to a wire of about 20 mm, which can then be used to haul out the boats carrying the larger anchor.

A bower anchor should, preferably, be carried out between two boats. The boats are brought parallel to one another, about one metre apart, and a heavy spar is lashed across them. The spar should be supported by timbers placed on the sidebenches so that the weight will not be taken by the gunwales. A lighter spar should also be lashed across the after ends of the boats to keep them parallel to one another.

The anchor is lowered into the water until the shackle is just clear of the surface then the boats are manoeuvred to bring the anchor between them and beneath the heavy spar. A good fibre rope lashing, or a wire strop with a senhouse slip, is used to secure the anchor to the spar before it is released from the derrick fall.

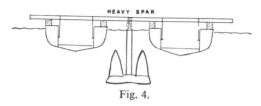

Fig. 4.

The boats are then hauled aft, along the ship's side, and the heavy wire is lowered on to them. It may be worth making a platform between the boats on which the wire can be flaked down. The end of the wire is shackled on to the anchor ring making sure that a bight can be easily paid out before the anchor is let go.

It is better to take out the full coil of wire and to bring the end back to the ship, rather than to carry out the end of the wire attached to the anchor. If the end of the wire is taken out there will be a bight of heavy wire between the boats and the ship which will make the task of carrying out the anchor even more difficult. The end of a messenger rope should be taken out so that the rope can be used to haul the boats, and the end of the wire, back to the ship.

When all is ready, the anchor is carried away from the ship's side as far as the length of wire will permit. It must not be dropped too close to the ship as the anchor will lose much of its holding power if the pull is not horizontal (see page 185). The rope messenger can be used to measure the distance from the ship.

As the boats approach the position at which the anchor is to be dropped a bight of wire is lowered over half way down to the sea bed. The lashing is cut, or the slip released, to let go the anchor. The messenger is hauled on and the wire is paid out until the boats are brought back under the stern of the ship. The end of the wire is then taken aboard through an appropriate fairlead.

If a purchase is to be used to exert a strong pull on the wire it will be necessary to devise a satisfactory connection between the wire and the moving block. This could be achieved by passing the wire around a short stout piece of timber of sufficient strength, known as a toggle, and seizing it back on its own part using chain stoppers.

The moving block is secured to the toggle with a strop of heavy wire or chain. The standing block must be taken to a strong pair of bitts.

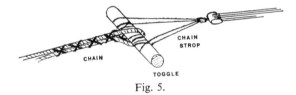

Fig. 5.

TOWING A DISABLED VESSEL

When a vessel becomes disabled at sea salvage tugs are often used to tow her to a repair port, but occasionally another merchant ship may undertake the task. The towage of one merchant ship by another will be considered in this section.

A ship is not obliged to take another vessel in tow, even though that vessel may be in distress, unless the safety of those on board depends upon it. The legal requirement is to render assistance to persons aboard a ship in distress. Before agreeing to tow another vessel the master should check whether he is allowed to do so by the terms of the charter party and/or bills of lading and obtain per-mission from the owners. He should also be satisfied that his ship is of sufficient power and is provided with the necessary equipment. There must also be sufficient bunkers for the proposed voyage.

The master of the disabled ship should preferably seek assistance from a vessel of the same company, or of the same nationality. He should be satisfied that the towing vessel is of sufficient power. A merchant ship will usually be capable of towing another vessel of up to twice her own size. An approximate rule is that a vessel can exert a pull of one tonne in the tow-line for every 75 KW (100 H.P.) of engine power. The pull required may be in excess of 100 tonnes for large vessels in load condition, but should not exceed 25 tonnes for vessels of less than 15,000 tonnes displacement towed at speeds of less than 10 knots in reasonable weather conditions.

For both vessels the most satisfactory salvage agreement will normally be Lloyd's Standard Form which is on the basis of "no cure, no pay". It will be sufficient to agree terms by radio as there will be evidence to this effect in the radio log. Lloyd's Form need not be signed until the voyage is completed.

Tow-line. The tow-line must have good elasticity as well as con-siderable strength. Fibre rope has good elasticity but a ship's fibre mooring ropes are unlikely to be strong enough for this purpose. Wire rope has greater strength but has practically no elasticity. Cable, in the form of anchor chain has considerable strength and, because its weight causes it to form a shallow curve between the two ships known as a catenary, gives sufficient resilience to absorb the changing stresses in the tow-line. All cable tow-lines have been used to tow relatively small ships but they are difficult to set up on the towing vessel and are unlikely to be of sufficient length.

The most suitable form of tow-line is generally considered to be a combination of the anchor cable from the disabled ship shackled to the heavy wire of the towing vessel. This arrangement has been used on numerous occasions for towing vessels of all sizes including a fully laden 200,000 tonne deadweight tanker.

Preparations. In order to set up such a tow-line the disabled vessel should if possible, land the anchor on deck and disconnect the cable ready for shackling to the heavy wire from the other ship. If this is not possible, due to rough weather or othei causes, the anchor should be either hung off or jettisonned, rather than lashed in the hawse pipe, as if the cable is passed through a fairlead there will be a bad nip. However, passing the cable through a fairlead may be satisfactory for towing over a short distance in good weather conditions.

On the towing vessel the inner end of the wire should be secured using several sets of bitts to distribute the load, or by some alternative method such as passing the wire around a coaming or housing. Careful thought should be given to the method of paying out the end of the heavy wire. On large vessels the most satisfactory method will probably be to reeve the bight through a snatch block which is shackled to the end of a mooring rope. The mooring rope is then taken forward to a winch so that the wire can be sent out under full control (see Fig. 6).

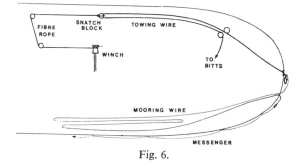

Fig. 6.

Connecting the tow. The tow-line should be passed across in daylight, and if the seas are rough it may be worth waiting for the weather to improve. The usual method of making the connection is to fire a rocket line across. The disabled vessel will probably be lying, stopped, beam on to wind and sea. If time permits the towing vessel should first determine whether there is any appreciable differ-ence between the rates of drift of the two vessels by taking up a position in line with the other ship.

In good weather conditions the towing vessel should be able to approach from fine on the other vessel's quarter and move in parallel to her sending a rocket line across when the two vessels are abreast of one another. The towing vessel then takes up a position slightly ahead of the disabled ship to pass the tow-line across.

In rough weather it may be necessary for the towing vessel to take up a position stern to wind, off the end of the disabled ship (see Fig. 5 on page 155) as the vessels are likely to have a different rate of drift.

The rocket line should be attached to a fibre messenger rope which is then secured to a wire or synthetic fibre rope of sufficient strength to haul the heavy wire across. The wires will usually be hauled from the towing vessel to the disabled vessel, but if the latter is without power she should send her heavy wire across to the towing vessel. The eye of the heavy wire should be left clear ready for shackling on to the cable so the messenger is secured as illustrated in Fig. 7.

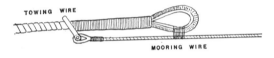

Fig. 7.

Commencing to tow. When the heavy wire has been shackled to the end of the disabled vessel's cable, and secured aboard the towing vessel, the cable is veered to get the required length of tow-line. At least three shackles of cable should be used to give a long tow-line with a sufficient sag to absorb shocks. More cable is needed for towing large ships, and for bad weather conditions. The cable should be secured by tightly screwing up the brake and using the bow stopper.

Aboard the towing vessel the wire must be well greased where it passes through the fairlead. Some vessels have protected the wire at this point by making a sleeve consisting of an inner sheet of lead and outer sheets of copper clamped on to the wire. The lower part of the fairlead should also be lined with soft wood covered by several thicknesses of canvas which have been well greased. Considerable loads will be imposed on the fairlead so it may be necessary to shore up from each side.

It is essential that the stress on the tow-line should be imposed gradually with the towing vessel increasing speed a few revolutions at a time. It is probably best for the towing ship to move ahead in line with the disabled vessel then turn slowly on to the required course. An alternative method is for the towing vessel to move off at 90° to the disabled vessel's heading so that the initial stress is used to pivot the tow rather than to overcome the inertia.

Towing voyage. The towing speed is governed by a number of factors including the size of the vessel towed, strength of tow-line and weather conditions. It should usually be less than 10 knots even if the weather is good. The tow-line should never be allowed to come completely out of the water. The lowest part should preferably be kept between 6 and 12 metres below the surface.

CABLE   6 – 12 m   WIRE

Fig. 8.

The stress on the tow-line can be appreciably reduced by un-coupling the shafting of the disabled ship forward of the thrust block to allow the propeller to rotate freely. The towed vessel should be trimmed by the stern as much as possible and steered, in order to reduce the tendency to yaw. In rough weather oil should be distributed by the towing ship (see page 156).

A watch must be kept on the tow-line at all times, and for signals from the other vessel. If possible the V.H.F. radiotelephone should be used for communication. The fairlead must be kept well greased and the nip should be freshened if there is any sign of chafe.

Before arriving at the destination it will usually be advantageous to arrange for harbour tugs to bring the disabled vessel into port under an ordinary contract of towage. Speed must be reduced gradually on approaching port. If possible the two vessels should be anchored simultaneously before disconnecting the tow.

CHAPTER XI

CARGO WORK AND MAINTENANCE

Cargo Handling Equipment

CARGO handling equipment commonly in use includes:

Slings which are made of 24 mm to 36 mm fibre rope, 10 to 16 metres being cut from a coil and the ends joined by a short splice.

Snotters which may be either of rope or wire, 4 to 8 metres in length, with an eye spliced in each end. The middle of the rope is passed under the package, one end is rove through the eye at the other end and placed on the hook of the derrick fall. The weight tightens the snotter round the package.

Nets which are suitable for small packages, bags, etc.

Strong Wooden Trays which are used for lifting a number of small articles such as drums of paint or oil, cases containing bottles or cans and other packages that can be lifted conveniently by one man and placed on the tray. The trays are constructed to lift a load of up to about $1\frac{1}{2}$ tonnes and are slung with a four-legged bridle.

The Bridle is made of four legs of equal lengths of either fibre or wire rope. One end of each leg is spliced into an iron ring, the other end into the eye of a hook, with one hook for each of the eyebolts at the corners of the tray. The derrick fall is hooked on to the ring and the tray of goods hoisted.

Can Hooks are used for lifting casks but not, as a rule, when they contain liquid. The sling of the can hook may be of rope or chain. The hooks catch under the chine of the cask, and the heavier the weight the better they grip.

Chain Slings have a hook at one end and a big link at the other end. They are used to sling heavy coarse goods, such as iron bars, sheet iron, structural and agricultural materials. The chain is passed round the material once, or twice if necessary, and the end hooked round the chain. The derrick fall is hooked on to the big link and the weight tightens the turns of chain around the load.

Spreaders may have to be used for lifting difficult loads. The function of a spreader is to hold the wires apart over the load to prevent damage. It has a number of hooks attached. A special design is the container spreader which is fitted with twist locks designed to grip the container. Safety locks prevent the container being lifted until all four locks are engaged.

Bull Ropes are used in the holds when goods have to be dragged from the ends or sides of the cargo spaces into the square of the hatch before hoisting. One end is made fast to a pillar or some secure

* Fig. 1. Loading general cargo. When closed the hatch covers are designed to lie flush with the deck to give a clear area for fork lift trucks to work in.

foundation, the other end is passed round the derrick fall then back to the pillar, around which a turn is taken, leaving the bight of the bull rope slack enough to keep the fall from rasping on the underside of the hatch coaming and to drag the sling of goods more or less horizontally to the hatchway. The end of the bull rope is then let go and the goods hoisted.

Fork Lift Trucks. In many trades the fork lift truck is an important piece of cargo handling equipment. Some ships carry a number of their own trucks while others rely on the stevedores to supply them. For a ship to make use of fork lift trucks, the tween decks must be adequately strengthened, the decks level and free from obstruction. The cargo is loaded and stowed on pallets which can be picked up and transported by the trucks. Although cargo loaded on pallets takes up more room than when each piece is separately stowed the speed of handling is considered to give more than adequate compensation for the loss of cargo space.

*Fig. 2. A pallet of frozen lamb on board the P&O ship *Zaida*. The brackets at the bottom of the pallet take the prongs of a fork lift truck.

When using petrol-driven or diesel trucks some sort of mechanical ventilation must be used because of the dangerous fumes given off. For this reason trucks powered by battery are more popular for use in the ship's hold. Some ships are specially designed to be loaded and discharged by fork lift trucks. Instead of the conventional hatch these ships have side or stern doors, and elevators inside the ship which take the pallets to different deck levels.

Maintenance

The Health and Safety at Work Act, and the equivalent foreign legislation, place a heavy responsibility on the ship's officers to ensure that all equipment is maintained in good order. The equipment should be overhauled at sea, where runners and topping lifts are taken down, wires examined and oiled, blocks taken apart, greased and examined and the derrick heels taken out of the goosenecks and greased.

Certain equipment needs to be annealed. This process consists of heating the equipment up slowly in a furnace and allowing it to cool. Annealing restores the crystal structure of the metal and prevents it from becoming brittle.

The Act lays down requirements for fencing around hatchways, construction of ladders and gangways and lighting of holds. It is very important that the ship's officers check that these safety requirements are complied with. (see pages 349–350).

Dunnage

Most conventional cargo vessels have permanent dunnage or ceiling covering the tank tops consisting of 8 cm planking resting on bearers about 5 cm deep, which form an air space between the tank top and the ceiling to dry up moisture.

Portable Side Battens consisting of boards about 15 cm broad and 5 cm thick spaced about 23 cm apart, are fitted into cleats on the side framing of the ship; the battens may be arranged horizontally or vertically and sometimes diagonally. This permanent dunnage is usually sufficient for rough cargoes and for goods that are not liable to absorb moisture.

Additional Dunnage should be laid at the bilges where water is likely to accumulate, also on stringers and stringer plates where moisture from condensation may trickle down the shell plating and lodge on the stringer.

Plastic Dunnage, plastic bags inflated by compressed air, and polythene sheeting are also used.

Matting should always be laid on the ceiling for bale goods and bag cargoes. If the nature of the cargo is likely to draw moisture an additional 5 or 8 cm of dunnage should be laid on the ceiling and at the turn of the bilges.

The Dunnage Wood is of various lengths and thicknesses, and it should be kept clean and dry, as many cargoes, especially foodstuffs in bags, generate heat and absorb moisture, dirt and oil stains from dirty dunnage wood.

Regulations regarding the dunnaging, stowing and ventilating of particular cargoes are enforced at some ports, particularly for rice and grain, and the conditions of loading them must be complied with.

Bulk Carriers

These ships are designed to be able to carry a wide range of different cargoes, they are given large hatches so that they can carry containers and timber while at the same time the holds are strengthened to carry the high density bulk cargoes like iron ore. The bulk carrier has developed into three main types:

(*a*) *The handy sized bulk carrier.* This ship has a deadweight of up to about 40,000 tonnes. It will usually have its own cargo gear which will either be derricks, cranes or the more expensive gantry equipment such as the Munck Loader.

(*b*) *The large bulk carrier.* These ships are designed to carry heavy ore or coal cargoes. They are specially strengthened with small holds to raise the height of the cargo so preventing the ship from becoming unduly stiff when carrying this heavy ore.

The additional space is used for water ballast, the system being designed to allow for the handling of ballast at the same time as the cargo is being worked.

(*c*) *Combination ships.* There are two types in this category: Firstly the ore/oil carrier, secondly the oil/bulk/ore (O.B.O.) carrier.

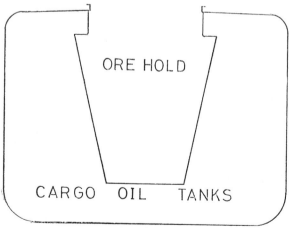

Fig. 3. Section of Ore/Oil Carrier.

The ore/oil carrier is usually a very large ship, over 150,000 tonnes dwt. In this ship the ballast tanks can also be used to carry oil, and the relationship between the hold and tank space is such that these ships can carry a full cargo of ore or oil. Ore/oil ships can be used in whatever trade is the most profitable at any one time or they can reduce unprofitable ballast time by carrying different cargoes on different stages of the voyage.

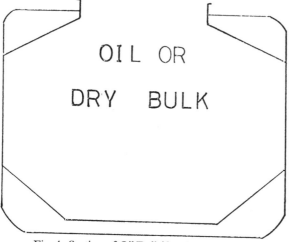

Fig. 4. Section of Oil/Bulk/Ore (OBO) Carrier.

The oil/bulk/ore ships differ from the larger ore/oil ships in that they can carry either ore or oil in the same holds. This gives the ship the advantage of greater hold space to carry a wider range of bulk cargoes, i.e. grain, than the ore/oil ship with her small holds. When changing over from an oil to a dry bulk cargo, the holds must first be cleaned and gas freed and the heating coils lifted. These ships have to carry water ballast in their holds and, to prevent free surface from endangering stability, can only sail with their holds full or empty. They have large hatch coamings and a liquid cargo must be filled up into these spaces to reduce free surface.

Other types of ships which are not generally considered as bulk carriers are the container and L.A.S.H. ships. In each case by loading exactly similar containers or lighters in bulk they give the advantage of the larger ship and faster turnround.

Ore. This is the form in which most metals are mined. The size of the particles shipped depends on the process of mining and whether any purification has previously been carried out. The main ores traded are iron, aluminium (known as bauxite), copper, manganese and chrome. These ores all have a very high density, iron stowing around 0·5 m³/tonne. When loaded into specially designed ore carriers there is no difficulty as the holds are sufficiently strengthened while the shape of the hold will provide an adequate pile height to prevent the ship from being too stiff.

*Fig. 5.   Oil/Bulk/Ore Carrier.   Note the deep hatch coamings.

When ores are carried in general cargo ships the dangers are inadequate stability and excessive weight concentration. Many ore cargoes are liable to shift, the governing factor being the angle of repose. When a sample of the ore is poured on to a flat surface, the sides of the cone so formed will make an angle with the base, this is known as the angle of repose. A cargo with a low angle of repose is particularly liable to shift. In the I.M.O. code of safe practice, 35° or less is considered a cargo that needs special precautions. When

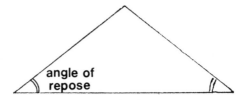

Fig. 6. Angle of Repose.

carrying cargoes with a low angle of repose, shifting boards and bins are advised. Bearing in mind the very high density of this cargo, strongly constructed boards and bins are needed. With any cargo liable to shift the sensible precaution is to maintain maximum stability by keeping free surface to a minimum and loading the smallest amount of cargo possible in the tween deck. It should be noted that with bulk cargoes a relatively large GM is desirable, as this will reduce the amount of list in the event of a shift in the cargo. Should the ship then take a list she will still have adequate stability. A general cargo ship is normally designed to carry cargo with a stowage factor of between 1·4–1·7 m³/tonne. With a high density cargo, serious damage can occur to the ship's structure from over-loading. To prevent this the ship's capacity plan should be consulted to find the maximum wt. per m² that can be loaded in any part of the ship, and in any case it is important to trim the cargo as level as possible in order to distribute the weight evenly.

Pellets. This is a semi-refined form of iron ore, of more regular size and greater density than ordinary ore.

Concentrates. These are ores that have been partially refined. In addition to the dangers of dry movement they can under certain conditions become liquefied, so presenting the additional hazards of liquid movement. A concentrate is only capable of liquid movement when the moisture content is above a certain level known as the transportable moisture limit (T.M.L.). The IMO code of safe practice for solid bulk cargoes, which gives a list of the concentrates and their T.M.L., should be consulted before they are shipped.

Concentrates with their moisture content above the T.M.L. should only be carried in specially designed ships.

If concentrates are shipped in too dry a state they will also be subject to oxidization and spontaneous heating so a spray may have to be used to cool them.

Coal. This is generally carried in bulk carriers or special colliers designed for short voyages.

Surface Ventilation is essential with a coal cargo as the gas is lighter than air and must be given an opportunity of escaping upwards through the ventilators and a hatch should be left off in fine weather. Through ventilation is to be avoided as a current of air passing through the mass of coal might stimulate into activity any dormant gases into spontaneous combustion.

It is recommended that vessels carrying coal on long passages should unship the side dunnage battens and so remove this avoidable source of providing air pockets and the supply of oxygen necessary for combustion.

All kinds of coal, even anthracite, are liable to spontaneous heating and combustion, though some are more dangerous than others.

All coal gives off inflammable gas when freshly worked or when freshly broken, and the gas becomes explosive when mixed with certain proportions of air.

Heating of coal does not proceed from the presence of gas, but is caused by the absorption of oxygen from the air.

This absorption and the accompanying development of heat is greater at high than at low temperatures, so that when once commenced it proceeds at an increasing rate if the supply of air is maintained.

Danger of over heating and spontaneous combustion increases with the length of time the coal remains in the ship, 38°C being a critical temperature.

When loading the coal should be trimmed level to reduce the area exposed to the air.

Wet coal can be dangerous for three reasons, firstly the moisture can cause heating and a possible fire risk, secondly the moisture can with high sulphur coals cause corrosion of the ships structure and finally with small ships there is the risk of liquid movement of the cargo endangering the ship's stability.

Grain. As grain is a foodstuff a high standard of cleanliness is required in its handling. The holds must be cleaned to the satisfaction of a surveyor before it can be loaded, depending on the previous cargo the hold will have to be swept and washed out. The bilges must be cleaned and made graintight and there must be no strong smells to taint the grain. During the voyage the grain can germinate so the cargo must be loaded dry.

During the voyage the cargo will settle and with the ship's movement it can shift to one side and so cause a loss of stability. To prevent this the grain must be loaded according to the Merchant Shipping (Grain) (Regulations) 1980 grain rules. With these rules the loss of stability due to a possible shift of grain is calculated and then, if necessary, shifting boards, bagged grain or other methods are used to prevent the cargo from shifting to a dangerous extent. In most tankers and bulk carriers there is adequate stability without having to take any extra precautions so these ships are popular in the grain trade.

Rice is an expensive cargo to carry as the holds have to be fitted up with an elaborate system of ventilation on the principle of a drainage scheme, so that air may pass freely throughout the whole cargo The ventilators are box-shaped and made of two planks of wood kept about 0·2 m distance apart by pieces of wood. They are laid fore and aft on top of a tier of bags from bulkhead to bulkhead and also athwartships from side to side. These ventilators communicate with a series of vertical vents extending from the ceiling to the top deck. This horizontal system is laid at every third tier of bags. In addition to all this the side battens and bulkheads are covered with sticks or bamboos tied criss-cross or lattice fashion and all bare iron and dunnage is covered with rush mats.

The purpose is to secure a current of air through the cargo to carry away the carbonic acid gas given off by the rice and also to keep the hold from **sweating**. An air space is left between the top tier of bags and the underside of the deck and also round the inside of the hatch coamings. During the latter part of the rice season when the grain is more mature the ventilation is reduced a little. The cargo is loaded under the supervision of official surveyors.

In Fig. 7, *A* indicates the fore-and-aft ventilators, *B* the athwartship ventilators, *C* the five bag spacing of ventilators. The arrows indicate the air current flowing to the vertical ventilators.

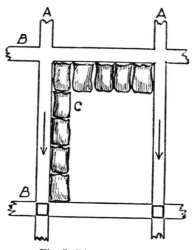

Fig. 7. Rice Ventilation.

Containers. Containers are carried either on specially designed container ships or as a part cargo in general ships. The advantage claimed for containers is that the goods are not disturbed after being packed into the container until it is unpacked at the destination. When the cargo from one source is not sufficient to make a full container load several consignments are packed into one container at inland depots, before being shipped on as full containers. As the cargo now comes in uniform shapes and sizes, it is possible to carry it in specially designed ships, and cranes capable of handling the

*Fig. 8. OCL Container Ship *Botany Bay*.

containers at high speeds bring the advantages of bulk handling to the liner trade.

When loading containers, the positions on the ship which the containers are to occupy are decided ashore as she starts loading and discharging simultaneously almost as soon as she berths. The officer must check that the containers are being loaded according to plan; that those on deck are loaded with their doors facing aft and that any

*Fig. 9.   P&O Roll on/Roll off Ship *Dragon*. The design of these ships makes the handling of awkward loads reasonably simple.

*Fig. 10. Container handling at Brisbane. The cranes are able to lift two 20 foot containers simultaneously.

containing dangerous goods are placed in position according to regulations. Refrigerated containers are used to carry meat and fruit. The advantage claimed is that the cargo is packed at a freezer depot and not opened until it reaches its destination and therefore will arrive in good condition. There are two main types of refrigerated containers in use. One type has a refrigeration unit attached and all that is required is to connect these units to the ship's

*Fig. 11. Containers on board the P&O ship *Remuera*. The vertical guides in the hold locate the containers in their cells.

electricity supply. With this type the ship's officer must check that they are connected and functioning correctly. The other type of unit relies on a supply of cold air from the ship's refrigerated supply. A portable clip-on refrigerator unit is used when this container is ashore.

To load containers efficiently the ship must be kept within narrow limits of list and trim so that they fit in the guides. On some ships this is controlled automatically, on others it is the officer's responsibility to prevent a list from developing.

Roll on Roll off (RoRo). These ships are fitted with large stern doors and on some ships stern ramps. This makes for a flexible cargo carrier, there is a large clear space for different types of cargo, containers trailers, and general cargo loaded on specially designed low loaders.

Most RoRo ships can carry cargo on several decks connected by movable ramps. The advantage of these ships is that they are able to operate with only a jetty for port facilities, but there are problems with stability as the clear cargo decks do not have any sub-division. (Fig. 9)

Dangerous Goods. It is an offence to ship a dangerous cargo without declaring it to the ship. The declaration must give the chemical name and class as well as any trade name that the manufacturer may wish to use. The class to which the goods belong, details regarding fire-fighting and any other relevant information are required. If any undeclared goods are found the master may dispose of them without any compensation to the owners if he considers them a danger to either ship or crew.

Dangerous goods are divided into 10 classes:—

1. Explosives
2. Gasses: compressed, liquefied or dissolved under pressure.
3. Inflammable liquids.
4. Inflammable solids.
5. Oxidizing substances.
6. Poisonous or infectious substances.
7. Radioactive substances.
8. Corrosives.
9. Miscellaneous dangerous substances.
10. Dangerous chemicals in limited quantities.

In the "Carriage of dangerous goods in ships", known as the "Blue Book", detailed information is provided on the stowage of dangerous goods and segregation requirements are set out. Class 1, explosives, are covered in greater detail. There are specific goods listed in the "Blue Book" that may not be carried on a ship with explosives on board. Further regulations for the carriage of dangerous goods are found in the IMDG codes (International

Maritime Dangerous Goods code, published by IMCO), which must be used in conjunction with the 'Blue Book'. Explosives must be carried in a magazine constructed according to the requirements. Outline requirements are for close-fitting boards, 25 mm thick, secured to 75 mm×75 mm uprights, three non-ferrous nails per plank. If the ship's side forms part of the magazine and is not already protected, it must be covered with 75 mm×25 mm boards up to the deckheads. One or more doors secured by padlocks must be fitted. All electrical connections leading to the magazine must be broken, it is not sufficient to remove the fuse. Ventilators should be well protected by a gauze screen and an efficient fire detection system provided. Steam will make some explosives unstable, so steam smothering is now allowed in a hold where there is a magazine. In many cases suitably approved portable magazines are now used, instead of building magazines specifically for the purpose on board.

Deep Tank Liquids. Before any liquid cargo is loaded into a deep tank, the tank must be tested to ensure that it will not leak and damage other cargo. The tank lid is screwed down tightly and the tank filled with water to the top of the filling pipes. It is then checked for leaks, paying particular attention to the packing around the lid. The tank is then pumped out, the double bottom tanks are pressed up and the deep tank inspected internally for any signs of leakage. A surveyor will then issue a certificate stating that the tank is tight and capable of carrying liquid cargo.

After the tightness tests, the tank must be thoroughly cleaned out. If the tank is coated the cleaning consists of washing down the sides with fresh water and a cleaning solution. If the tank is not coated it will have to be cleaned out with caustic. Some caustic is placed in a perforated drum and a steam hose inserted producing a fine caustic spray. While the tank is still hot it is hosed down with fresh water. Staging is then built and the sides are carefully scraped and wire brushed. All loose scale must be removed. The heating coils must be tested under pressure for leaks and bilge and CO_2 lines blanked off.

When carrying latex the tank is coated with wax to prevent any contact between the latex and the steelwork. Contact with the air must be reduced to a minimum by completely filling the tank and using special pressure valves instead of ventilators.

Before any liquid cargo is loaded the tank must be passed by a surveyor for cleanliness and suitability for that particular cargo.

Temperatures. Any heating instructions must be complied with. It is normal practice to take and record temperatures of the cargo twice daily and a copy of the record is then sent to the consignee. If the required temperature is exceeded scorching can result thus making the cargo worthless, or at least reduced in quality; conversely if the cargo is not up to the required temperature it thickens and becomes very difficult to discharge. If not heated some liquids will solidify and no amount of subsequent heating will return them to a liquid state.

Documents

1. **Cargo Plans.** Cargo plans are necessary to provide information in advance of the ship regarding the disposition of the cargo, thus making it possible to plan the labour efficiently. The ship's copy is required so that the stowage of cargo in further ports can be planned, a check kept on the stability and the possibility of overcarriage reduced. The custom with cargo plans is to show the holds in elevation and the tween decks in plan. Different colours are used to distinguish between different ports. If too much detail is shown on a cargo plan it will be confusing; if not enough detail is shown the plan loses its value.

2. **Boat Note.** This is an advance note from the shipper giving details of the cargo being offered for shipment.

3. **Mate's Receipt.** When the cargo is shipped, the shipper obtains a receipt that the cargo is loaded. It is important that the exact amount and condition of the cargo is noted on the receipt. The Mate's receipt as the name implies is signed by the Chief Officer.

4. **Bill of Lading.** The Bill of Lading is made up from the Mates' receipt and is a legal document giving the possessor title to the goods. It is for this reason that it is important that all details of the cargo are shown correctly, otherwise the shipowner is liable to be sued for any discrepancy between the bill of lading and the actual condition. Bills of Lading are subject to the Carriage of Goods by Sea Act.

General Cargo. Before commencement of loading the hold must be adequately prepared. It must be swept, and hosed out if necessary. The fire detection system is tested by holding a source of smoke under each outlet in turn while observing the alarm cabinet at the same time. The pipes from the CO_2 room are tested by pumping air through the connections and checking that it is passing through the outlets, thus establishing that the pipes are clear.

Safety requirements must also be complied with:—ladders and handrails to be checked and put in order and adequate lighting for the hold provided. This is a suitable occasion to replace any faulty lightbulbs.

Any repairs to hatches or hatchboards should be attended to at this time. All these checks must be logged and if there is likely to be any dispute a surveyor will be employed to inspect the hold. If a cargo of food is to be carried it may be necessary to comply with Public Health requirements as well.

The great variety of cargo being carried at sea makes it impossible to give details of stowage of every type to be encountered. For details of specific cargoes there are reference books available.

The following considerations should be borne in mind when planning stowage:

1. **Damage.** Do not overstow a light cargo with a heavier cargo. Do not stow anything between cars. Some packages must be stowed in a particular position, e.g. plate glass must always be stowed on end. In some cases the cargo will have to be lashed to prevent any movement in bad weather.

2. **Taint.** Some commodities give off a strong odour that can affect other materials, e.g. tea and rubber. Butter and eggs are liable to be damaged by taint.

3. **Pilferage.** Many types of goods are of sufficient value to provide temptation to a potential thief. Spirits, cigarettes and clothing are amongst the many in this category. As a check, any valuable cargo should be tallied into a lockable compartment by a ship's officer or other reliable personnel.

4. **Discharge.** Stow cargoes to give as quick a discharge as possible. This generally means distributing cargo destined for each port between as many different holds as practicable. In this way the optimum use may be made of the labour available in any port.

5. **Stability.** The ship must have adequate stability for every stage of the voyage. This means that the metacentric height (GM) must always be at an acceptable value and the trim be maintained within reasonable limits. When planning for metacentric height the worst possible stage of the voyage should be considered; this normally occurs when most of the oil in the double bottom tank is consumed, reducing the bottom weight. A rule of thumb is to distribute the weight $\frac{2}{3}$ in the lower hold and $\frac{1}{3}$ in the tween deck. It is desirable for a ship to trim as near to an even keel as possible, as extreme trim by the head can make a ship difficult to steer and liable to take seas over the foredeck. Most ports charge pilotage according to the deepest draft and too deep a draft can result in a ship having to wait for a tide before entering or leaving port.

Ventilation. Sweat is a common cause of damage to cargo. To prevent this it is necessary to ensure that ventilation is attended to at all times. Ship sweat occurs when the temperature of the outside air is below the dewpoint of the air in the hold. Air entering the hold deposits moisture on the ship's structure where it can drip on to the cargo. This situation is likely to occur when a ship passes from a warm to a cooler climate. When a ship passes from a cold to a warmer climate, the temperature of the hold will be below the dewpoint of the outside air and unless ventilation is stopped, moisture will be deposited on the cargo. This is known as cargo sweat.

All vegetable materials give off moisture to a certain extent. With many types of produce it is necessary to ventilate to prevent this moisture from damaging the cargo. With some varieties of bagged cargo it is necessary to stow so as to allow some form of natural ventilation. In many ships mechanical ventilation is provided for all holds. "Cargocaire" and "Drihold" are two such devices. These either allow outside air to be used to ventilate the hold or, where this is not suitable, artificially dried dry air can be circulated around the holds.

Refrigerated Cargo. Meat, dairy products and fruit, unless carried in refrigerated compartments would very quickly deteriorate. Ships designed to carry refrigerated cargo have insulated holds with pipes and machinery to cool the air. A system of fans and ducts distributes the cold air around the hold to maintain the low temperature. In some ships the hold space is entirely refrigerated, in others only some compartments are suitable for refrigerated cargo.

When preparing a hold for a refrigerated cargo it is most important to ensure that the hold is clean enough to load the unprotected carcasses. The hold must be thoroughly swept out and wiped down with cloths soaked in disinfectant. If there is any danger of taint, the hold is deodorised with ozone. The gratings must be scrubbed and disinfected and any fat spots scraped off. The tween deck scuppers must be tested and then brine poured into them. As brine has a low freezing point, it will stay in the "S" bend and seal off the tween decks. This will keep the scupper unblocked whilst still allowing water to drain into the bilge.

The dunnage should be inspected and if there is any doubt about its condition it must be landed and replaced with new dunnage. In some trades the dunnage is automatically replaced. If chilled cargo is to be loaded the hooks and chains for hanging the meat are sent ashore to be sterilised.

Before loading, the hold is cooled down to the carrying temperature and the thermometer stands placed in position. A Lloyds surveyor will inspect the refrigeration machinery to ensure that it is capable of maintaining the temperature for the voyage. This is known as a loading port survey. The hold is also inspected for cleanliness by a representative of the shippers. When loading meat, a close watch must be kept on the hold temperatures. If they rise too high the hatch should be covered until the temperature drops. As the carcasses are loaded they should be inspected and any bloodstained or soft carcasses rejected. The temperature of the meat must be checked as it is loaded, returning any that are above the required temperature. Frozen carcasses are stacked in the hold and lockers. The stevedores must wear protective overboots to prevent contamination. Chilled meat must be hung from the deckhead and ships that carry this have a large number of tween decks to hang the meat. As a result, the ship when loaded becomes rather tender and it is important to watch the stability of the ship during the voyage. After loading, the holds must be secured. If any other cargo is loaded in the hold the locker doors must be sealed to prevent warm air from entering.

Deck Cargo. Deck stowage is used for cargo that is too dangerous or too bulky to stow below decks, or when the cargo is of a density that fills the hold without loading the ship down to her marks. Examples of the latter are containers and timber. The carriage of deck cargo is covered by the Merchant Shipping Deck Cargo Regulations. These are in two parts.

Part One applies to all deck cargo. It requires that the cargo must be stowed to prevent damage to the ship, and in such a way as to provide access to parts of the ship required for working or accommodation. Lashings must be adequate for the weather conditions expected on the voyage and there must be a safe margin of stability at all times. If there is no safe access, above or below decks, between crew quarters and their places of work, then a gangway or catwalk over the cargo must be provided. It must be 1 metre wide and fitted with guard rails 1 metre high.

Part Two applies to timber carried as deck cargo. During the winter season the height of a timber deck cargo must not exceed one third of the extreme breadth of the ship. The cargo must be lashed with a system of overall lashings and uprights used to prevent any movement of the cargo. Ships that are especially strengthened may have a timber load line assigned, and load deeper than would otherwise be the case. For ships to take advantage of this regulation, the cargo must be compactly stowed over the complete area to a height of not less than that of the forecastle. The cargo must be lashed with separate chains to eye plates attached to the sheerstrake at stipulated intervals.

BULK OIL

Two distinct types of tanker exist:

The Crude Oil Tanker. These are large ships, some are more than 400,000 tonnes dwt. while 200,000 tonnes dwt. is a common size. They are employed in transporting the crude oil from the oil fields where it is produced, mainly in the Middle East to the oil refineries.

The crude oil tanker has a relatively simple pipeline system and high capacity pumps to reduce time spent in port discharging cargo. Heating coils may be fitted.

The Product Tanker. The specialised product tanker carries refined oil from the refineries to storage tanks in ports throughout the world. The average size is about 30,000 tonnes deadweight.

Refined products are sub-divided into black products such as fuel oil and heavy diesel, and white products which include petrol, kerosene, gas oil and lubricating oil.

Separation of the different grades is most important when carrying

*Fig. 12. Crude Oil Tanker, 214,000 tons dwt.

refined products. Contamination would make the product useless and possibly dangerous. A complicated pipeline system is therefore fitted to a product tanker so that several grades can be carried with less risk of contamination.

Pipeline Systems. Three main types of pipeline system are fitted. The layout will also differ in detail in accordance with the owner's requirements and the type of cargo for which the ship is designed.

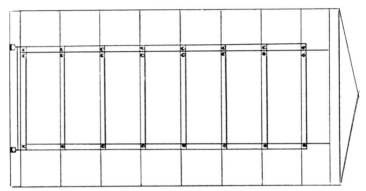

Fig. 13. Ring Main Pipeline System.

DIRECT LINES

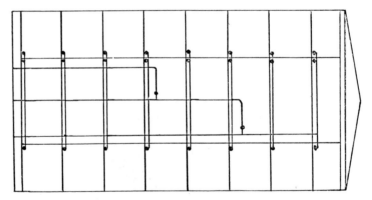

Fig. 14. Direct Loading Lines.

(*a*) **The Ring Main System** is used in product tankers. Oil may be loaded or discharged through either the port or starboard pipelines as the pipelines run the full length on each side. (Figures 13 and 14).

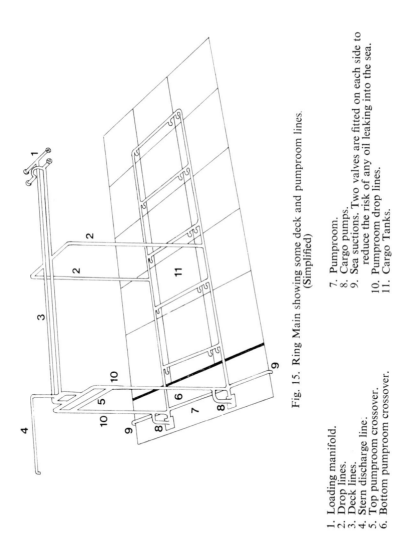

Fig. 15. Ring Main showing some deck and pumproom lines.
(Simplified)

1. Loading manifold.
2. Drop lines.
3. Deck lines.
4. Stern discharge line.
5. Top pumproom crossover.
6. Bottom pumproom crossover.

7. Pumproom.
8. Cargo pumps.
9. Sea suctions. Two valves are fitted on each side to reduce the risk of any oil leaking into the sea.
10. Pumproom drop lines.
11. Cargo Tanks.

There are two variations to the system. Older tankers may have pumprooms arranged so that the system is divided into three ring mains. New product tankers may have a double ring main with four lines running the length of the ship to give a choice of four lines for loading or discharging.

(b) **Block System (or direct system).** A separate pipeline is provided for each pump leading directly to the cargo tanks. Greater pumping rates are possible. This system is used mainly for crude oil but, as some segregation is possible, it is also in use in some product tankers. (Fig. 15)

(c) **Free Flow.** In this system the suctions are fitted in the aftermost centre cargo tank and the oil is allowed to drain through to this tank through power operated bulkhead valves without passing through a pipeline. A ring main system is fitted to control the final stages of loading or discharging. Lines are led directly to the different tanks from the loading connections on deck in order to control the trim during loading. This system is used only in crude oil tankers as segregation is not possible. (Fig. 16)

FREE FLOW

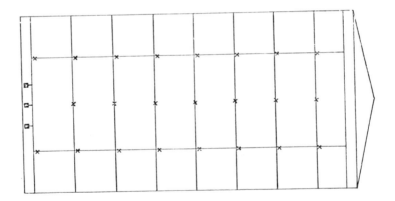

× BULKHEAD VALVE

Fig. 16. Free Flow System.

Stripping Line. This is a small ring main connected to stripping pumps which are used for discharging when the level of the oil has reached about half a metre. The main pumps are shut off at this stage as the introduction of air into the centrifugal pumps may cause them to overspeed and be stopped by the operation of the safety trips. Improvements in cargo pump design have made it possible for the main cargo pumps to discharge the cargo completely, but stripping lines are still fitted.

Direct Loading Lines, or drop lines, are fitted to connect the deck manifold to the bottom pipelines without passing through the pump-rooms. Direct loading lines may also be fitted to selected tanks in product tankers to increase segregation.

Loading Manifold. This is the term used to describe the loading connections which usually run athwartships across the deck at about the amidships point. There are likely to be three or four connections for the main cargo lines of a crude oil tanker in addition to bunker and stripping line connections. A more complicated manifold is fitted to product tankers.

Valves. The flow of oil through the pipelines is controlled by valves. A valve for a bottom pipeline is controlled from on deck by a wheel or powered actuator, which is connected to the valve by means of a spindle.

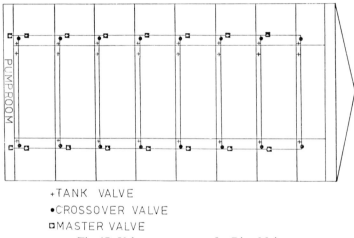

+TANK VALVE
•CROSSOVER VALVE
□MASTER VALVE

Fig. 17. Valve arrangements for Ring Main.

Master valves are fitted to the main line so that sections of the line can be isolated.

Crossover valves connect athwartships sections with the main pipelines running fore and aft.

Stripping valves for the stripping line are usually smaller than those on the main line.

Manifold valves are fitted at the loading connections on deck.

Sea valves are fitted to allow sea water to be loaded or discharged through the pipeline system.

Sluice valves are large power operated valves situated in the bulkheads of free flow ships.

Cargo pumps are placed at a low level as it is not possible to raise the oil from a depth of more than about 10 metres by means of a vacuum.

Reciprocating Pumps, or positive displacement pumps, draw liquid in by suction then force it out through valves into the pipeline. They are incapable of pumping oil at a high rate but can be operated on low pressure steam. As they are able to pump mixtures of air and liquid they are often used as stripping pumps.

Centrifugal Pumps are more efficient than reciprocating pumps and are used for the main cargo tanks of modern tankers. The oil flows into the impeller which rotates at high speed forcing the oil through outlets into the discharge lines by centrifugal force. Steam turbines or electric motors are used for the high power driving units and these are located in the engine room. The pumproom is situated aft when this type of pump is used so that the pumps can be driven by spindles passing through gas-tight glands in the engine room bulkhead.

Gas Lines. Ventilation is not required for an oil cargo but as an excessive pressure can build up due to gas being given off it is necessary to fit gaslines. The gas lines lead up from all tanks, through the tank coaming or deck, to a vent high up on the mast. Pressure/vacuum valves (P.V. valves) are fitted to control the rate at which gas can escape, or air can enter the tank. They are set to operate at a pressure differential of 0.1 kg/cm^2. The operation of the P.V. valves should be checked at regular intervals.

Gas lines are designed to allow the gas to escape at the anticipated rate of loading. They are usually divided into several sections with the line from the forward tanks leading to the foremast and two separate lines from the middle and after sections venting up a derrick post. Screens are fitted to the vents to prevent sparks from entering. It is important to ensure that the screens remain intact, and that they do not get blocked with paint or dirt.

The P.V. valves must be by-passed when loading or discharging as they are not capable of allowing large quantities of gas and air to pass through.

Contamination through the gas lines must be avoided when carrying different grades of refined oil. Product tankers may have a separate vent for each tank with its own P.V. valve. An alternative method is to have a P.V. valve for each set of tanks and to ensure that the by-pass is kept shut when cargo is not being loaded into the tanks concerned.

Inert Gas. To reduce the risk of fire and explosion, the air in the cargo tanks is replaced by an inert gas that will not support combustion. This inert gas is produced by burning oil in the ship's boiler where the oxygen in the air is converted into carbon dioxide. This gas is then cooled and any solids are removed by passing it through a scrubber containing sea-water. The gas is then passed into the cargo tanks where it displaces the air and the tank is then inert. Seals and non-return valves prevent any gas from the cargo tanks passing back through the cargo lines into the ship's boiler, where a serious explosion could occur. By keeping the inert gas at a pressure slightly above atmospheric, any leaks will cause the inert gas to escape, and not the outside air to enter the tanks. For the atmosphere to remain safe, it is important to test frequently to ensure that the oxygen content does not rise above 8 %; should this occur then the tank must be purged by pumping in more inert gas from the gas plant to displace the mixture in the tank.

Loading Operations

Orders will be received by the master before arrival at the loading port giving information about the amount and type of oil to be loaded. A shore representative will come on board to discuss the loading plan with the chief officer on arrival. The representative will inspect the ships' tanks after the ballast has been discharged to ensure that they are empty. A more thorough inspection will be made if refined products are to be carried.

The loading order for each grade is decided then the loading sequence for the tanks. With a small number of tanks loading may be started in all but one of the tanks so that when these are full and the final tank is being loaded a check can be made on the amount of oil in the other tanks.

A method of loading a homogeneous cargo is to fill the wing tanks first then all but one or two of the centre tanks. The last centre tank to be loaded should preferably be close to the centre of flotation so that the trim will not be changed during the final stages whilst the amount of oil in the remaining tanks is being determined.

With a large tanker the loading will start while some ballast remains on board to reduce hull stresses. The order of loading and discharging has to be carefully controlled to keep the stresses within acceptable limits.

After the tanks have been passed the lines are set for loading. In a crude oil tanker this is a relatively simple operation. The direct loading lines are opened to by-pass the pumproom and the valves to the tanks are opened. A more complicated procedure will usually have to be followed in a product carrier to avoid contamination. At least two valves, in addition to tank valves, must be kept closed between any two grades. The master list of valves, kept by the chief

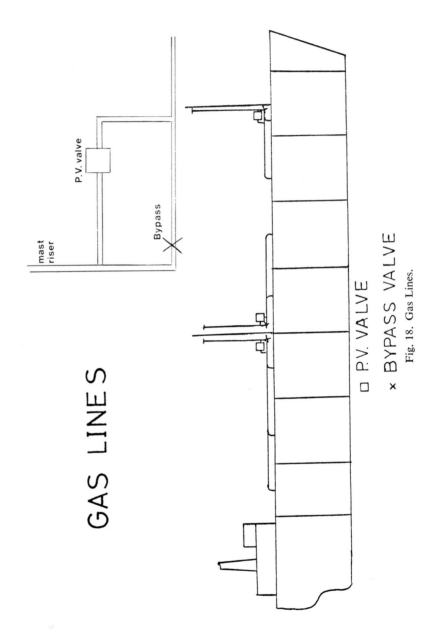

Fig. 18. Gas Lines.

officer, must be checked off before loading is commenced. Sea valves must be checked to see that they are properly closed and in some ports they may have to be sealed.

The gas lines will also have to be set, opening the by-pass lines and, if necessary, closing lines to certain tanks to prevent contamination. Relief valves are normally fitted to prevent excessive build up of gas pressure but if there is any doubt the sighting ports should be unscrewed and covered with a sandbag so that they will be forced up by excessive pressure.

An adequate method of communicating with the shore must be arranged before loading is commenced. The loading should be started at a low speed to reduce the risk of an explosion caused by static electricity and to give time for checking that the oil is entering the selected tanks. The maximum rate of loading will vary with the cargo and the ship.

The temperature and relative density (R.D.) of the oil is taken during loading and the amount of oil to be loaded in each tank is computed to an ullage.

As the oil level in each tank reaches the required ullage the valve is shut. This is known as "topping off". Excess pressure must not be allowed to build up in the cargo lines so as the last tank of a particular set reaches the correct ullage and is shut off the first tank of the next set must be opened simultaneously. An empty tank can be partially opened when topping off an intermediate tank if it is necessary to slow down the rate at which the ullage is decreasing. When loading the final tank the loading rate is reduced and the loading is finally stopped from ashore. The valves in the ship are not closed until the contents of the shore pipeline have been allowed to run into the ship's tank.

Ullages, samples and water dips are taken at all tanks when loading has been completed. All cargo valves are closed, the P.V. valves set to operate. Ullage openings and sighting ports are secured. The pipelines are disconnected and any oil spills cleaned up.

When cargo tonnages have been agreed between ship and shore representatives the documents can be completed and the ship will be free to sail.

Discharging

On arrival at the discharging port, ullages, temperatures and water dips are taken and the amount of cargo on board is again determined. Samples will also be taken by shore representatives before any cargo can be discharged.

When the pipelines have been connected the safety check is carried out before discharging is commenced. As in the case of loading, discharging is begun at a slow rate in case there has been any mistake in setting the lines, and as a precaution against a possible build up of static in the shore tanks.

The order of discharge must be arranged to ensure a trim by the stern as the tanks are being drained. With a homogeneous cargo it is usual to open between a half and one-third of the tanks at once. The gas lines must be set to by-pass the P.V. valves.

The draining and stripping of tanks must be done at a slow rate otherwise the pumps will draw in air and lose suction. Small tankers may be given a list to cause the oil to move towards the suctions but in vessels with separate stripping lines the main pumps are shut off and the stripping pumps started. As the stripping pumps have a relatively low capacity it is not usually possible to discharge through the same lines as the main pumps so the normal practice is to strip into an empty tank on board.

The final tank is discharged using the main pumps and finishing off with a stripping pump. A shore representative will check that all tanks are empty when discharging has been completed.

BALLASTING

Before the empty tanker can put to sea, it is necessary to ballast to a suitable draft to make her seaworthy for the next voyage. Seawater ballast has to be pumped into selected tanks. As these tanks will be full of gas from the previous cargo, the displaced gas makes this a potentially dangerous operation and the same safety precautions as those required for loading must be observed. The amount of ballast required depends on the anticipated weather conditions. If bad weather is expected a tanker could ballast to about half her deadweight, i.e. a 100,000-tonne tanker might carry 50,000 tonnes of ballast but if fine weather is expected the amount of ballast will be reduced. As a bad choice of ballast tanks can impose heavy stresses on the hull, and in extreme cases cause a tanker to break up, it is important that the ship's stability information is consulted before deciding on a particular ballast arrangement. To prevent any oil in the ship's lines from running out into the harbour when the sea valves are opened, the pump is first started slowly before opening the sea valves and the resulting suction will prevent any oil from escaping.

Segregated Ballast. In order to reduce the requirement for tank cleaning, and hence the amount of oil discharged into the sea, all new tankers will be required to have ballast tanks, pipes and pumps that are totally independent from those used for cargo. This will ensure that the ballast system will never contain any oil, and ballast can be discharged without any fear of pollution. These tanks will be arranged along the ship's side so that in the event of an accident the escape of oil can be minimised.

Tank Cleaning. Before a tanker can start to load a cargo, she must first discharge her ballast. In many cases this will have to be into the harbour, so it is vital that the ballast does not contain any oil or other polluting substance. To ensure this the ballast tanks must first be cleaned. Unless the ship has a segregated ballast system the normal procedure is for the ship to leave the loading port with ballast in dirty tanks while the other tanks are cleaned. Once the final ballast tanks have been cleaned and ballasted, the dirty ballast water is discharged into a slop tank. Apart from the need to have clean ballast tanks, sludge can build up in cargo tanks and, unless this is removed by cleaning, it will be very difficult to drain the tanks.

Crude Oil Tank Cleaning. After a cargo of crude oil is discharged the residues normally consist of heavier particles that have settled during the voyage, and these have to be removed by tank cleaning. If the tanks are cleaned with crude oil pumped through fixed tank-cleaning machines as the cargo is discharged, much of these residues will be mixed back in the cargo and discharged with it. This will substantially reduce the amount left behind after discharging the cargo, and reduce the amount of tank cleaning. Because of the gas produced and the dangers from static electricity, crude oil tank cleaning should only be carried out on ships fitted with inert gas. Crude oil tank cleaning will be fitted on all new tankers and it is now being fitted to some existing ships.

Prevention of Pollution Act, 1971. This Act prohibits the discharge of crude, fuel, lubricating and heavy diesel oil or any mixture containing these oils by a British ship anywhere at sea. It is also an offence to discharge any oil, however small the amount, into U.K. territorial waters. The Owner or Master is liable to a fine not exceeding £50,000 for either of the above offences.

The outline exceptions to these are that tankers may discharge oil on a passage at sea provided:—

The ship is more than 50 miles from land.
The rate of discharge does not exceed 60 litres per mile.
The quantity of oil discharged does not exceed 1/15,000-part of the ship's total carrying capacity.

Any ship may discharge a mixture of oil and water from her bilges if she is on a passage and as far as practicable from land, provided the rate of discharge does not exceed 60 litres per mile and the oil content of the mixture is less than 100 parts per million parts of water.

Oil Record Book. All ships must keep a record of all operations connected with loading, discharging, ballasting and cleaning tanks. There are two books provided, one for tankers and the other for dry-cargo ships.

Load on Top

The oil in the dirty ballast tanks will float to the top of the sea water. Most of the water from each tank can therefore be discharged into the sea but the top layer is pumped into a slop tank. Dirty water from line washing and tank cleaning is also pumped into a slop tank as it is an offence to discharge dirty oils anywhere at sea. The mixture in the slop tank is allowed to separate and the clean water is pumped into the sea. The oil on the top is retained on board and discharged with the next cargo.

⚓   ⚓   ⚓   ⚓

THE PROPERTIES AND USES OF PAINTS

Corrosion. When steel is exposed to the action of air, or of moisture, particularly if it be salt-laden, rust soon appears on its surface which penetrates into the plating and corrodes it away. Oxygen is necessary to the formation of rust, hence the reason why it is necessary to exclude air from direct contact with iron and steel by keeping it well coated with paint. New ships should be well coated, especially round rivet heads, butts and laps.

When corrosion sets in all rust must be scaled or hammered off, the bare metal thoroughly scraped, cleaned and dried before applying a priming coat of paint. Several coats should be given in succession, allowing sufficient time between each to allow for thorough drying.

Sometimes butt straps and plate landings show signs of moisture and when this occurs the "weeping" joints are made tight by cleaning out the crevices with a wire brush and caulking the edges which is just burring up the edges of the plating with a chisel and hammer to close up the joint.

Electrolytic Corrosion. If two dissimilar metals are placed in a suitable electrolyte and a wire is connected between them, an electric current flows from one "pole" to the other. The movement of electric current is accompanied by a wastage of the metal at one pole, the anode.

A similar process occurs in ships when dissimilar metals are in contact in the presence of sea water, which forms the electrolyte. Examples are seen in submarines where steel, brass and zinc are in close proximity; also on the forward end of the rudder on single-screw vessels when a phosphor-bronze propeller is used.

The "working" of steel during fabrication or the presence of impurities or scale are sufficient to produce variations which act in the same way as dissimilar metals in the presence of an electrolyte (e.g.

sea water). Thus, a series of "cells" are set up at various points on the surface, with consequent wastage or corrosion of the steel. In certain conditions, sodium chloride in the sea water is converted to sodium hydroxide (caustic soda); this is a powerful paint remover and may remove paint from adjacent areas and expose the metal to fresh attack.

So far as paint is concerned there are two ways of approaching the problem of protecting the metal:

(a) By providing a barrier to prevent the electroylte (sea water) from coming in contact with the metal, thus preventing cell formations. Normal paints are not sufficiently impervious to water to do this but bituminous materials applied sufficiently thickly (about 2·5 mm=at least five coats) are reasonably water resistant. However, if the coating is damaged, exposing the metal, attack is highly concentrated; further, rust will tend to form behind the coating.

(b) By including in the paint, materials which stifle the electrochemical action. For this purpose, rust-inhibitive pigments, e.g. red lead, zinc chromate, are used. Paints of this type depend for their effectiveness on the passage of water through the film in small amounts. They will not prevent corrosion completely, but they have the advantage over bituminous coatings of helping to stifle corrosion should the film be damaged.

What Paint Is. Most paints consist of a liquid (called the *vehicle* or *medium*) in which is suspended solid material (pigment).

The vehicles at present in use may be divided into a number of broad groups, the most common of which are as follows:

(a) Emulsions of oils or resins and water.
(b) Drying oils, e.g. linseed oil.
(c) Varnishes.
(d) Cellulose solutions.
(e) Special solutions, e.g. vehicles based on natural or synthetic rubber.
(f) Bituminous solutions.

Of the above, only (b) and (c) are widely used in ships' paints; paints in groups (e) and (f) are used to a lesser extent for certain types of work.

In general, the solution types form a solid film mainly by evaporation of the solvent. The remainder dry mainly by chemical change induced by absorption of oxygen and the action of light, although evaporation of the solvent assists drying.

The vehicle acts as a "binder" for the pigment and ensures its adhesion to the surface to which the paint is applied. In addition, the vehicle used largely determines the nature and behaviour of the paint. For instance, some vehicles possess good water resistance and others good chemical resistance, whilst others may be chosen for their quick drying properties or superior flexibility.

Linseed oil and certain other vegetable oils used in paint manufacture have the property of drying to form a tough coating; mineral oils do not have this property and must not be added to paint or its drying will be retarded or prevented altogether.

The toughness, gloss and durability of linseed and other oils can be increased by various ways, including heating, and vehicles of this type are widely used for protective paints.

Gloss and protective value can be increased further by combining the treated oil with a resin to form a varnish. The resin may be natural or synthetic.

Drying oils dry comparatively slowly; in order to speed up the process materials termed "driers" are added during manufacture. "Driers" are sometimes made available to the painter (e.g. "Liquid Driers," "Terebene," etc.) who often adds them to the paint in order to hasten drying under adverse conditions. Over-addition of driers many actually retard drying or cause paint failure. An adequate supply of fresh air is necessary for good drying.

Solvents or "thinners" are added to the paint during manufacture in order to make it workable and to assist drying. If the paint thickens, because of long storage or failure to replace lids, for example it may be necessary to add more thinner. The paint must not be over-thinned and the right type of thinner must be used; paraffin and similar "greasy" thinners will retard drying and spoil the paint.

Pigments give paint its colour and opacity; they also help to give it thickness or "body". In addition certain pigments impart specific properties to the paint. Some pigments, e.g. red lead, zinc chromate help to inhibit rust and are thus of special value in marine painting. Others are used to advantage in chemical resistant finishes. Flow and brushing properties can be affected by the use of particular pigments.

Many important pigments are produced from titanium, lead, zinc and other metals, some are derived from natural oxides or coloured earths, whilst others are made chemically. Metallic pigments, e.g. lead, zinc and aluminium in powder or flake form are also used as pigments in special types of paint.

What Paint Does. The chief functions of ships' paints are:

Protection. If unprotected by a coating of suitable paint, metal would corrode and timber would decay. In marine conditions attack by weather and water is especially severe.

Anti-fouling. Marine growths on hulls and ships' bottoms reduce speed and increase fuel consumption. Suitable paints discourage growths.

Appearance. A smart appearance helps morale and encourages pride in the ship.

Paint is also used to:

Help prevent condensation (sweating).

Give a rough surface to metal decks and so prevent skidding.

No single paint will perform all the functions mentioned above; different types of paint are available and it is important to use the one designed for the job.

Preparation and Priming Generally. Sound preparation is essential to successful painting. Dirt, moisture, rust, salt deposits, grease and oil prevent the paint from adhering properly and additionally may cause slow drying and other defects.

Paint does not adhere well to smooth, shiny surfaces, e.g. glossy paint which has aged and hardened but not weathered. Adhesion to certain metals, e.g. zinc and aluminium, is poor also, unless the surface is pretreated.

The methods normally available for the cleaning of *steelwork* are:—

(*a*) Mechanical or manual wirebrushing, chipping, etc.

(*b*) Flame cleaning.

(*c*) Grit or wet sand blasting.

Of these, grit or wet sand blasting is probably the most effective but it is expensive and often not practicable because of difficulties of access, inconvenience caused by residues of grit or sand, etc.

By force of circumstances, most steelwork is prepared for painting by manual or mechanical chipping, scraping and wirebrushing. This method will not remove tightly adherent scale but, if conscientiously done, is reasonably effective in removing loose scale and rust. When metal is to be chipped especially with mechanical tools, it should be ensured that the metal itself is not excessively chipped, indented or "burred", thus producing high spots and sharp edges which protrude through the paint film.

Oil and grease must be removed by washing with white spirit or other suitable solvent (not paraffin). Where contamination is heavy, repeated washing, with repeated changes of solvent and rag or waste, will be necessary.

Salt and similar deposited material must be removed. Usually, this can be done by washing with clean water, preferably before the surface is wirebrushed so that any rusting induced by wetting the surface is removed.

In all cases, the steelwork must be primed as soon as possible after preparation and the work should be so planned that prepared surfaces are primed the same day. With flame cleaning, the metal should be primed whilst still warm.

Whenever possible, at least two coats of primer should be applied to ensure that sharp edges and "holidays" in the first coat are properly covered.

Primers for Iron and Steel. Iron and steel rust rapidly if not protected, especially in marine conditions. Complete exclusion of air and moisture from perfectly cleaned steel would prevent rusting, but, in practice, complete removal of rust is rarely possible and most paint films will not exclude air and moisture altogether. Primers for iron and steel must, therefore, help to stifle or "inhibit" rust and they usually contain "rust inhibitive" pigments in a suitable vehicle. Rust inhibitive pigments include:

Red and white lead.
Basic lead sulphate.
Chromates of lead and zinc.
Metallic (dust) lead and zinc.

It must be made clear that the vehicle plays an important part; a rust inhibitive pigment would be of little value in a poor quality or unsuitable vehicle.

Lead based paints should not be applied to surfaces in refrigerated spaces and spaces used for foodstuffs and drinking water. They are also unsuitable for use on galvanised metal.

Aluminium, Copper, etc. The adhesion of paint to these surfaces is usually poor. Aluminium should be pretreated or wash primed if possible; if not, the surface should be abraded with glasspaper or wire wool, using white spirit as a lubricant. *Lead-containing primers must not be used*; zinc chromate primers are suitable.

Copper, brass, lead, etc., give adhesion troubles; abrasion, followed by priming with a zinc chromate primer or direct application of gloss finish, gives best results but some flaking must always be expected.

Fouling. The study of marine growth is a specialised subject, and the development of suitable anti-fouling paints requires close co-operation with marine biologists. The latter have devoted much time to investigation of the life-cycles and habits of marine growths; knowledge of this kind is essential if satisfactory anti-fouling paints are to be devised.

It is found, for example, that anti-fouling agents which are effective in temperate waters are less so in tropical waters; even local conditions such as the discharge of warm effluents into tidal rivers, can greatly affect rates of growth and degree of fouling.

Anti-fouling paints operate by the slow release of substances poisonous to marine growths.

Painting. Underwater paints are applied in drydock. They are classed as anti-corrosive, anti-fouling and boot-topping. They are specially manufactured with heavy pigments which settle rapidly and have to be kept stirred continuously during application and a quickly evaporating vehicle which causes the paint to dry almost as quickly as it is put on.

The anti-corrosive is applied as a primer and in the case of a new ship three coats are given. The anti-fouling composition is applied over the anti-corrosive and usually carried up to the light load line. Anti-fouling paint must not be applied to bare metal. Some anti-fouling paints must be applied within a period from four to twenty-four hours before the dock is filled with water but longer periods may be allowed with modern high duty paints. A cheaper paint called boot-topping is applied between the light and load water marks when the ship is afloat. The boot-top area has to be frequently painted due to the paint being often damaged by chafing the ship's side against quay walls and barges when handling cargo.

Black bituminous compositions are usually applied at the stern plates, stern post and rudder in order to counteract the electrolitic action between the bronze propeller and the adjacent steelwork.

Red Lead paint is used as a primer for the topsides but as this is slow drying paint in cold weather, chromate primers are used when the time available for applying the finishing coat is short.

Special paints are manufactured to suit special requirements, such as heat-resisting funnel paints, non-slip (or sanded) Deck paint, Black Varnish to protect Chain Lockers, Double Bottoms and Bunker spaces, and paint to withstand long immersion for fresh water tanks.

There are several types of paint which have a high resistance to chemical attack. These include:

Epoxide-Resin Paints which consist of two solutions which are mixed together when required. Coatings of this paint possess considerable resistance to mechanical damage.

Chlorinated Rubber Paints consist of chlorinated rubber and a plasticiser together with extenders and inert pigments. Advantages, apart from chemical resistance, are fast drying and good adhesion.

CHAPTER XII

SHIP CONSTRUCTION

Structural Stresses. A ship is subjected to stresses from a complex system of forces and the structure must be braced and supported to withstand any reasonable combinations of load at a given time. The design and fabrication must be aimed at reducing the overall cost and yet conform to the standards required by the statutory bodies and the classification societies. Also the structure should be as light in weight as possible, consistent with strength, rigidity, seaworthiness and the required cargo capacity.

To study the problems of the structural stresses in ship construction a number of simplifications can be made. The forces applied to the structure are divided into two categories, Static Forces and Dynamic Forces. Static forces are produced by the acceleration of gravity, for example the forces of weight and water pressure. Since the water pressure acts perpendicular to the hull it can be split into horizontal and vertical components. The vertical component is the force of buoyancy. Dynamic forces are due to any other acceleration such as those due to rolling, pitching or heaving.

These forces produce various stresses which can be subdivided into three groups, longitudinal, transverse and local stresses.

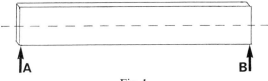

A   B

Fig. 1.

Longitudinal Stresses. Fig. 1 represents a narrow steel plate standing on its edge, the ends resting on supports *A* and *B*. It is a simple girder. If a heavy load *C* is applied at its middle point

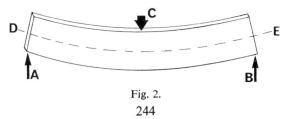

Fig. 2.

244

(Fig. 2), the girder will bend and suffer from bending stresses as it tries to resist this effect. The upper edge is under compression and the lower edge is in tension. Along the line, *DE*, or neutral axis the girder is not subjected to bending stress. Should the load be excessive the upper edge will buckle and the lower edge fracture or at least show signs of strain.

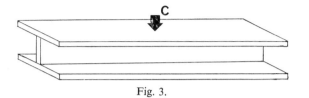

Fig. 3.

By stiffening the edges of the plate with flanges as in Fig. 3, the girder will now be able to resist distortion due to the weight *C*. The vertical plate is called the web of the girder and the edge plates its flanges. The web could now be made thinner and the arrangement gives a more efficient girder than the simple plate. Similarly a more efficient girder could be produced by forming a box girder with two webs and two flanges.

If the girder was supported at its middle point *A*, with loads *B* and *C* at each end as in Fig. 4, the girder will bend in the other direction.

Fig. 4.

The upper edge will now be under tension and the lower edge under compression, with the neutral axis *DE* between.

A ship when afloat is subjected to similar stresses. The loads are due to the difference in the distribution of the weight and buoyancy in the various sections of the ship's length. There may be a concentration of weight amidships whilst for a particular waterline the buoyancy distribution may be greater at the ends.

Fig. 5 represents such a case in still water. The resulting bending causes compression in the upper flange or upper deck, and tension in the lower flange or keel, with the neutral axis between them. This condition is called "sagging".

When the vessel is in a seaway the waterline follows the shape of the waves. This causes a change in the distribution of the force of buoyancy.

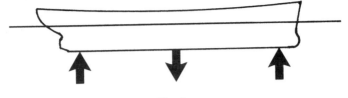

Fig. 5.

Fig. 6 represents a ship supported at each end on the crests of two waves. The increase in buoyancy at the ends and the decrease in the middle produces a sagging condition. The vessel must be capable of withstanding the combination of the stresses produced by this wave together with the sagging in still water.

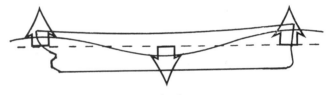

Fig. 6.

In many cases the weight distribution may be reversed. An excess of weight may occur at the ends with an excess of buoyancy amidships.

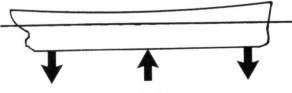

Fig. 7.

Now in still water there will be a tendency to bend in the opposite direction. This causes tension in the upper deck and compression in the keel, and is called "hogging".

When the vessel is supported amidships on the crest of a wave (Fig. 8), with the ends in troughs, there is an increase in the upthrust in the mid-length and a decrease at the end. This is called a hogging wave.

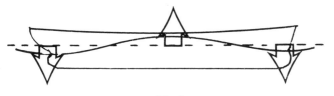

Fig. 8.

If the vessel is hogged in still water then those stresses will be combined with the stresses due to the standard hogging wave to see if the ship will suffer excessive stresses. Since the upper and lower flange experience the greatest stresses due to longitudinal bending, special attention must be paid to the longitudinal strength of the upper deck and the keel. Only the continuous longitudinal members resist this bending. This is no problem on the lower flange since the keel plating, bilge strakes, centre girders, side girders, longitudinals and the inner bottom are continuous. However problems may arise in ships with wide hatchways since only the structure outside the line of hatches will be continuous. The effective upper flange consists of the continuous sections of the upper deck, the underdeck longitudinals, the longitudinal girders and the sheer strakes. Tankers are particularly strong since the upper deck is almost continuous and further longitudinal strength is provided by twin longitudinal bulkheads.

Another effect of the differences in the distribution of the weight and the buoyancy along the length is vertical shear forces. At most points along the length, the load on one side will be upwards and on the other side an equal but downwards force. The effect is to cause shear stresses. The worst effect occurs at a transverse bulkhead between a loaded compartment and one which is empty.

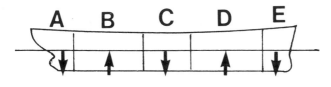

Fig. 9.

In Fig. 9 the loads *A*, *C* and *E* indicate when the weight is greater than the buoyancy whilst *B* and *D* indicate that the buoyancy is greater perhaps because the compartments are empty or only part full. Suppose it were possible to disconnect the several compartments. Each compartment would float at a waterline where the buoyancy of each section would support its weight. The the compartments A, C and E would float at a deeper draught than the initial draught, whilst the compartments B and D would float at a lighter draught (Fig. 10).

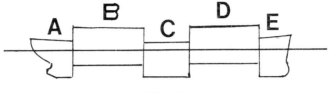

Fig. 10.

To resist this shearing effect the continuity of strength must be maintained between each compartment and the next. In order to avoid exceeding the maximum values of shear and bending stress, information is supplied on the safe distribution of the weights of cargo, ballast, bunkers and fresh water. Large bulk carriers and tankers are equipped with electronic calculators to determine these stresses.

Transverse stresses. When the ship is rolling in a seaway the transverse section will try to distort at the corners due to racking stresses (Fig. 11).

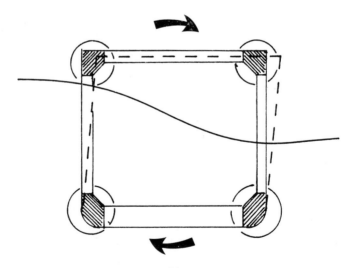

Fig. 11.

The solid lines represent the original shape of the cross-section and the pecked lines show the distorted shape due to the wave. The strain occurs mostly at the corners which must be strengthened. Transverse bulkheads are important in resisting any attempt to change the transverse form. Between the transverse bulkheads the shape is maintained by a series of transverse rings formed by the floors, side frames or webs and the transverse beams or girders. To resist racking stresses adequate brackets must be provided in way of the bilge strakes and between the deck stringer and the sheer strakes. Since the continuity of the transverse strength is reduced on the upper deck due to hatch openings, greater attention must be paid to the upper deck beam knees than to the bilge bracket which forms part of a rigid bottom structure. Racking stresses are a problem for Roll-on Roll-off ships which have a reduced number of transverse bulkheads.

Water pressure acts perpendicular to the surface of the submerged hull and increases with depth at the rate of 1·025 tonnes for every metre. This produces collapsing stresses which must be resisted (Fig. 12).

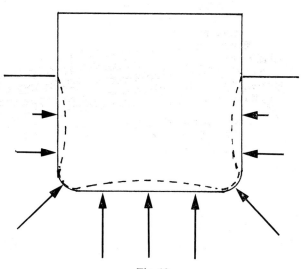

Fig. 12.

The hull plating forms a comparatively thin watertight envelope which would not resist the collapsing stresses. Reinforcement is provided by the bulkheads, the side frames and the plate floors which together with the centre girder, side girders, longitudinals and stringers, form panels of sufficient strength to withstand the pressure of the water.

When the ship is drydocked the thrust from the water is removed. The weight is now supported by the keel blocks (Fig. 13).

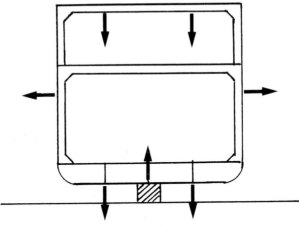

Fig. 13.

An upthrust acts along the keel due to the reaction between the ship and the keel blocks. The hull on either side of the keel strake tends to sag downwards, the sides bulge outwards and the beams are in tension. Sufficient strength must be provided in the bottom structure to resist the distortion due to the upthrusts and the tendency to sag. Ships with a double bottom have a strong aitch girder which will provide sufficient rigidity. Those without double bottoms have heavy centre girders supported by docking brackets. External support can be supplied by bilge blocks and side shores.

Local stresses. Additional structural strength must be provided in certain parts of the ship which are subjected to localised loads.

When the ship is under way in a seaway, the water pressure varies with the changing depth of water. A combination of the waves and the pitching of the vessel means that there are great variations in pressure at the ends of the vessel. This produces a tendency to vibrate due to the panting stresses. The structure forward of the collision bulkhead and aft of the after peak bulkhead are strengthened to cope with these alternations of tension and compression. Panting arrangements consist of additional panting beams and stringers or perforated flats with wash plate bulkheads on the centre line.

As the ship pitches into a head sea excessive pounding may occur in the forward section if the vessel is not fully loaded. Extra strengthening is required in the pounding area, aft of the collision bulkhead where the bottom plating becomes flat. Additional plate floors and side girders are provided.

The concentration of heavy weights along the middle line of the hold causes the sides to tend to collapse inwards (Fig. 14).

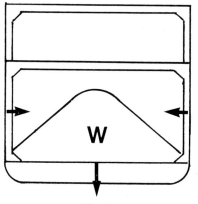

Fig. 14.

Where this is a typical method of loading extra side girders, longitudinals and plate floors are required to cope with these concentrations of weight.

Other localised stresses in way of deck machinery such as windlass, winches, derricks, steering gear, etc., and the structure in their vicinity is stiffened by thickening the plating, putting in additional or stronger beams so that the local stresses may be distributed to adjacent parts.

This very general and brief reference to the stresses applied to the ship's hull when considered as a girder indicates that the longitudinal and transverse framework of the ship is designed to enable the shell plating to keep its form and to resist any distortion and strain. The structure must be made rigid enough longitudinally and transversely to withstand all the normal stresses to be expected when the ship is labouring at sea with her cargo intelligently distributed and securely stowed.

The longitudinal framing consists principally of keel, stem and stern posts, centre girder, side girders, top and bottom longitudinals, margin plates and stringers. The transverse framing consists of plate and bracket floors, side and web frames, tank side brackets, beams, beam knees and pillars. The shell, inner bottom and deck plating also add considerably to the strength of the ship and form the most important part of the structure, not merely because they make the hull watertight but because the plating is the heaviest item of all the components·

The traditional methods of connecting the parts of the ship's structure are riveting and welding. In modern ship construction the predominant method is welding and only a limited amount of riveting is used.

Welding. This method of joining two pieces of metal together by the process of heat fusion has the advantages that less steel is required to build the ship, watertightness can be obtained without caulking, and a smooth underwater hull reduces friction and saves horse power.

Electric arc welding is a fusion process in which a wire or electrode is connected to an electricity supply which passes through the plates to be welded. On touching the plates with the electrode, the circuit is completed and the current flows. The electrode is then withdrawn a short distance, about 6 mm to form an air gap which the current can jump. The increased resistance across the air gap causes an intensely hot arc to be generated which melts both plates and electrode to form the weld.

The electrode plays a most important part in the welding process. For manual welding the electrode has a chemical coating which on melting, releases gases to protect the weld metal from oxidation, stabilises the arc and produces a slag coating over the weld metal to reduce the cooling rate. With machine welding these chemicals are usually added to the weld separately.

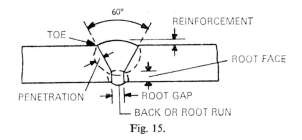
Fig. 15.

Type of Welded Connection. The two main types of connection are (1) Butt Weld. (2) Fillet Weld.

The Butt weld joining two plates in the same plane is shown in Fig. 15; the plates have been bevelled to form a single *V* and the weld metal lies internally to the parts to be joined. A sealing run of weld metal is usually required on the face opposite the *V*.

The fillet weld is used for joining plates at right angles and in overlapped joints. The weld metal in a fillet weld is usually roughly like a right angled triangle lying outside the plates or metal to be joined.

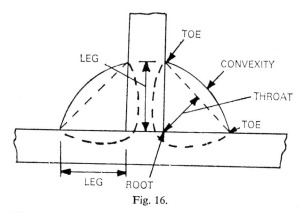

Fig. 16.

Short fillet welds 75 mm long and spaced 150 mm apart are used to secure stiffeners to plating and may be "staggered" on each side of the stiffener or they may be "chain intermittent" meaning that the welds are opposite each other.

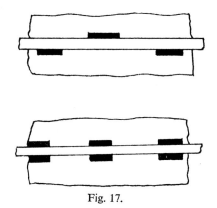

Fig. 17.

Intermittent welds with "scallops" are frequently found at the frame to shell connection, the main purpose being to relieve stress and brittleness that a continuous weld might produce.

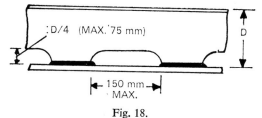

Fig. 18.

Some of the section commonly used in construction are illustrated in Fig. 19.

These are called:—

A. Slab section.   B. Bulb section.
C. Angle section.   D. "T" section.

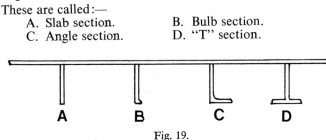

Fig. 19.

The Cellular Double Bottom. Double Bottom structures are illustrated in Fig. 20 and Fig. 21. Fig. 20 shows the older structure of dry cargo vessels which has transverse framing throughout. Fig. 20(a) shows a plate floor which is fitted at every other frame space except under the machinery space and in the area forward strengthened to withstand pounding. At the alternate frame spaces are fitted bracket floors as shown in Fig. 20(b). In ships over 120 m in length Lloyd's now recommend longitudinal framing in the double bottom (Fig. 21). As can be seen from the figures it is usual in dry cargo vessels to combine longitudinal framing in the double bottom with transverse framing on the side shell. In this system the plate floors occur at every three or four frame spaces (Fig. 21(a)) with bracket floors (Fig. 21(b)) in between. Plate floors are fitted at every frame space under main engines and at every other frame space in the area forward strengthened against pounding.

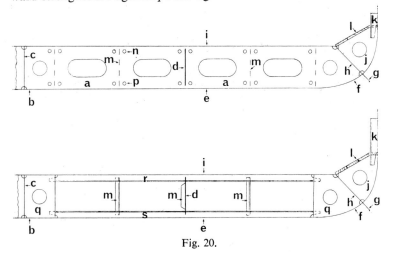

Fig. 20.

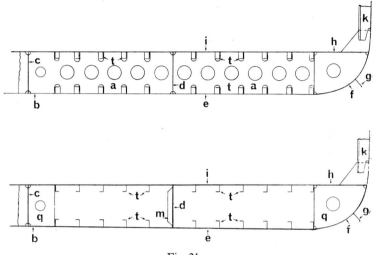

Fig. 21.

Key to Figs. 20 and 21.

(a) Plate floor   (b) Keel plate
(c) Continuous centre girder   (d) Intercostal side girder
(e) Outer bottom shell plating   (f) Bilge plate
(g) Bilge keel   (h) Margin plate
(i) Inner bottom plating   (j) Bilge bracket
(k) Side frames   (l) Bilge limbers
(m) Stiffeners   (n) Air holes
(p) Drain holes   (q) Bracket floors
(r) Inner bottom frame   (s) Outer bottom frame
(t) Longitudinal frames

Beams. The top ends of the port and starboard frames are tied together by means of a beam, the beam being efficiently connected to the frames by a "knee". The beams are slightly rounded upwards, thus forming a "camber" to shed water off the deck; the camber is usually about one fiftieth of the breadth of the vessel. The lower deck beams are similar to the upper deck beams.

At the upper deck a watertight connection is made between the upper strake of the side shell, the sheer strake, and the outboard strake of the deck plating, the deck stringer plate (Fig. 22).

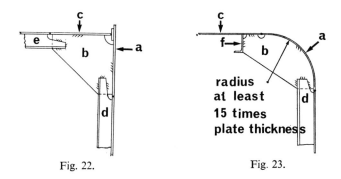

Fig. 22.   Fig. 23.

In large tankers and bulk carriers the sheer strake is rounded (Fig. 23). This improves the continuity of strength at the upper corners of the hull.

Sheer strake to deck stringer plate connection (Figs. 22 and 23.)

(a) sheer strake
(b) beam knee or bracket
(c) deck stringer plate
(d) side frame
(e) transverse beam
(f) longitudinals

Watertight Flats. It is necessary to get watertight work where the frames pass up through a side stringer plate of a watertight deck. The most common method is to cut the frame at the under side of the watertight flat so that the stringer plate resting on the beams may be fitted close against the shell plating and be connected thereto by means of a continuous fore-and-aft angle bar or weld.

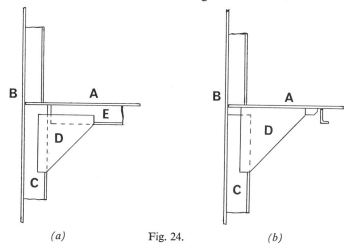

(a)   Fig. 24.   (b)

In Figure 24, *A* is the stringer plate lying on beam *E*, with its connection to the shell strake *B* by means of a continuous weld. The frame *C* is cut at the beam and continued again above the deck as shown. The bracket *D* is welded to the frame and beam in Fig. 24(a) and to the bottom of the stringer plate in Fig. 24(b) where the under-deck structure is longitudinal.

Bulkheads are vertical partitions arranged transversely or longitudinally to form walls to subdivide the ship into convenient sections for stores, living accommodation, cargo, etc.

Transverse Watertight Bulkheads, however, enter largely into the main structure of the vessel, their principal function being to impart strength and to add to the safety of the vessel by subdividing the hull into self-contained watertight compartments so that in the event of one or more compartments being flooded there would still be left sufficient reserve buoyancy to keep the ship afloat. They also serve to reduce the risks from fire by confining an outbreak to one hold.

The minimum number of watertight bulkheads required by law is four; the collision bulkhead placed not less than 5 and not greater than 8 per cent of the ship's length from the fore end of the load waterline; the after peak bulkhead which encloses the shaft tubes in a watertight compartment; and bulkheads at the fore and after end of the machinery space to enclose the engines and boilers in a self-contained compartment.

Passenger ships are required by law to be provided with adequate subdivision so that if the ship receives reasonable damage it will survive flooding, without excessive list. This is provided by the calculation of the maximum permissible length between watertight bulkheads. There is no such requirement for the cargo ship. However in types of ships with superior subdivision, such as oil tankers and ore carriers, this is recognised by the reduction of the freeboard assigned under the Loadline Rules.

The classification societies specify the minimum number of bulkheads based on the length of the vessel:—when the length is over 90 metres, 5 bulkheads should be fitted; over 105 metres, 6; over 125 metres, 7; over 145 metres, 8; over 165 metres, 9; over 190 metres the number is considered individually. However these are not requirements of law so that where watertight bulkheads interfere with the working of the ship, as in Roll-on Roll-off ships, the number may be less than the guidelines.

Watertight bulkheads extend to the shell plating on each side and from the floor to the upper deck. Such a large area of plating must be efficiently stiffened, not merely to prevent it buckling under normal structural stresses but more particularly to withstand the great pressure of a body of water on one side when a compartment is flooded through stranding or collision. The plating of a bulkhead is generally welded in horizontal strakes, increasing in plate thickness with depth below the top of the bulkhead. Vertical stiffeners are fitted to bulkheads with adequate connections at the top and bottom. The thickness of the bulkhead plating also depends on the spacing and strength of the stiffeners fitted. The stronger the stiffeners and the closer they are spaced the thinner may be the plating.

The Collision Bulkhead and the stiffeners are stronger than for other bulkheads, to withstand the pressures that would be applied to it if the ship was proceeding with the forward section laid open to the sea by collision.

Bulkheads make the section where they occur perfectly rigid and overstrong so that the excessive local strength has to be distributed by means of brackets to the adjoining members of the hull, to stringers, girders, shell plating, deck plating, and these components pass it on throughout the structure and maintain a continuity of strength.

Bulkheads. The plating may be arranged transversely or vertically and suitably stiffened by rolled sections, swedges or corrugations. Fig. 25 shows the connection between the stiffener and the ship structure when (a) transverse beams are fitted and (b) when longitudinal construction is used.

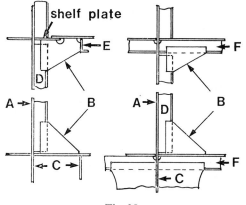

Fig. 25.

In the figure, A is the bulkhead to which the vertical stiffener D has been welded. The stiffener is connected to the deck and tank top by brackets B. The bulkhead is over a watertight floor C. Transverse beam E is shown in Fig. (a) and longitudinals F in Fig. (b). A shelf plate may be used to assist fabrication.

Fig. 26 shows a corrugated bulkhead (a) and swedged section in (b).

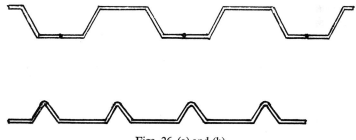

Figs. 26. (a) and (b)

The swedges and corrugation provide sufficient rigidity so that the normal stiffeners are not required.

Deep tanks (Fig. 27) may be fitted in a general cargo ship to provide a compartment which is suitable for dry cargo or liquids. The liquids may be liquid cargo or water ballast. Arrangements must be made to provide a system for pumping out the cargo or ballast. Heating coils may be required for certain liquid cargoes but these may have to be blanked off and removed when dry cargo is carried. When they are needed to increase the mean draught of the vessel the tank will be near to midships. If they are used to trim the ship then the deep tank will be placed nearer to the end of the vessel. Fore peak and after peak tanks for water ballast serve as trimming tanks in addition to increasing the displacement of the ship when filled.

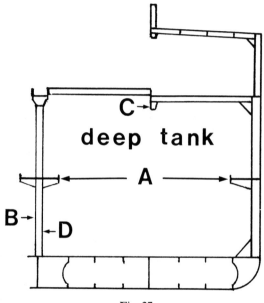

Fig. 27.

The construction of a deep tank must have greater structural strength than a conventional cargo hold to withstand the internal pressure due to a head of liquid. The thickness of the plating of the bulkheads is increased. Vertical stiffeners are increased in size and horizontal stringers fitted. To increase the strength and reduce the effects of free surface a centreline bulkhead is fitted. As an alternative to plate bulkheads with stiffeners corrugated bulkheads may be used both for the centreline and end bulkheads. The figure shows the stringer *A*, centreline bulkhead *B* and vertical stiffener *D*. A deep girder *C* is fitted along the side of the tank opening with a similar hatch end girder.

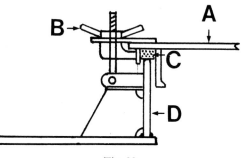

Fig. 28.

Deep tanks are fitted with liquid or watertight hatch covers (Fig. 28). The steel hatch cover A is made liquidtight by tightening a bolt or toggle B to make an effective joint between the hatch coaming D and the gasket C.

Shell Plating. It is modern practice for the shell to be flush welded but the following points should be noted.

As a general rule the thickness of the shell plating increases with depth to cope with the greater water pressure. However the sheer strake and the bottom plating make important contribution to the longitudinal strength of a ship. The thickness of the sheer strake is greater than the other side plating particularly within the 40 per cent of the ship's length about midships.

The upper edge of the sheer strake is dressed smooth to avoid notches. Where rounded sheer strakes are adopted guardrails and fairleads must be kept off the radiused plate. Any openings in the shell, such as cargo doors, must have rounded corners and be fully compensated for any loss of strength. Sea suctions and discharges should be kept clear of the turn of the bilge and any opening in this region must be elliptical in shape.

Additional thickness is required at the ends of the ship, near propeller brackets and hawse pipes, and in areas of local stress.

Bilge keels should be fitted to a continuous flat bar welded to the shell and gradually tapered at their ends.

Lloyd's grade steel with the letters A to E. The basic grade is A. In areas of high tension and low service temperatures steels of greater notch ductility are used. Higher tensile steels of greater strength may also be used in these highly stressed areas.

Strakes are traditionally given identity letters starting with A for the garboard strake next to the keel strake. Each plate within a strake is numbered starting from aft. Each shell plate is thus identified and shown on a Shell Expansion Plan.

A stealer plate is introduced in the shell and deck plating towards the ends of the vessel where the reduced breadth of the plating makes it convenient to merge two strakes into one. The single strake is the stealer and takes the letter of the strake nearest the keel.

Pillars are fitted to transfer the load on the deck to the bottom structure and at the same time tie the top and the bottom of the ship together. Pillars (Fig. 29) may be constructed of solid round bars, tubes *A*, octagonal pillars *B*, hollow square pillars *C* and built-up "I" web frames *D*. The small round pillars are used in areas of local stress such as beneath the windlass. The hollow section pillars are used in hatches. Such pillars are kept to a minimum since they interfere with cargo stowage. Usually these pillars are placed at the hatch corners but in some cases are placed at the mid-length or on the centreline. Web frames are used extensively in machinery spaces.

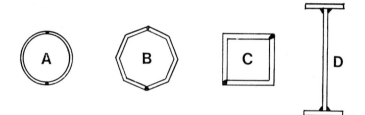

Fig. 29.

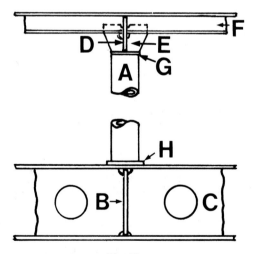

Fig. 30.

Fig. 30 illustrates the attachments of a tubular pillar. Where possible the pillar *A* should be over the intersection of the side girder *B* and a plate floor *C*. At the head the pillar should be connected to the hatch side girder *D*. This in turn is connected by brackets *E* to the transverse beam *F*. The load at the top of the pillar is transferred through a head plate *G* and at the bottom by a doubling plate *H*. By using heavy web frames and cantilever brackets it is possible to produce a hatch construction which does not use pillars.

Bulwarks. Protection of open deck is provided at the ship's side by guard rails and bulwarks. The plates of the bulwarks give protection for crew working on the deck but any water shipped in heavy seas becomes entrapped. To clear the decks of this water, openings or freeing ports are fitted in the bulwarks. Fig. 31 shows a bulwark *A* with gunwale *B*, stay *C*, deck stringer plate *D*, sheer strake *E* and the freeing port *F*.

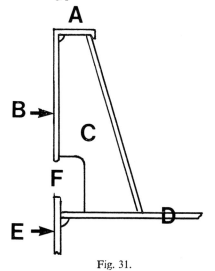

Fig. 31.

The lower edge of the freeing port should be as near as possible with the gap not more than 230 mm above the deck. In some ships the freeing ports were fitted with hinged doors that open to allow the seas to clear the deck but remain closed to incoming seas.

The area of the freeing ports is based on a formula contained in the Load Line Rules. Two-thirds of the freeing port area must be in the half of the well nearest the low point of the sheer. In tankers no more than half the length of exposed decks can be fitted with bulwarks.

Cargo Hatches are needed for the vertical handling of cargo through the decks. The size of the hatchway has increased to facilitate the rapidity in loading and discharging. These large openings in the deck necessitate cutting many of the transverse beams and girders, thus reducing considerably the transverse strength. In ships with very wide hatchways the area of continuous plating outside the line of hatches is greatly reduced, which considerably reduces the longitudinal strength.

The Hatch Openings not only weaken the vessel structurally but also affect her seaworthiness. The lost strength must be restored by means of additional girders and hatch coamings, hatch covers and tarpaulins to maintain the watertight integrity of the hull when heavy seas break on board.

The coamings of upper deck hatches should have a minimum height above the deck of 600 mm but if the hatch cover is steel and a surveyor is satisfied that the safety of the ship is not impaired, the height of the coaming may be reduced or eliminated.

Fig. 32(a) shows a traditional coaming for wood covers supported by a portable hatch beam. Under the Load Line Rules this method is penalised by an increased freeboard. Fig. 32(b) shows the equivalent modern structure.

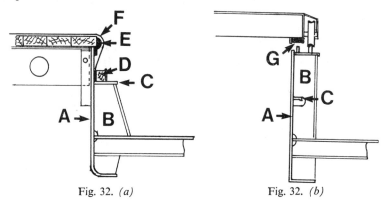

Fig. 32. (a)   Fig. 32. (b)

The coaming plate A is supported by a vertical stay or stiffener B and a horizontal stiffener C, which in the case of the wood covers carries the battens and wedge cleats D. A half-round moulding E is fitted at the landing over which the tarpaulins F is stretched. In the case of steel covers a gasket G is provided to ensure watertightness when the cover is lowered and secured.

The dimensions of the wood covers are specified in the Load Line Rules. Two good tarpaulins must be provided to cover the hatchway secured by battens and wedges in cleats. Locking bars must be fitted.

Steel covers must meet the standard of structural strength required by the Load Line Rules and be provided with watertight gaskets and clamping devices. Securing cleats must be placed about 2 m apart around the sides and cross joint wedges 1·5 m apart between the panels unless some other efficient method is used.

Fig. 33.—Macgregor Side Rolling Hatch Covers.

The nine hatches of the bulk carrier shown in the above figure are operated by hydraulic chain drive powered by two pumps which normally work simultaneously and each one can act as a stand-by to the other in case of an emergency. When the covers are in the closed position the wheels are lowered into slots in the coaming.

Hatchways to cargo tanks on oil tankers are the same height as other coamings but of small size and closed by watertight gasketed covers of steel (Fig. 34). Such covers provide greater watertightness and this is recognised by reduced freeboard for oil tankers.

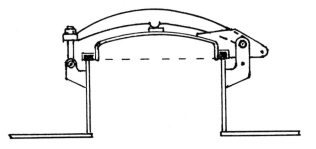

Fig. 34.

The Stem Bar in modern ships consists of a solid round bar which is fitted from the keel to the waterline region. The stem bar is welded inside the keel plating at the lower end. The shell plating is welded to the stem bar (Fig. 35). The stem bar A is connected to the shell B and supported by breasthook C and the frame D.

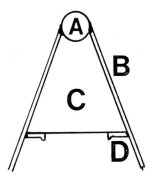

Fig. 35.

Above the waterline modern vessels are fitted with a "soft nosed" bow designed to collapse on impact and reduce the damage caused to both vessels. Fig. 36 shows this type with the bow shape formed by a radiused plate E supported on the centre line by a stiffener F and a breasthook J. The side plating is connected on either side by flush welds H and then to the ship's frames D.

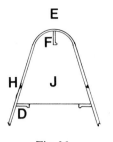

Fig. 36.

Additional strengthening is required in the forward section to resist the panting stresses.

Panting Beams are fitted across the interior of the vessel on the fore side of the collision bulkhead as well as abaft the after peak bulkhead. Their strength is distributed over the frames and shell plating by means of the panting stringers to which they are connected.

Fig. 37 shows a typical arrangement with the panting beams *A* passing across the vessel at alternate frame spaces. The stringer *B* incorporates the breasthook to form the bow shape *E* and is notched to allow the frames *D* and bow stiffener *F* to pass through. The beams are supported on the centre line by pillars or a wash bulkhead *G* and connected to the frames *D* by a bracket. The collision bulkhead *C* forms an important boundary to the main panting area.

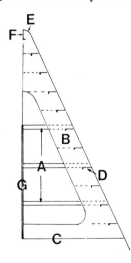

Fig. 37.

This structure is repeated at 2 m vertical intervals in the fore end of the vessel and at 2·5 m intervals abaft the after peak bulkhead. A perforated flat may be fitted as an alternative to the panting beams. The area of the perforations must be sufficient to reduce the water pressure on the flat. Aft of the collision bulkhead the panting stringer is extended for 15 per cent of the vessel's length from forward. However they may be omitted if they cause broken stowage of cargo and the strength in this area is compensated by increasing the thickness of the shell plating.

The Stern Frame may be forged, cast, or fabricated from steel plate and sections. The vibrations from the propeller set up stresses in the after structure. To withstand these the structure must be strengthened by a substantial stern frame, connected to the hull and stiffened by deep floors. The sterntube is supported at the after end by the stern frame and a rudder post forms the upper part of this section.

Fig. 38 shows a typical stern frame and rudder from a large single screw tanker. The frame has been cast in three parts with joins at *A*. The upper part *B* has extensions cast on to give rigid attachment to the deep floors of the vessel. These are the vibration post *C* and the rudder post *D* respectively. The centre part contains the propeller shaft boss *E* and is provided with cast webs on the forward side to locate the crutches within the hull. The lower part forms the sole of the frame with the rocker *F* about which the vessel trims when dry docking.

The stern post, or in this case the rudder axle post *G*, forms a rigid connection between the top and bottom of the frame. It is of round forged section and secured by a bolted connection *H* at the top and a taper with a nut *J* through the sole. The rudder stock *K* swings the rudder blade on bearings *L* consisting of lignum vitae or tufnol strips in brass liners with the load being carried on metal washers *M*.

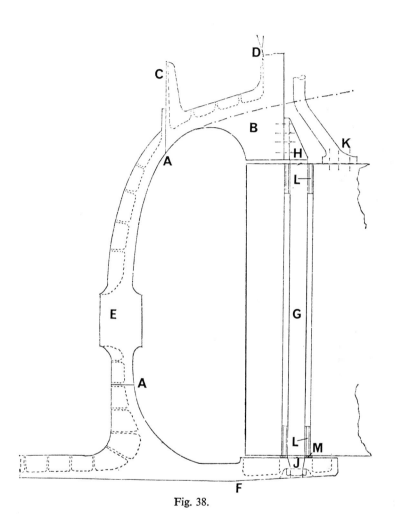

Fig. 38.

Rudder blades are hollow and built up on streamlined sections with vertical stiffeners. The natural buoyancy of the blade largely compensates for its weight leaving little to be borne by the carrier and the sole. A hollow tube allows the axle to pass through and contains the upper and lower bearings. With the blade swung to one side the axle can be removed from the frame and the two lifted away complete.

Fig. 39 shows the form of an "open water" stern frame found on many high speed vessels. Notice the absence of a stern post so the rocker is now at the after end of the hull *F* and the rudder blade is steadied by bearings *L* in the skeg or horn of the frame *N*.

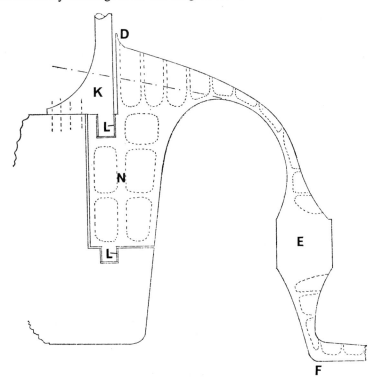

Fig. 39.

Rudder carrier and rudder gland (Figs. 40 and 41). The rudder is supported by the carrier *A* through a collar *B* keyed through a hard steel key *C* to the rudder stock *D*. A grease nipple is used to supply a lubrication space *F* between the faces of the collar and the carrier. The weight of this structure is taken by the steering flat deck *E*.

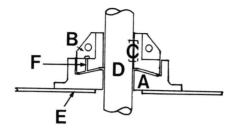

Fig. 40.

Any water in the rudder trunk must be prevented from entering the hull by a rudder gland. This consists of a split gland collar G, which can be hardened up by stud bolts tapped into the cast steady H on to stuffing or packing I. There is a lower bearing J between the cast and the rudder stock. In the figure the rudder carrier and rudder gland are shown separately. However, where the rudder trunk is short they may be combined in one unit.

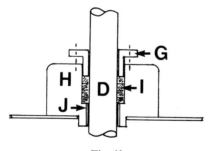

Fig. 41.

The Stern Tube. The propeller post is expanded to form a boss for the stern tube. The tail shaft A passes through the stern tube B, which carries the bearings C for the shaft to revolve upon. The stern tube is of cast iron or gunmetal with a flange D on its forward end bolted to the after peak bulkhead. A stern gland E is fitted to prevent water entering the ship. The outer end of the stern tube passes through the stern post and is secured thereto by a screw nut F on the end of the tube. The bearings work in strips of lignum vitae recessed into the bush and kept in position by means of a check plate G. The lubricant is sea water and a drain pipe is led through the bulkhead with a cock on it to enable the engineer to draw water from the stern tube, so that its temperature may be tested to ascertain if the bearings are working cool. H, a strong massive nut screwed on to the end of the shaft prevents the propeller from working off.

outer end of the stern tube passes through the stern post and is secured thereto by a screw nut *F* on the end of the tube. The bearings work in strips of lignum vitae recessed into the bush and kept in position by means of a check plate *G*. The lubricant is sea water and a drain pipe is led through the bulkhead with a cock on it to enable the engineer to draw water from the stern tube, so that its temperature may be tested to ascertain if the bearings are working cool. *H*, a strong massive nut screwed on to the end of the shaft prevents the propeller from working off.

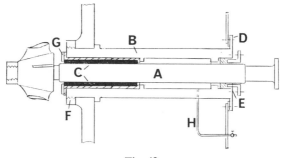

Fig. 42.

To unship a propeller in drydock the nut must be unscrewed and the propeller slung by tackles hooked on to eyebolts for the purpose on each side of the ship's stern. The gland is unscrewed and the tail shaft uncoupled from its adjoining length of shafting, and which has also to be removed to allow of the tail shaft being drawn straight forward, leaving the propeller suspended by the tackles. Repairs and rebushing of the tail shaft can then be executed.

The other lengths of shafting pass through bearings supported on widely spaced stools, the forward length being coupled to the thrust shaft at the thrust block, which takes up the fore-and-aft pressure of propeller and passes the thrust on to the hull.

The shaftings and stern tubes for the propellers of a twin screw ship are arranged in the same way as for a single screw ship.

The tail end bearing is supported either by a cast spectacle frame, Fig. 43, or by struts in the form of an "A" bracket, Fig. 44.

The cast spectacle frame *A* is a heavy structure projecting out from the shell *C* and supporting the tail end bearing *B* on either side. It is heavily supported on the centre line and strongly attached to the surrounding frame and floors. In most cases the whole of the tail end shafting is enclosed by plating.

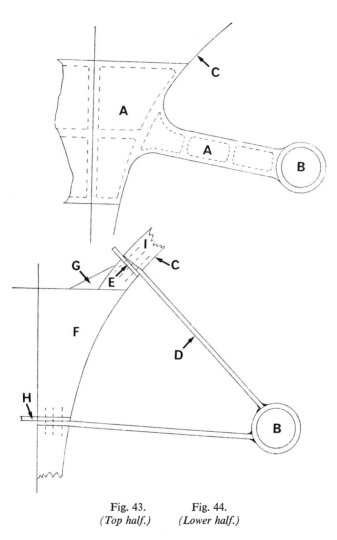

Fig. 43.   Fig. 44.
(Top half.)   *(Lower half.)*

On the other hand the shafting is not enclosed with the "A" bracket. Here the tail end bearing *B* is supported by two struts *D*. The upper inboard end of the struts are attached to carling stringers *E*. The load is transferred to the solid floor *F* through brackets *G* and the frame *I*. The lower strut is attached to an intercostal web *H* which transfers the load to the floor. The struts must be watertight where they pass through the shell *C*.

Oil tanker.

The tank section is divided by twin longitudinal bulkheads into port, starboard and centre tanks. In most cases there is no double bottom. Longitudinals strengthen the main deck and the outer bottom. In some cases the side shell is also stiffened by longitudinals but in the figure the side shell is strengthened by transverse frames. At the half length of the tank a heavy transverse web is fitted. Along the centre girder docking brackets are fitted at regular intervals.

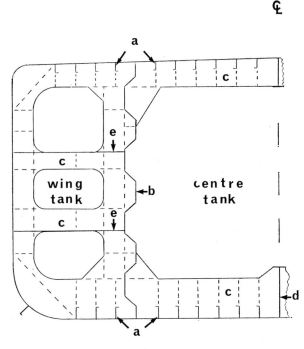

Fig. 53.

a longitudinals.
b longitudinal bulkhead, horizontally corrugated (note these bulkheads need not be corrugated).
c transverse webs, dotted lines indicate stiffeners.
d centre girder.
e stringers.

Dry Cargo Vessel.

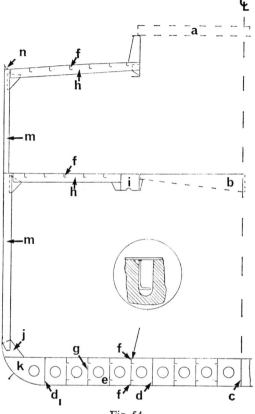

Fig. 54.

a   weather deck pontoon hatch cover.
b   flush tween deck pontoon hatch cover.
c   centre girder, continuous and watertight.
d   d₁ side girders; d is intercostal between floors,
                    d₁ is continuous and watertight at bilge, called the margin
                    plate.
e   solid floor.
f   longitudinals.
g   stiffeners between longitudinals in double bottom.
h   transversals.
i   box type hatch slide girder.
j   tank side bracket.
k   bilge bracket.
m   ship side frames, note the reduction in scantlings in tween deck
n   deck stringer angle.

Detail shows how a longitudinal passes through a transversal or plate floor.

Container vessel.

These ships are designed to carry containers. The hull structure is either a single hull with heavy web frames and cantilevers or a double hull as shown in the figure. Hatchways are as large as possible covering up to 80% of the breadth of the main deck.

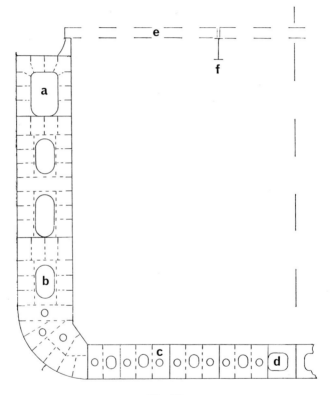

Fig. 55.

a underdeck passageway.
b side wing tank showing web plate, longitudinals and stiffeners (dotted lines).
c double bottom, showing plate floor and longitudinals.
d pipe duct.
e hatch cover, in this case three abreast.
f longitudinal hatch girder.

Bulk Carrier.

These ships are designed to carry dry cargo in bulk. The structural features include upper wing tanks, wide hatchways and strengthened inner bottoms.

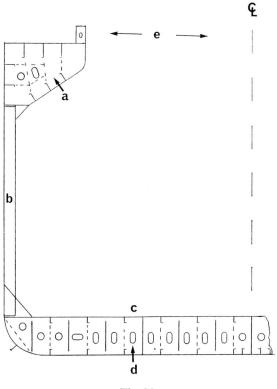

Fig. 56.

a upper wing tank showing longitudinals and web. Used for ballast but not connected to double bottom.

b transverse web frames.

c inner bottom strengthened to withstand the impact of loading bulk cargoes such as ores.

d double bottom showing plate floor with longitudinals as well as continuous and intercostal side girders.

e hatchway.

Liquefied Natural Gas (LNG) tankers.

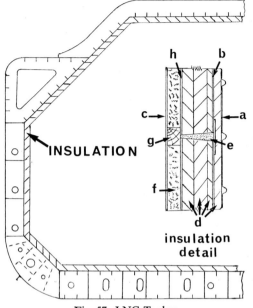

Fig. 57. LNG Tanker.

a	corrugated stainless steel tank.	*e*	PVC wedge.
b	plywood secondary barrier.	*f*	glassfibre.
c	steel inner hull.	*g*	wood ground.
d	balsa wood insulation.	*h*	plywood facing.

Natural gas can be liquefied at atmospheric pressure if cooled to a temperature of −164°C. The volume of the liquid is 0·158% of the original volume of gas which is a considerable reduction in the size of the storage tanks.

If LNG was loaded into an ordinary tanker two things would occur which would have serious effects. Firstly the very low temperature of the cargo would cause the mild steel structure to crystalise and fracture. Secondly the heat entering the cargo spaces through the hull would raise the temperature of the liquid above its boiling point causing excessive evaporation and "boil-off" losses. The construction and the materials used of an LNG tanker must take both of these points into account. A steel doubled hull structure is provided to stiffen the hull and provide adequate water-ballast space. Between the inner hull and the tank is placed insulation, usually balsa wood.

The inner surface of the tank must be constructed of a metal which will stand up to these low temperatures. Materials used include stainless steel, aluminium and Invar. In case the tank fractures a secondary barrier of plywood is fitted to contain any spillage of LNG.

Roll on roll off ship. (RoRo)

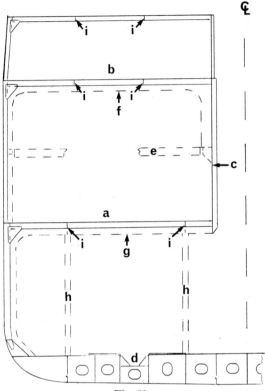

Fig. 58.

a   main or freeboard deck which is the floor of the vehicle deck.
b   accommodation deck.
c   casings which are constructed and stiffened as a superstructure and act as a
    trunk for services and engine room exhausts.
d   engine bed, twin screw vessel.
e   gallery deck used for cars which can be stowed out of the way.
f   strong beam and web frames to support gallery deck.
g   E.R. strong beam and web frame spaced every 14 feet.
h   E.R. pillars spaced every 14 feet.
i   tripping girders.

These ships fall into two main types. The first is mainly concerned
with the transport of passenger vehicles and must provide separate
spaces for vehicles and passenger accommodation. The other type
carries trailers with cargo. Many vessels are a mix of both types. Both
types must be provided with suitable access for the vehicles to be driven
on board. This may be through bow, stern or side doors. Ramps or
elevators are often fitted to provide internal access between decks.

CHAPTER XIII

SHIP STABILITY

Displacement (W). The weight of the ship at all times equals the weight of the water she displaces. The volume of the ship below each waterline can be calculated from the Naval Architect's plans allowing tables of displacement to be drawn up against a scale of true mean draft. The values for both sea and fresh water are usually given as the weight of any fixed volume of water will vary as its relative density.

Relative Density (RD). The density of a substance is its mass per unit volume. It can be measured in tonnes/m³, lbs/ft³ or in any other required combination. Relative Density is the ratio of the density of a substance divided by the density of fresh water, and being a ratio it has no units.

The density of fresh water is 1 tonne/m³ and that of sea water 1·025 tonnes/m³. From this we can deduce that the RD of sea water is 1·025.

Example. A tank contains 25 tonnes/tons of fresh water. How many tonnes/tons of fuel oil of RD 0·85 would it contain?

$$25 \times 0.85 = 21.25 \text{ tonnes/tons}$$

Note that the ratio holds good regardless of the units.

The Hydrometer. The marine hydrometer consists of a glass cylinder with a bulb at the lower end containing small lead shot acting as ballast to keep the instrument upright when floating. The cylinder supports a narrow stem which carries a scale of relative density. The scale is graduated from 0 at the top to 25 or more at the lower end, these values being read as 1·000 and 1·025 respectively. As the hydrometer displaces a greater volume when submerged the scale is not constant. Taking samples of the water about the ship, keeping well clear of any discharges, an average value of the relative density can be obtained by placing the hydrometer in the sample and spinning it round slightly to break down the surface tension about the stem. Corrections for the water temperature may be applied but these are usually ignored in practice.

Fresh Water Allowance (FWA). When a ship moves from fresh water (RD 1·000) into sea water (RD 1·025) she reduces her draft by

280

an amount that can be calculated in advance. The main purpose of the allowance is to deduce the distance by which the appropriate load line may be submerged in dock water, so that on entering sea water, the ship will regain her correct freeboard. It is usual to provide only the value for the Summer Displacement and this is referred to as the ship's fresh water allowance. Expressed in inches or millimetres it is represented by the distance between the summer and fresh water load lines on the ship's side.

Example. Assuming the ship has a FWA of 120 mm and requires to load to her summer marks in a dock of RD 1·015

$$\text{Allowance} = \text{FWA} \times \frac{(\text{RD sea water}) - (\text{RD dock water})}{(\text{RD sea water}) - (\text{RD fresh water})}$$

$$= \text{FWA} \times \frac{1\cdot025 - 1\cdot015}{1\cdot025 - 1\cdot000}$$

$$= 120 \times \frac{10}{25}$$

$$= 48 \text{ mm}$$

The summer load line may be submerged 48 mm when loading.

Centre of Buoyancy (B). The centre of buoyancy of the ship is the geometrical centre of the underwater volume. The position of B must be fixed relative to known points on the ship; vertically above the keel (KB); transversely about the centre line (BB_1); and longitudinally from amidships or from the after perpendicular (LCB).

Centre of Flotation (C of F). The centre of flotation of the ship is the geometrical centre of the waterplane area. It is the point about which the ship trims and is frequently referred to as the tipping centre. The centre of flotation may be forward or aft of amidships depending on the shape of the waterplane at different drafts.

Metacentre (M). The metacentre is the point through which the lines of upthrust through the initial (B), and slightly inclined (B_1), centres of buoyancy cut. It is the point about which the centres of buoyancy rotate as the ship inclines. Figure 1. For small angles *M*

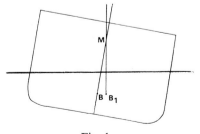

Fig. 1.

may be considered to be a fixed point but it does not however remain so and in general moves upward and away from the centre line as shown. Figures 2A, B and C.

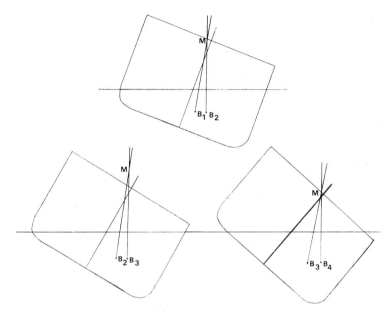

Figs. 2A, B and C.

This tendency continues until the deck edge is submerged when the metacentre moves downward again. During this period it is referred to as the Pro-metacentre.

Tonnes per Centimetre (TPC). This is the additional tonnage displaced when the draft is increased by 1 centimetre. Due to the changing underwater shape of the ship its value is not constant over the whole range of drafts. Figure 3.

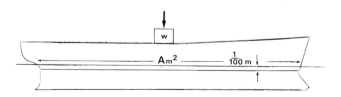

Fig. 3.

Let A = the area of the ship's waterplane in m²

When the ship increases her draft by 1 cm the volume of her displacement is increased by $A \times \frac{1}{100}$m³

Therefore $TPC = \frac{A}{100}$ in fresh water or $\frac{A}{100} \times 1.025$ in sea water.

Example. A ship has 4·2 cm to bring her to the loaded draft. If the *TPC* for this draft is 23·81, calculate the weight to be loaded.

Draft change in centimetres $\times$ *TPC* = Weight to be loaded

$$4.2 \times 23.81 = 100 \text{ tonnes}$$

Moment Change Trim (MCT). This is the moment required to change the ship's trim by 1 centimetre. Its value varies due to the changing underwater shape of the ship and must be calculated for each draft over the range of light to load displacement.

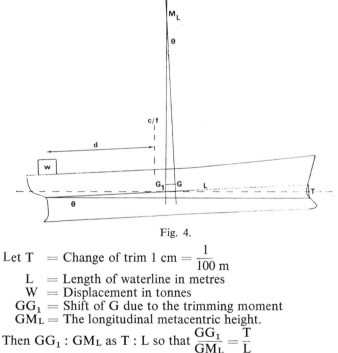

Fig. 4.

Let T   = Change of trim 1 cm = $\frac{1}{100}$ m

L   = Length of waterline in metres

W   = Displacement in tonnes

GG_1 = Shift of G due to the trimming moment

GM_L = The longitudinal metacentric height.

Then $GG_1 : GM_L$ as T : L so that $\dfrac{GG_1}{GM_L} = \dfrac{T}{L}$

$$GG_1 = \frac{T \times GM_L}{L}$$

$$= \frac{1 \times GM_L}{100L}$$

But GG_1 is the result of $\dfrac{\text{Trimming moment}}{\text{Displacement}}$

Therefore

Trimming moment 1 cm $= \dfrac{W \times GM_L}{100L}$

Hydrostatic Tables and Diagrams. Most of the information that we require for our ship can be calculated in advance. This information is governed by the overall dimensions and underwater shape of the ship, all of which are fixed from the moment she is built.

The information is presented in the form of tables or diagrams, one or both of which are included in the ship's stability booklet.

If one considers the numerous drafts and trims that the ship may assume, tables covering all these conditions would be very large and complex, so that certain restraints must be introduced.

It is therefore standard practice to assume that—

1. The ship is on even keel.
2. The ship is upright.
3. The ship is floating in sea water of RD 1·025 unless otherwise clearly stated.

HYDROSTATIC INFORMATION

Centres from amidships 76.241m forward of A. Perp. Salt Water RD 1.025

DRAFT	DISPLACEMENT	TPC	MCT	LCF	KM	KB	LCB
m	Tonnes			m	m	m	m
2.8	5563	22.24	150	0.48 F	13.21	1.47	0.52 F
3.0	6009	22.37	152	0.43 F	12.54	1.58	0.52 F
3.2	6458	22.52	154	0.38 F	12.00	1.69	0.51 F
3.4	6910	22.67	157	0.33 F	11.54	1.79	0.50 F
3.6	7364	22.81	159	0.27 F	11.54	1.90	0.49 F
3.8	7822	22.95	161·	0.21 F	10.80	2.01	0.47 F
4.0	8282	23.08	163	0.14 F	10.50	2.11	0.46 F
9.0	20623	26.49	235	3.54 A	8.82	4.77	0.66 A
9.2	21155	26.64	238	3.71 A	8.86	4.88	0.73 A
9.4	21689	26.78	242	3.87 A	8.89	4.99	0.81 A
9.6	22226	26.96	246	4.10 A	8.94	5.10	0.88 A
9.8	22767	27.11	250	4.27 A	8.98	5.21	0.96 A

Fig. 5.

In practice it is, of course, unnecessary to bring the ship to the three conditions above before entering the tables. In most cases the arithmetical mean draft will be all that is required but when the utmost accuracy is needed, for example the final displacement, draft and trim, then the true mean draft should be used.

True Mean Draft (TMD). The ship's hydrostatic information is given for the even keel condition so that to enter the tables the true mean, or even keel draft, must be found.

The ship does not trim about the mid-point of her length but about the centre of flotation or centre of the waterplane. This centre is not a fixed point but varies with changing waterplane shape. It may lie forward or aft of the mid-point and its exact location must first be obtained from the tables using the arithmetical mean draft.

In figure 6 the ship of length L is trimmed by the stern a total amount T. The total trim is the difference between the drafts forward and aft and the mean value, obtained by adding them together and dividing by two, is the arithmetical mean draft AMD.

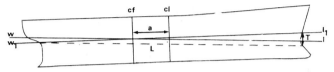

Fig. 6.

When $c =$ correction from arithmetical to true draft
$\quad a =$ distance between C of F and the mid-point
$\quad T =$ the total trim and $L =$ the ship's length
Then $c: T$ as $a: L$
Therefore Correction $= \dfrac{a \times T}{L}$

Example. A ship at drafts of 7·75 m F and 9·25 m A and length 145 m has, from the hydrostatic tables, the C of F 4·07 m aft of amidships.
$7·75 + 9·25 = 17·00 \div 2 = 8·50$ m AMD
$9·25 - 7·75 = 1·50$ m total trim by the stern
Correction $= \dfrac{a \times T}{L} = \dfrac{4·07 \times 1·50}{145} = 0·04$ m
Therefore $8·50 + 0·04 = 8·54$ m TMD.

Note that in this case the correction was added but this is not always the case.

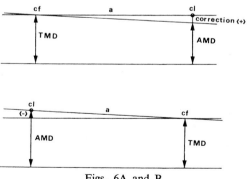

Figs. 6A and B.

Centre of Gravity (G). The centre of gravity of the ship is the point about which the total weight of the ship can be considered to act. The position of G must be fixed relative to known points on the ship; vertically above the keel (KG); transversely about the centre line (GG_1); and longitudinally from amidships or from the after perpendicular (LCG).

The Inclining Experiment. The purpose of the inclining experiment is to determine the displacement and the position of the ship's centre of gravity in an accurately known condition. This information, the KG, is the only value that cannot be calculated from the ship's plans and tabulated for our use at a later date.

The experiment is usually carried out when the ship is as nearly complete as possible, small corrections being made for any components missing or shipyard stores aboard at the time. It consists of moving weights across the deck under controlled conditions and measuring the resulting angle of list. The angles are deliberately kept small and are measured by long pendulums suspended down holds, tanks or engineroom skylights.

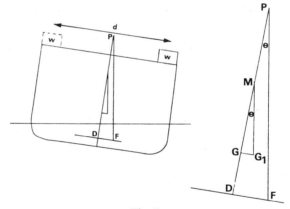

Fig. 7.

In the figure 7. $\dfrac{\text{Deflection}}{\text{Length of pendulum}} = \dfrac{DF}{PD} = \text{Tan } \theta$

and $\dfrac{GG_1}{GM} = \text{Tan } \theta$

therefore $\dfrac{DF}{PD} = \dfrac{GG_1}{GM}$ and $GM = \dfrac{GG_1 \times PD}{DF}$

Using the true mean draft at the time of the experiment to obtain the KM from the hydrostatic information then—

$$KM - GM = KG$$

Example. A ship of 4550 tonnes light displacement is inclined by moving a weight of 12 tonnes transversely 16 m. A plumb line 11 m long records a deflection of 13 cm. From the hydrostatic information at this displacement the *KM* is noted to be 9·3 m. Calculate the *KG*.

$$GG_1 = \frac{w \times d}{W} = \frac{12 \times 16}{4550} = 0 \cdot 0422 \text{ m}$$

$$GM = \frac{GG_1 \times \text{Plumb line}}{\text{Deflection}} = \frac{0 \cdot 0422 \times 11}{0 \cdot 13} = 3 \cdot 57 \text{ m}$$

$$KG = KM - GM = 9 \cdot 30 - 3 \cdot 57 = 5 \cdot 73 \text{ m}$$

The Capacity Plan. In order to establish the ship's *KG* for conditions of loading other than those at the time of the inclining experiment it will be necessary to know the Kg of each individual weight loaded or discharged.

Most ships are provided with a large scale plan, from which measurements can be taken for deck cargoes and large single loads, also tables of *KG*, *LCG* and the capacity of holds, stores, compartments and tanks.

The values for *KG* and *LCG* given assume the geometrical centre of the compartment or tank, that is that the tank is filled with a homogeneous solid or liquid. As this is not always the case some adjustment may have to be made but, as will be seen later, if no allowance is applied the error will be on the right side.

Stowage factor. The stowage factor of any commodity is the figure which expresses the number of cubic feet or metres which a ton or tonne will occupy in a hold or tank. It is not the actual volume of the commodity but a figure found, in practice, to include the expected broken stowage and dunnage as appropriate.

In the tables on the capacity plan will be found the volumes of each compartment for both grain and bale. The assumption is that grain will fill all the space available whilst bale or case goods will be restricted by frames, stiffeners, spar ceiling and beams.

Example. A refrigerated space has a bale capacity of 817 m³. Given that the stowage factor of cased butter is 1·59 calculate the approximate tonnage content.

Volume of compartment ÷ stowage factor = tonnage

$$817 \div 1 \cdot 59 = 513 \cdot 8 \text{ tonnes}$$

The principle of moments. The principle of moments can be used to determine the position of the centre of gravity of any system of weights. As the centre of gravity is the point through which the total weight may be considered to act, its position from any point may be found by dividing the resultant moments of all the individual weights about that point by the total weight.

Example. Four weights of 5 tonnes are suspended from *B, C, D* and *E* which are respectively 8, 6, 4 and 2 metres from *A*. The moments about *A* are—

$(5 \times 8) + (5 \times 6) + (5 \times 4) + (5 \times 2) = 100$ tonnes metres

$$\frac{\text{Total moments}}{\text{Total weight}} = \frac{100}{20} = 5 \text{ m}$$

Therefore the centre of gravity of the system lies 5 m from *A*, the point about which the moments were taken. Figure 8.

We should now select aboard our ship some point such that all the added weights will lie on the same side for the convenience of calculation. The most obvious choice is the keel.

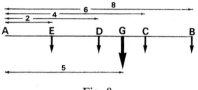

Fig. 8.

The vertical position of G. (*KG*) Whenever calculating the *KG* for a particular condition, such as arrival or departure, moments are taken about the keel of all the weights added to the light displacement for which the *KG* is known from the inclining experiment.

In most cases a large number of weights and their moments are involved so that it is most important to develop a layout which is simple but enables a systematic calculation of the sum of the moments. Such a layout is shown in the example.

Example. The ship's light displacement and *KG* were obtained from the hydrostatic information whilst the added weights and kg's came from loading figures, the capacity plan and tables.

Item	Weight	KG	Moment
Ship	4379	7·63	33412
No. 1 Tween Deck	144	10·42	1500
No. 2 Tween Deck	306	9·93	3039
No. 3 Tween Deck	141	9·67	1363
No. 4 Tween Deck	210	9·86	2071
No. 5 Tween Deck	107	10·30	1102
No. 1 Lower Hold	423	4·91	2077
No. 2 Lower Hold	940	4·58	4305
No. 3 Lower Hold	629	4·51	2837
No. 4 Lower Hold	834	4·98	4153
No. 5 Lower Hold	355	6·53	2318
No. 2 D.B. Tank	126	0·56	71

Item	Weight	KG	Moment
No. 5 D.B. Tank	150	0·77	116
No. 6 D.B. Tank	37	0·77	28
Stores	39	9·42	367
Heavy Oil	12	6·70	80
Dist. Water	10	6·55	66
Lub. Oil	16	6·55	105
Total	8858		59010

$$KG = \frac{\text{Total Moment}}{\text{Total Weight}} = \frac{59010}{8858} = 6\cdot66 \text{ m}$$

A full calculation based on the light displacement is not always necessary. If a previous calculation is known to be accurate then it can be adjusted by adding or subtracting the differences in weight and moment. Similarly if the above calculation was for departure then the totals could be adjusted for the fresh water, fuel and stores consumed on passage until arrival.

Example. Using the above departure condition an estimate for fresh water, fuel and stores used on voyage has been made. Calculate the ship's *KG* on arrival.

Item	Weight	KG	Moment
Ship	8858	6·66	59010
No. 2 D.B. Tank	−64	0·56	−36
No. 6 D.B. Tank	−18	0·77	−14
Stores	−3	9·42	−28
Total	8773		58932

$$KG = \frac{\text{Total Moment}}{\text{Total Weight}} = \frac{58932}{8773} = 6\cdot72 \text{ m}$$

Many ships are provided with printed loading sheets, or pro-forma, on which all the spaces available are listed with the *KG* and other information permanently recorded. For each voyage it is only necessary, therefore, to complete the column provided with the weights loaded or already aboard and then, with the aid of a calculator, enter and sum the moments.

The transverse position of G. (GG_1) When the ship is upright the centre of gravity lies on the centre line. The moments of the weights to port and starboard are equal and the ship is balanced transversely.

If the centre of gravity G_1 is not on the centre line then the ship will list as the moments about the centre line are no longer balanced and a listing moment results. Figure 9.

The weight of the ship acts through G_1 whilst the buoyancy acts through B causing a listing moment $W \times GG_1$.

As the ship lists B will move to B_1, the centre of the new underwater volume, directly below G_1 giving a new stable condition. Figure 10.

$$\text{The distance } GG_1 = \frac{\text{Listing Moment}}{\text{Weight}}$$

$$\text{Angle of list Tan } \theta = \frac{GG_1}{GM}$$

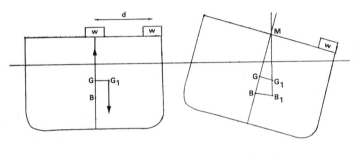

Fig. 9.   Fig. 10.

Example. A ship displaces 12,000 tonnes KG 6·54 m and is upright. A parcel of cargo weighing 140 tonnes is to be loaded at Kg 8·0 m and 6·0 m to starboard of the centre line. The final KM from the hydrostatic information is 7·37 m. Calculate the angle of list.

Item	Weight	KG	Moment	Dist.	Moment
Ship	12000	6·54	78480	0	0
Cargo	140	8·00	1120	6·0S	840S
Totals	12140		79600		840S

$$KG = \frac{\text{Total Moment}}{\text{Total Weight}} = \frac{79600}{12140} = 6\cdot55 \text{ m}$$

$$GG_1 = \frac{\text{Listing Moment}}{\text{Total Weight}} = \frac{840}{12140} = 0\cdot069 \text{ m}$$

$$GM = KM - KG = 7\cdot37 - 6\cdot55 = 0\cdot82 \text{ m}$$

$$\text{Tan } \theta = \frac{GG_1}{GM} = \frac{0\cdot069}{0\cdot820} = 0\cdot084 = 4\cdot8° \text{ to starboard}$$

As in the case of the KG, ships loading containers and other unsymmetrical cargoes may be provided with printed sheets to include moments to port and starboard.

Example. A ship displaces 10,920 tonnes *KG* 6·81 m and is upright. She is to load and discharge the following parcels of cargo. The final *KM* from the hydrostatic information is 7·33 m. Calculate the angle of list.

Item	*Weight*	*KG*	*Moment*	*Dist.*	*Mom. P.*	*Mom. S.*
Ship	10920	6·81	74365	0	0	0
Cargo	125	4·91	614	3·67P	459	0
Cargo	186	9·93	1847	0	0	0
Cargo	163	9·67	1576	3·10S	0	505
Cargo	−84	10·42	−875	4·80P	0	403*
Cargo	−42	4·51	−189	2·50S	105*	0
Totals	11268		77338		564	908
						564
						344S

*A weight discharged from the port side has the same listing effect as a weight loaded on the starboard side and vice versa.

$$KG = \frac{\text{Total Moment}}{\text{Total Weight}} = \frac{77338}{11268} = 6·68 \text{ m}$$

$$GG_1 = \frac{\text{Listing Moment}}{\text{Total Weight}} = \frac{344}{11268} = 0·03 \text{ m}$$

$$GM = KM - KG = 7·33 - 6·86 = 0·47 \text{ m}$$

$$\text{Tan } \theta = \frac{GG_1}{GM} = \frac{0·03}{0·47} = 0·064 = 3·7° \text{ to starboard.}$$

From our table of moments the greater, and therefore residual, moment was to starboard causing a final starboard list.

Correcting a list. For the ship to be upright the moments to port and starboard must be equal. In the previous example the ship has a list of 3·7° to starboard due to a listing moment of 344 tonne metres. If a final parcel of 120 tonnes of cargo is available where should it be placed to bring the ship upright?

Example. The ship has a listing moment of 344 tm to starboard and spaces are available 4·8 m to port and 3·2 m to starboard of the centre line. Given 120 tonnes of cargo how should this be distributed to leave the ship upright?

Let the weight to port = *w*
Port moments = Starboard moments
4·8 × *w* = 344 + 3·2 (120 − *w*)
4·8*w* = 344 + 384 − 3·2*w*
8·0*w* = 728
w = 91

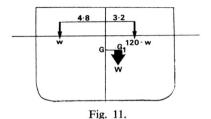

Fig. 11.

The cargo should be loaded 91 tonnes to port and $120-91=29$ tonnes to starboard.

When the ship is upright there is no GG_1 and we are not concerned with GM. Therefore there is no need for this purpose to calculate the final KG after the cargo is loaded.

Suspended weights. When any cargo is lifted by the ship's derrick the weight is effectively transferred to the derrick head at the instant that it is lifted off the deck or quay. The effect on the ship's centre of gravity G is to move it upward GG_1 and transversely G_1G_2. This results in the ship listing. Figure 12.

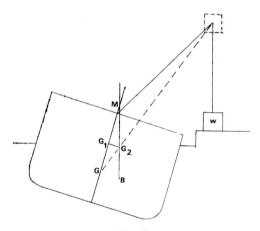

Fig. 12.

Example. A ship displaces 3900 tonnes, KG 4·25 m, KM 7·75 m and is upright. A weight of 100 tonnes is to be lifted from the quay 13·8 m from the centre line by a derrick, the height of the head, measured from the rigging plan, being 31·8 m above the keel. Calculate the angle of list as the weight is taken.

Vertical shift of G

Item	Weight	KG	Moment
Ship	3900	4·25	16575
Cargo	100	31·80	3180
Total	4000		19755

Transverse shift of G

Item	Weight	Dist.	Moment
Ship	3900	0	0
Cargo	100	13·8	1380
Total	4000		1380

$$KG = \frac{\text{Total Moment}}{\text{Total Weight}} = \frac{19755}{4000} = 4.94 \text{ m}$$

$$GG_1 = \frac{\text{Listing Moment}}{\text{Total Weight}} = \frac{1380}{4000} = 0.345 \text{ m}$$

$$GM = KM - KG = 7.75 - 4.94 = 2.81 \text{ m}$$

$$\text{Tan } \theta = \frac{GG_1}{GM} = \frac{0.345}{02.81} = 0.1228 = 7°$$

The Longitudinal position of G. (LCG) When the ship is floating in equilibrium the centre of gravity is in the same vertical plane as the centre of buoyancy. The longitudinal centre of buoyancy is tabulated in the hydrostatic information for the ship on even keel and this may be used to determine the position of the LCG.

Assume the ship to be on even keel and it is required to establish a trim by the stern. For this to happen a weight must be moved aft or a weight loaded aft or discharged from forward. In each case the ship's centre of gravity will move aft away from the centre of buoyancy causing a trimming moment $W \times GG_1$.

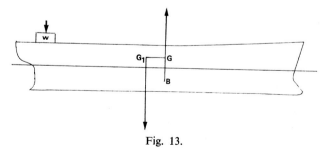

Fig. 13.

Example. A ship displaces 8858 tonnes and is trimmed 56 cm by the stern. From the hydrostatic information the LCB is 1·98 m forward of amidships and the MCT 125. Calculate the position of the LCG with respect to amidships.

$$\text{Trimming moment} = \text{Trim (cm)} \times MCT$$
$$8858 \times GG_1 = 56 \times 125$$
$$GG_1 = \frac{56 \times 125}{8858}$$
$$= 0·79 \text{ m}$$

The centre of gravity has moved aft 0·79 m from its initial position in the same vertical plane as the centre of buoyancy.

Position of $LCB - GG_1 =$ Position of LCG

1·98 − 0·79 = 1·19 m forward of amidships

The LCG having moved aft is now less distance forward of amidships.

The Longitudinal Metacentre. (M_L) As the ship trims, changes in the underwater shape cause the centre of buoyancy B to move to B_1 the new centre of the underwater volume. Since trim angles are relatively small the vertical lines through the various positions of B cut at a point M_L, the longitudinal metacentre.

In a similar manner to the transverse metacentre M it can be thought of as the point about which the ship rotates longitudinally.

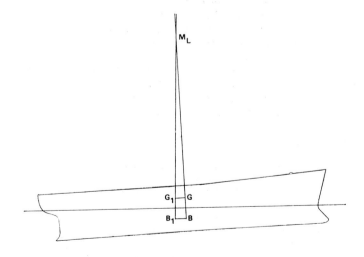

Fig. 14.

Trim. When a weight is loaded or discharged or moved longitud-inally, the ship's centre of gravity will respond about the longitudinal plane and a trimming moment produced. The effect of this moment on the ship's trim must be considered in one of two ways.

Trim by small weights. A small weight is one which, upon inspection of the hydrostatic information, does not substantially change the position of the centre of flotation about which the ship trims or the value of the MCT.

As the ship trims about the C of F, then the moments produced by loading or discharging weights must be taken about this point. A weight loaded aft of the C of F will produce a trim by the stern, and one forward of the C of F a trim by the head. In the case of a weight discharged the reverse trim will occur. A weight moved from forward to aft will cause a trim by the stern, regardless of its initial and final positions, the moment being the sum of the weight times the distance moved.

Example. A weight aboard the ship of 40 tonnes is moved aft a distance of 38·09 m. At the same time 100 tonnes is loaded 32·79 m forward of the C of F and 40 tonnes 1·54 m forward and 60 tonnes 31·55 m aft of the C of F discharged. Calculate the change of trim if the MCT is 137·6 for this condition.

Item	Weight	Distance	Moment	
			By head	By stern
Cargo	40	38·09A		1523·6
Cargo	100	32·79F	3279·0	
Cargo	−40	1·54F		61·6*
Cargo	−60	31·55A	1893·0*	
			5172·0	1585·2
			1585·2	
			3586·8	

Resultant moment=   3586·8 by the head

Change of trim $=\dfrac{\text{Trimming moment}}{\text{MCT}}=\dfrac{3586\cdot8}{137\cdot6}=26\cdot1$ cm by head.

*Note that the trimming moments are tabulated by the effect that they cause.

Trim by large weights. When loading or discharging a part or complete cargo careful note must be kept of the longitudinal position of each item in a similar manner to that adopted for the vertical shift of G. The initial position of the LCG can be found in the way already set out and this forms the starting point for the calculation.

Example.

Item	Weight	LCG	Moment	
			By head	By stern
Ship	4379	2·62A		11473
No. 1 T.D.	144	48·83F	7032	
No. 2 T.D.	306	31·25F	9563	
No. 3 T.D.	141	9·68F	1365	
No. 4 T.D.	210	33·09A		6949
No. 5 T.D.	107	47·28A		5059
No. 1 L.H.	423	47·62F	20143	
No. 2 L.H.	940	30·49F	28661	
No. 3 L.H.	629	14·25F	8963	
No. 4 L.H.	834	30·55A		25479
No. 5 L.H.	355	47·99A		17036
No. 2 D.B.	126	29·70F	3742	
No. 5 D.B.	150	8·38A		1257
No. 6 D.B.	37	18·17A		672
Stores	39	12·04A		470
Heavy Oil	12	21·33A		256
Water	10	10·26A		103
Lub. Oil	16	6·93A		111
Totals	8858		79469	68865
			68865	

Resultant moment   10604 by the head

$$\text{Final } LCG = \frac{\text{Total moment}}{\text{Total weight}} = \frac{10604}{8858} = 1 \cdot 197 \text{ m forward of amidships.}$$

Note that as there has been a very large change in displacement, the position of the centre of flotation could not be considered fixed and the moments have therefore been taken about the mid point. In some ships these distances are given from the after perpendicular (*AP*) in which case only one column of moments would be required. The final position of the *LCG* would then be with respect to the after perpendicular.

Example. From the hydrostatic information for a displacement of 8858 tonnes the *LCB* was 1·989 m forward of amidships and the *MCT* 124·9.

$$GG_1 = LCB \text{ (tabulated)} - LCG \text{ (actual)}$$
$$= 1 \cdot 989 - 1 \cdot 197$$
$$= 0 \cdot 792 \text{ m by the stern.}$$

The actual *LCG* is aft of the *LCB*, it is therefore less far forward of amidships, so that the final trim will be by the stern.

$$\text{Trim}=\frac{W\times GG_1}{MCT}$$

$$=\frac{8858\times0\cdot792}{124\cdot9}=56\cdot2 \text{ cm by the stern.}$$

Trim correction. If a ship trimmed about her mid point then the change of trim would be equally divided about the two ends. When, as in practice, the ship trims about the centre of flotation then this equality is no longer true.

When $t_f=$trim forward $l_f=$length forward of C of F
      $t_a=$trim aft $l_a=$length aft of C of F
      $T=$Total trim $L=$Total length

Then $t_f: l_f$ as $t_a: l_a$ and $T: L$

Therefore $t_f=l_f\times\dfrac{T}{L}$ and $t_a=l_a\times\dfrac{T}{L}$

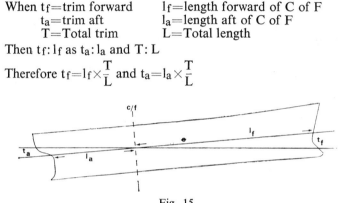

Fig. 15.

Example. A ship of length 145 m has a *TMD* of 8·54 m and is trimmed 1·50 m by the stern. From the hydrostatic information the *LCF* is 4·07 m aft of amidships. Calculate the drafts forward and aft.

$t_f=l_f\times\dfrac{T}{L}$ $\qquad\qquad$ $t_a=l_a\times\dfrac{T}{L}$

$=(72\cdot5+4\cdot07)\times\dfrac{1\cdot50}{145}$ $\qquad$ $=(72\cdot5-4\cdot07)\times\dfrac{1\cdot50}{145}$

$=0\cdot79$ m $\qquad\qquad\qquad$ $=0\cdot71$ m

Final drafts$=8\cdot54-0\cdot79=7\cdot75$ mF
                $=8\cdot54+0\cdot71=9\cdot25$ mA

Trimming tables. Most ships are provided with sets of trimming tables which should more correctly be referred to as change of draft tables. These tables predict the change of draft at each end of the ship as the result of loading or discharging small weights from various fixed positions aboard.

As the values of *MCT*, *TPC* and the C of F cannot be considered fixed if the change of displacement is large then it follows that these tables can only be produced for some nominated draft. In practice a selection of drafts are given between the light and load displacements or graphs are used on the axis of draft and change from which any intermediate value can be lifted.

The prime function of these tables is to allow fine changes in trim and draft to be made by ballasting or small parcels of cargo when this is important as, for example, entering drydock.

The Righting Lever. (*GZ*) When the ship is in a stable condition the weight acting vertically downward is exactly balanced by the upthrust due to buoyancy. Figure 16. If the ship is heeled by an

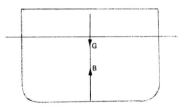

Fig. 16.

external force, such as the wind or sea, the centre of buoyancy moves to the centre of the new underwater form whilst *G* remains in a fixed

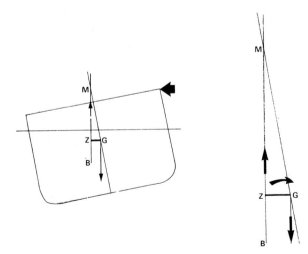

Fig. 17.

position. Figure 17. The lines of action of the forces of weight and buoyancy are now separated by a perpendicular distance GZ which is known as the righting lever and, acting as a couple between the forces, tends to rotate the ship back to her original position.

The Metacentric Height. (GM) As a measure of the ship's stability it has become common practice to quote the metacentric height GM. If, from previous experience, a suitable value for GM, or initial stability as it is sometimes called, is known then by reference to the hydrostatic information for the loaded displacement the KM can be obtained. From this is deducted the required GM to establish what

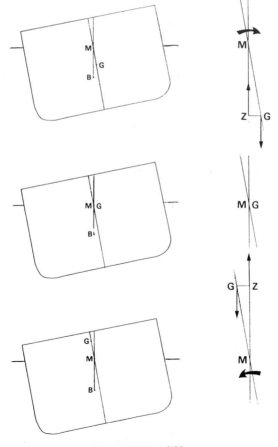

Figs. 18, 19 and 20.

is now the maximum *KG* to be aimed for when planning the cargo distribution. The figures show the three conditions of initial stability. In figure 18, *G* is below *M* and the righting lever formed will return the ship to her initial position giving positive stability.

In figure 19, *G* and *M* are coincident so that no righting lever is formed and the ship is said to have neutral stability. This is a transient condition due to the fact that the metacentre is not stationary as the ship heels. In figure 20, *G* is above *M* and a capsizing lever will be formed tending to increase the heel further and the ship is said to have negative stability.

The Righting Moment. The righting moment, or moment of statical stability, is a measure of the ship's resistance to further inclination at any given angle of heel. It is the product of the righting lever and the ship's displacement $GZ \times W$.

For any given displacement and angle of heel, the righting moment will vary as the length of the righting lever which is governed by the position of *G*. In figure 21 it will be seen that if *G* is lowered to G_1 the length of the lever is increased and hence the moment. In this condition the ship will respond readily to a heeling force and she i s said to be stiff.

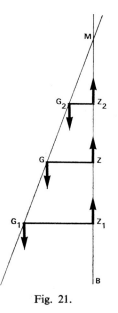

Fig. 21.

If *G* is raised to G_2 the lever is much reduced as is the moment and the ship will now respond weakly to any disturbing forces. In this

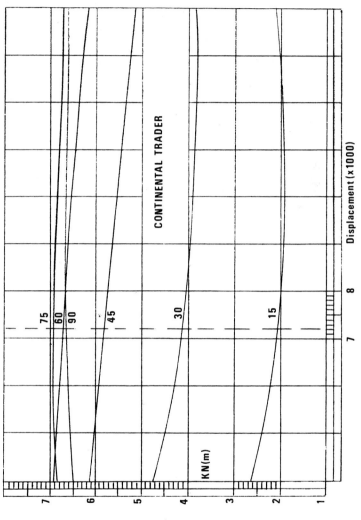

Fig. 22.

condition she is said to be tender and although more comfortable to those aboard it is preferable to aim toward a stiff ship as the effect of using bunkers and fresh water will reduce this tendency during the voyage.

The cross curves of stability. The values of the righting levers GZ at angles of heel from 0 to 90°, or in some cases 0 to 120°, are calculated in advance for a full range of displacements covering the light to loaded drafts.

Whilst it used to be the practice to plot the values of GZ direct for an assumed KG this method has now been superseded by the introduction of the KN curves.

Using the KN curves. These curves assume the ship's centre of gravity to be at the keel, an impossible state of affairs but one giving, theoretically, the largest righting levers. The curves are drawn on a framework of two scales, the horizontal one being tonnes, from below the light to above the load displacement, and the vertical KN in metres. The displacement is usually given in 100 tonne steps, this being sufficient for our purpose, and the KN in 0·1 or 0·05 steps from which two decimal places can be reasonably estimated. Figure 22.

As the curves have a KG of zero, then the ship's actual KG must always exceed this by an amount equal to the KG. From figure 23 it will be seen that the GZ will be less than the KN such that
$$GZ = KN - KX$$
thus the corrected righting lever is at all times
$$GZ = KN - KG \text{ Sine } \theta$$
Values for angles of heel at 10° or 15° intervals are given and these are sufficient for the construction of a curve from which the GZ at any other angle may be obtained.

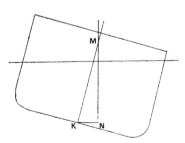

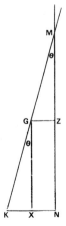

Fig. 23.

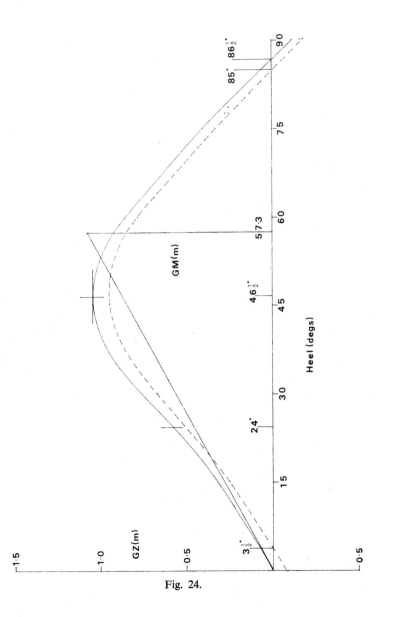

Fig. 24.

Example. On completion of loading the ship has a displacement of 7200 tonnes and KG 6·75 m. Construct the curve of righting levers for this condition.

From the curve at 7200 tonnes the values of KN are taken.

Angle of Heel	KN	$-$	KG Sine θ	$=$	GZ
0	0		6·75 Sine 0	=	0
15	2·07		6·75 Sine 15	=	0·32
30	4·14		6·75 Sine 30	=	0·76
45	5·81		6·75 Sine 45	=	1·04
60	6·71		6·75 Sine 60	=	0·86
75	6·92		6·75 Sine 75	=	0·40
90	6·64		6·75 Sine 90	=	−0·11

The curve may now be constructed on the axis of heel and GZ, Figure 24.

Reading the GZ curve. Inspection of the curve of righting levers shows:

(*a*) The range of positive stability extends from 0 to $86\frac{1}{2}°$.

(*b*) The maximum righting lever occurs at $46\frac{1}{2}°$.

(*c*) The point of deck edge immersion which appears in the curve as a change of direction from the initial rise to a folding over toward the peak. Approximately 24°.

(*d*) The slope of the origin of the curve which is found in the following manner. At an angle whose circular measure is unity, 57·3°, erect a perpendicular of length equal to the initial stability GM. Join the end of this line to the origin of the curve which will tend to lie along it as a tangent.

(*e*) The moment of statical stability at any required angle.

Moment of statical stability $= W \times GZ$

At $35° = 7200 \times 0·9$

$= 6480$ tonne metres

The effect of shifting cargo. The effect of ballasting or cargo shifting vertically will be to change the ship's KG such that our curve is no longer true. If the change is relatively small then a correction can be applied to the table of GZs. Figure 25.

If G has been lowered by an amount GG_1 then the correction will be positive as the lever has been increased from GZ to G_1Z_1. If G has been raised by an amount GG_2 then the correction will be negative as the lever has been reduced from GZ to G_2Z_2. In both cases the amount of the correction will be

Correction to $GZ =$ Shift of $G \times$ Sine θ

The effect of ballast or cargo moving transversely such that the ship is listed will cause G to move to G_1 reducing the lever GZ to G_1Z_1 an amount equal to GX. Figure 26.

In all cases this correction is negative, we only consider the low side, and its amount will be

Correction to $GZ=$ Shift of $G \times$ Cosine θ

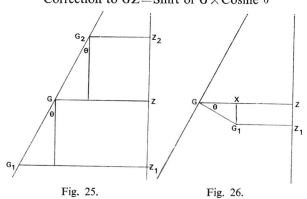

Fig. 25.   Fig. 26.

From the character of the ratio of the angle we can see that the vertical shift of G mainly effects the larger angles of our stability curve whilst a transverse shift of G effects the smaller or initial angles. A ship should not be allowed to sail in the listed condition unless adequate compensation has been made to the curve of righting levers.

Example. A heavy lift of 100 tonnes is loaded on deck Kg 10·3 m and 5·2 m from the centre line. Correct the curve of righting levers previously obtained.

Item	Weight	KG	Moment	Dist.	Moment
Ship	7200	6·75	48600	0	0
Cargo	100	10·30	1030	5·20	520
Totals	7300		49630		520

$$\text{New } KG = \frac{\text{Total Moment}}{\text{Total Weight}} = \frac{49630}{7300} = 6·80 \text{ m}$$

$$GG_1 = \frac{\text{Listing Moment}}{\text{Total Weight}} = \frac{520}{7300} = 0·07 \text{ m}$$

Vertical shift of $G=6·80-6·75=0·05$ m rise

Angle of Heel	$GZ-GG_V$	Sine $\theta-GG_H$	Cosine $\theta=$New GZ	
0	0	0	0·07	$=-0·07$
15	0·32	0·01	0·07	$= 0·24$
30	0·76	0·025	0·06	$= 0·67$
45	1·04	0·035	0·05	$= 0·95$
60	0·86	0·04	0·035	$= 0·78$
75	0·40	0·05	0·02	$= 0·33$
90	$-0·11$	0·05	0	$=-0·16$

From the new curve of righting levers. (Dashed on figure 24)

(a) The range of positive stability extends from $3\frac{1}{2}°$ to 85°.

(b) The angle of repose, that is the angle of list from which the curve now starts, is $3\frac{1}{2}°$.

Dynamical stability. This is the total work done in heeling the ship through some nominated angle at constant displacement.

If we stop the ship during a roll we can, from the righting lever curves, calculate the resistance at this point. This is statical stability and exists only at that angle for once the ship moves on again into her roll other resistances are brought into play.

The sum of all the moments of statical stability can be represented by the area under the curve of righting levers as it can be considered to be made up of an infinite number of levers all placed tightly together.

This is known as the area under the curve method.

Example. Using the original curve of righting levers, figure 24, lift off values at 5° intervals.

Angle of Heel	GZ	SM	Product of area
0	0	1	0
5	0·10	4	0·40
10	0·21	2	0·42
15	0·32	4	1·28
20	0·45	2	0·90
25	0·60	4	2·40
30	0·76	1	0·76
			6·16

Area under the curve $=\frac{1}{3}\times 5\times 6\cdot16=10\cdot26$ metre degrees

$$or=\frac{10\cdot26}{57\cdot3}=0\cdot179 \text{ metre radians}$$

The requirements of The Merchant Shipping (Load Line) Rules 1968 are expressed in the second form. The required value from 0 to 30°, as calculated above, is 0·055 metre radians so that our ship has adequate stability.

The total work done in heeling the ship to this angle is

Area under the curve $\times W=$ Work done

$0\cdot179\times 7200=1288\cdot8$ metre radian tonnes

For guidance on the use of Simpson's Rule for calculating the area under the curve refer to the later part of this chapter.

To illustrate the sequence of events recorded by the curve of righting levers refer to figure 27. The ship is shown in the six positions

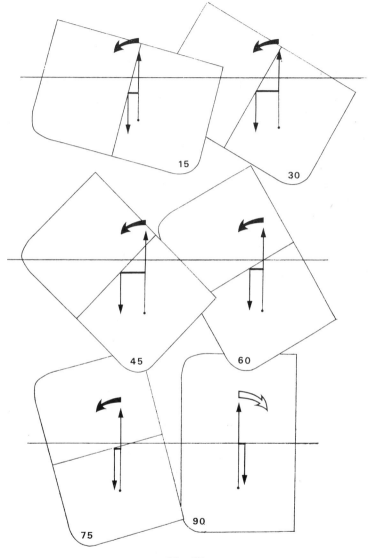

Fig. 27.

corresponding to the points plotted and it can be seen that the deck edge submerged between 15 and 30 degrees. At 45 degrees the righting lever is reaching its maximum value but subsequently the lines of action of the two forces move closer together until between 75 and 90 degrees they pass and a negative lever is formed. This is typical of the average cargo ship in a satisfactory condition of stability bearing in mind that, beyond 60 degrees, items aboard the ship may begin to move, completely changing the character of the curve and reducing the range of stability.

Negative stability. A ship with negative stability will, when listed, generate negative righting levers causing the list to increase. Figure 28. At some point, due to the change in the underwater shape, the forces of buoyancy and gravity will be once again in the same vertical line and the ship will be in a stable condition. Figure 29. This is referred to as the angle of loll and the ship will lie in this position unless she is taken back through the upright by a sea, or cargo loaded, when she will fall without resistance to a similar angle on the other side.

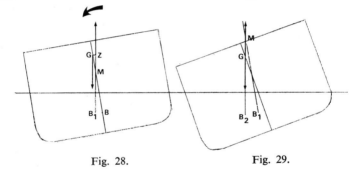

Fig. 28.   Fig. 29.

Increasing the list beyond the angle of loll will cause positive righting levers to form and the ship will tend to return to the loll position. Figure 30.

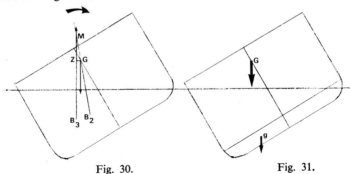

Fig. 30.   Fig. 31.

If it is determined that the list is due to instability, and not to off centre weights, then all cargo work should cease until the matter is rectified. Weight in the form of bottom ballast should be added on the low side where, being furthest from the ship's centre of gravity, it will have maximum effect. Figure 31.

This may initially increase the list but, as the ship becomes stable, ballast can be added to the high side to bring her upright. A ship approaching negative stability will readily list, and in fact begin to roll on the berth, as cargo is swung in on the derricks or landed by crane. This should provide ample warning to an observer who recognises its cause.

Remember that if water ballast is used to correct this condition there will be initially a further loss of stability due to the free surface effect.

Simplified stability information. As the result of a Court recommendation in 1971 shipowners were advised to provide stability information for small ships that their officers could readily understand and use. The ship is provided with a Deadweight Moment Curve, figure 32, and a simple capacity plan showing the Kg of each compartment. On loading, the officer calculates the moment of each unit of cargo, fuel, stores and water to produce a total deadweight moment. Note that the ship itself is a constant and is left out of the calculation, its moment being allowed for in the curve.

When the deadweight moment is plotted against displacement or draft the resultant should fall in the clear area of the diagram indicating adequate stability.

Basically the curve can be thought of as being one of safe KGs, that is the values at each draft that will produce a curve of righting levers meeting the requirements of the Load Line Rules.

Example. A small ship of 1200 tonnes load displacement, 500 tonnes light displacement, has the following weights aboard. Using the Kgs obtained from the capacity plan calculate the deadweight moment and, by plotting the result on the curve provided, ascertain that the ship has positive stability.

Item	Weight	Kg	Moment
Cargo No. 1 Hold	150	2·1	315
Cargo No. 2 Hold	250	2·25	562·5
Cargo No. 3 Hold	200	2·15	430
Fresh Water	10	2·5	25
Stores	8	3·6	28·8
Fuel No. 2 D.B.	38	0·5	19
Fuel No. 3 D.B.	44	0·5	22
Light Ship Displacement	500		
Total Displacement	1200	D.W. Moment	1402·3

Plotting the deadweight moment against the displacement we find that this load provides a safe stability condition. Figure 32.

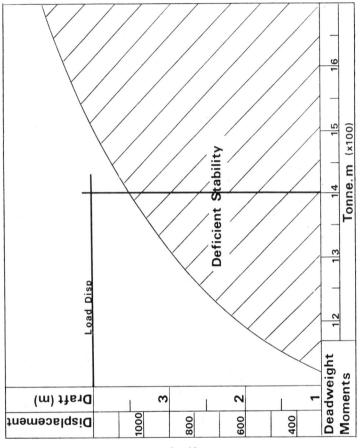

Fig. 32.

The effect of a free surface. Any tank aboard the ship which is not completely full of the liquid it contains is said to have a free surface. Any space above the surface will allow the liquid to move from side to side as the ship rolls in a seaway. This movement of the liquid produces an apparent loss of GM which is said to be greatest when the tank if half full, this value being the one given in the free surface information.

In figure 33, one side of a deep tank has a free surface such that a wedge of liquid has transferred to the low side as the ship rolls. The weight of the wedge has moved transversely a distance gg_1 and the ship's centre of gravity responds by moving from G to G_1. The effect on the righting lever GZ is the same as if G had risen to G_V, the virtual position of G, producing an apparent loss of GM. Figure 34.

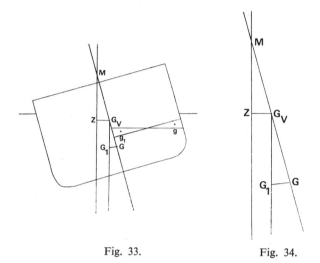

Fig. 33.   Fig. 34.

The position of the tank within the ship does not change this effect in any way. The apparent loss depends only on the shape and size of the free surface and the density of the liquid.

All tanks aboard the ship should be used in a regular and controlled manner so that corrections to GM can be made in advance and the effect of the free surface allowed for. Clearly all ballast tanks when used should be full before sailing and if ballast is taken at sea the result due to the sudden apparent loss of GM could well be dangerous.

The allowance for free surface. Tables for the effect of free surface in every tank aboard the ship are given in the hydrostatic information booklet. A worked example of their use is also provided.

In the past there has been a lack of standardisation in the presentation of these tables but it is now recommended that the free surface moment, FSM, be used.

For each tank the free surface moment, assuming fresh water of RD 1·000, is calculated and then applied in the following manner.

Example. From the free surface tables the *FSM* has been obtained for each tank found by sounding to be slack. Calculate the total apparent loss of *GM*. Displacement 10510 tonnes.

Tank	FSM	×	RD of liquid	=	Corrected FSM
No. 2 D.B.	714·73		1·025		732·60
No. 7 D.B.	367·27		0·850		312·18
F.W. Tank	10·52		1·000		10·52
Fore Peak	37·16		1·025		38·09

Total FSM   1093·39

$$\text{Loss of GM } (GGv) = \frac{\text{Total FSM}}{\text{Displacement}} = \frac{1093 \cdot 39}{10510} = 0 \cdot 104 \text{ m}$$

As can be seen in the above example the weight of the wedge is allowed for by applying the relative density.

Stability at small angles. At small angles of list and heel, by which is meant angles that may be experienced during the normal working of the ship through cargo or ballast, we can consider the metacentre to be a fixed point.

Under the condition set out above the following statements can be made.

From figure 35

The righting lever $GZ = GM$ Sine θ

and from figure 36

The transverse shift of $G = GM$ Tangent θ

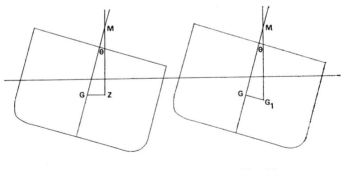

Fig. 35.   Fig. 36.

Example. A ship of 10000 tonnes is listed 7° by a heavy lift. Calculate the moment of statical stability and the listing moment at this angle if the *GM* is 1·5 m.

Moment of statical stability $= W \times GZ$
$= W \times GM$ Sine θ
$= 10000 \times 1 \cdot 5 \times$ Sine $7°$
$= 1828 \cdot 04$ tonne metres

Listing moment $\qquad = W \times GG_1$
$= W \times GM$ Tangent θ
$= 10000 \times 1 \cdot 5 \times$ Tangent $7°$
$= 1841 \cdot 77$ tonne metres

It would appear from the above example that the moment causing the list is greater than the ship's resistance to further inclination, a state of affairs that requires inspection.

Consider that the transverse shift of G was caused by a weight moved within the ship. The moment of the weight, $w \times d$, acts in a plane perpendicular to the ship's upright position and the shift of G is parallel to it whereas the righting lever is perpendicular to the listed position.

From figure 37 it can be seen that the horizontal component of the listing moment, parallel to the righting lever when listed, is $w \times d$ Cosine θ.

Although it will require an equal and opposite moment to bring the ship back to the upright, at this time—

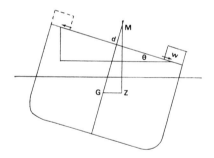

Fig. 37.

Moment of statical stability $=$ Listing moment $\times$ Cosine θ
$= 1841 \cdot 77 \times$ Cosine $7°$
$= 1828 \cdot 04$ tonne metres

The box shaped vessel. For the purpose of examination it is useful to consider our ship to have a simple box shape form as this allows a number of more advanced calculations to be carried out.

The Metacentric Radius. (BM) The position of the metacentre with respect to the centre of buoyancy is obtained from the expression

$$BM = \frac{I}{V}$$

where I = the second moment of the waterplane area (m⁴)
    V = the ship's volume of displacement (m³)

For the simple rectangular shape of our box ship's waterplane the second moment of its area, or moment of inertia, about the longitudinal or listing axis is given by—

$$I = \frac{LB^3}{12}$$

where L and B are the length and breadth of the waterplane respectively.

The full expression may now be written as—

$$BM = \frac{LB^3}{12} \times \frac{1}{L \times B \times draft}$$

Example. A box shaped ship 50 m × 10 m × 5 m floats at an even keel draft of 3 m. Calculate the metacentric radius.

$$BM = \frac{I}{V}$$
$$= \frac{LB^3}{12} \times \frac{1}{L \times B \times draft}$$
$$= \frac{50 \times 10^3 \times 1}{12 \times 50 \times 10 \times 3}$$
$$= 2 \cdot 78 \text{ m}$$

The Longitudinal Metacentric Radius. (BM_L) The position of the longitudinal metacentre with respect to the centre of buoyancy is obtained from the expression—

$$BM_L = \frac{I_L}{V}$$

where I_L = the second moment of the waterplane area (m⁴)
    V = the ship's volume of displacement (m³)

For the simple rectangular shape of our box ship's waterplane the second moment of its area, or moment of inertia, about the transverse or trim axis is given by—

$$I_L = \frac{BL^3}{12}$$

where L and B are the length and breadth of the waterplane respectively.

The full expression may now be written as—

$$BM_L = \frac{BL^3}{12} \times \frac{1}{L \times B \times draft}$$

Example. A box shaped ship 50 m × 10 m × 5 m floats at an even keel draft of 3m. Calculate the longitudinal metacentric radius.

$$BM_L = \frac{I_L}{V}$$

$$= \frac{BL^3}{12} \times \frac{1}{L \times B \times draft}$$

$$= \frac{10 \times 50^3 \times 1}{12 \times 50 \times 10 \times 3}$$

$$= 69.44 \text{ m}$$

Another advantage of our box shape is that, when on even keel, the KB is at the half draft. In the two previous examples this can be used to convert the BM to KM, the normally tabulated value.

$$KM = BM + KB$$

$$= 2.78 + \frac{3}{2}$$

$$= 4.28 \text{ m}$$

similarly

$$KM_L = BM_L + KB$$

$$= 69.44 + \frac{3}{2}$$

$$= 70.94 \text{ m}$$

Example. A box shaped ship 100 m × 20 m × 10 m floats on even keel at a draft of 5 m in sea water. Calculate the hydrostatic information for this draft. Assume KG 7 m.

Displacement = Volume of displacement × RD
$$= 100 \times 20 \times 5 \times 1.025$$
$$= 10250 \text{ tonnes}$$

C of F amidships. LCB amidships. $KB = \frac{Draft}{2} = \frac{5}{2} = 2.5 \text{ m}$

$$BM = \frac{I}{V} = \frac{LB^3}{12} \times \frac{1}{L \times B \times draft} = \frac{100 \times 20^3}{12 \times 100 \times 20 \times 5} = 6.67 \text{ m}$$

$$KM = BM + KB = 6.67 + 2.5 = 9.17 \text{ m}$$

$$BM_L = \frac{I_L}{V} = \frac{BL^3}{12} \times \frac{1}{L \times B \times draft} = \frac{20 \times 100^3}{12 \times 100 \times 20 \times 5} = 166.67 \text{ m}$$

$$KM_L = BM_L + KB = 166.67 + 2.5 = 169.17 \text{ m}$$

$$TPC = \frac{A}{100} \times RD = \frac{100 \times 20 \times 1.025}{100} = 20.5$$

$$MCT = \frac{W \times GM_L}{100 \times L} = \frac{10250 \times (169.17 - 7)}{100 \times 100} = 166.22$$

Note that $GM_L = KM_L - KG$ but in the absence of a value for KG the BM_L may be used as a close approximation.

Example. Using the hydrostatic information for the above condition, calculate the final drafts fore and aft when a weight of 82 tonnes is loaded 40·54 m aft of amidships.

$$\text{Sinkage} = \frac{\text{Weight}}{\text{TPC}} = \frac{82}{20 \cdot 5} = 4 \text{ cm} \qquad \text{Trim} = \frac{\text{Trim. moment about C of F}}{\text{MCT}}$$

$$= \frac{82 \times 40 \cdot 54}{166 \cdot 22} = 20 \text{ cm by stern}$$

Old draft	5·00 mF	5·00 mA
Sinkage	0·04	0·04
	5·04	5·04
Trim	− 0·10	+ 0·10
Final	4·94 m	5·14 m

Free Surface Moment. (*FSM*) The calculation of the free surface moment can be carried out if we consider tanks of simple rectangular form.

As the ship heels a wedge of liquid is transferred to the low side, its weight moving a distance gg_1. The centre of gravity of the tank b moves to the point b_1 in the line $b_1 m$, and its effect on the ship is just the same as if it were a solid weight concentrated at the point m. Although b_1 is the actual centre of gravity of the liquid, the point m is the virtual centre of gravity and the ship's centre of gravity G responds by rising to G_V its virtual position. Figure 38.

Some similarity will be seen to the expression considered before in this chapter for the metacentric radius.

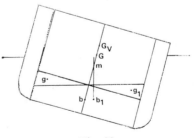

Fig. 38.

Apparent rise of $G = \dfrac{i}{V}$

where $i =$ the second moment of the tank's waterplane area (m⁴)
and $V =$ the ship's volume of displacement (m³)

For the simple rectangular shape of our tank's waterplane the second moment of its area, or moment of inertia, about the longitudinal or listing axis is given by—

$$i=\frac{lb^3}{12}$$

where l and b are the length and breadth of the tank's waterplane respectively.

The full expression can now be written—

$$\text{Apparent rise of } G=\frac{lb^3}{12}\times\frac{1}{\text{Volume of ship's displacement}}$$

Unless the liquid contained in the tank is the same as that in which the ship is floating then the rise in G will be in the relation to their relative density.

$$\text{Apparent rise in } G=\frac{lb^3}{12}\times\frac{1}{V}\times\frac{\text{RD (tank)}}{\text{RD (ship)}}$$

$$\text{The volume of the ship's displacement}=\frac{\text{displacement (tonnes)}}{\text{RD (sea water)}}$$

and this can be substituted to give—

$$\text{Apparent rise of } G=\frac{lb^3}{12}\times\frac{\text{RD (ship)}}{W}\times\frac{\text{RD (tank)}}{\text{RD (ship)}}$$

giving

$$\text{Apparent rise of } G=\frac{lb^3}{12}\times\frac{\text{RD (tank)}}{W}$$

or

$$=\frac{\text{Free surface moment}\times\text{RD (tank)}}{\text{Displacement}}$$

To summarise, the free surface moment varies directly as the length and as the cube of the breadth of the tank surface. Longitudinal liquid tight subdivision is therefore most beneficial as it reduces the breadth and hence the free surface moment by the square of the number of divisions; for example if the tank is divided into two then the effect is reduced to a quarter.

The volume of liquid and the position of the tank in the ship does not alter the effect, only the size and shape of the free surface is of importance.

Example. A tank of surface $10 \text{ m} \times 5 \text{ m}$ is partially filled with fuel oil of RD 0·95. If the ship displaces 5000 tonnes, calculate the apparent rise in G.

$$\text{Apparent rise of } G=\frac{lb^3}{12}\times\frac{\text{RD (tank)}}{W}$$
$$=\frac{10\times5^3}{12}\times\frac{0\cdot95}{5000}$$
$$=0\cdot02 \text{ m}$$

If the tank is now divided equally by an oil tight longitudinal bulkhead show the reduction in the free surface effect.

$$\text{Apparent rise of } G = 2 \times \frac{lb^3}{12} \times \frac{RD \text{ (tank)}}{W}$$

$$= 2 \times \frac{10 \times 2 \cdot 5^3}{12} \times \frac{0 \cdot 95}{5000}$$

$$= 0 \cdot 005 \text{ m}$$

By halving the tank we have reduced the free surface effect by a quarter.

Areas and volumes of ship shapes. By the application of various simple rules we are able to calculate the areas and volumes of ship shaped bodies. The first requirement is that the shape in question be divided into a number of equally spaced positions from which measurements can be taken. These equal spaces are called common intervals and the value chosen is given the symbol h.

In figure 39 a ship's waterplane has been divided into six common intervals giving seven breadths, or ordinates, lettered a to g and these are carefully measured.

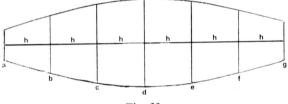

Fig. 39.

Using a base line of length equal to that of the waterplane in question, the ordinates are set up to give a curve, the area under which is equal to that of the waterplane. This curve is shown in figure 40 but note that as our ship is symmetrical about its centre line only half or semi-ordinates need be used and the result multiplied by two to get the same result.

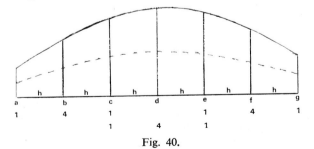

Fig. 40.

Although lettered *a* to *g* in this figure it is common practice to refer to these plotting points as stations and number them, in this case 0 to 7, starting from the stern.

Simpson's first rule. This rule provides us with three multipliers, 1, 4 and 1, which can be applied to the first three ordinates *a*, *b* and *c* to obtain the area contained between them. This process will have to be repeated throughout the figure to obtain the total area and the multipliers are so placed in figure 40.

Area$=(1a+4b+1c)+(1c+4d+1e)+(1e+4f+1g)$

Note that in the above series stations *c* and *e*, the boundry ordinates, are repeated and that the expression may be more conveniently written—

Area$=(1a+4b+2c+4d+2e+4f+1g)$

This progression may be extended to cover any number of ordinates with the provision that this number is three or greater and odd in total.

To complete the rule the sum of the product of the ordinates times the multipliers is itself multiplied by $\frac{h}{3}$, this being a constant.

Simpson's First Rule $\frac{h}{3}(1a+4b+1c)$

Example. Given the following ordinates of the waterplane in figure 39 calculate its area using Simpson's First Rule.

Station	Ordinate	S. M.	Product Area	
a	6 m	1	6	
b	12 m	4	48	
c	16 m	2	32	The ship's waterplane
d	18 m	4	72	length was 60 m and a
e	17 m	2	34	common interval of
f	13 m	4	52	10 m was chosen to
g	8 m	1	8	give the correct
			——	number of ordinates.
Sum of the products of area			252	

$$\text{Area} = \frac{h}{3}(\text{Sum of the products of area})$$

$$= \frac{10}{3} \times 252$$

$$= 840 \text{ m}^2$$

If, in place of the ordinates of the waterplane, the area of an imaginary bulkhead from the waterplane to the keel had been taken and these values set up on the baseline, as in figure 40, then by the same method we can obtain the volume of our figure.

Example. Given the following areas at each station below the waterplane in figure 39 calculate the volume of the body using Simpson's First Rule.

Station	Area	S. M.	Product Volume
a	12 m²	1	12
b	24 m²	4	96
c	32 m²	2	64
d	36 m²	4	144
e	34 m²	2	68
f	26 m²	4	104
g	16 m²	1	16

Sum of the product of volume   504

$$\text{Volume} = \frac{h}{3} \text{ (Sum of the products of volume)}$$

$$= \frac{10}{3} \times 504$$

$$= 1680 \text{ m}^3$$

Simpson's Second Rule. This rule provides us with four multipliers, 1, 3, 3 and 1, which can be applied to the first four ordinates *a*, *b*, *c* and *d* to obtain the area contained between them. This process will have to be repeated again to obtain the total area and the multipliers are so placed in figure 41.

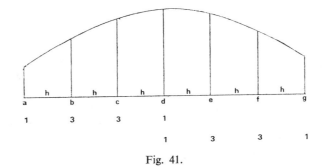

Fig. 41.

$$\text{Area} = (1a + 3b + 3c + 1d) + (1d + 3e + 3f + 1g)$$

Note that in the above series station d, the boundary ordinate, is repeated and that the expression may be more conveniently written—

$$\text{Area} = (1a + 3b + 3c + 2d + 3e + 3f + 1g)$$

This expression may be extended to cover any number of ordinates with the provision that this number is four plus increments of three.

To complete the rule the sum of the product of the ordinates times the multipliers is itself multiplied by $\dfrac{3h}{8}$, this being a constant.

Simpson's Second Rule $\quad \dfrac{3h}{8}(1a+3b+3c+1d)$

Example. Given the following ordinates of the waterplane in figure 39, calculate its area using Simpson's Second Rule.

Station	Ordinate	S. M.	Product Area
a	6 m	1	6
b	12 m	3	36
c	16 m	3	48
d	18 m	2	36
e	17 m	3	51
f	13 m	3	39
g	8 m	1	8

The ship's waterplane length was 60 m and a common interval of 10 m was chosen to give the correct number of ordinates.

Sum of the products of area   224

$\text{Area} = \dfrac{3h}{8}$ (Sum of the products of area)

$\quad = \dfrac{3}{8} \times 10 \times 224$

$\quad = 840 \text{ m}^2$

The use of the two rules on the same figure does not always produce an exact common answer as their basic approach to the solution is not the same. As a general policy use the First Rule for preference when starting from scratch or if the choice presents itself.

Intermediate Ordinates. When the curve of the waterplane is changing rapidly or in direction, as at the bow and stern, additional ordinates may be used to obtain a more accurate result. Figure 42.

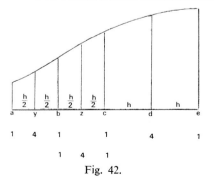

Fig. 42.

In the figure additional ordinates have been inserted at half intervals between stations a, b and c. The multipliers for the First Rule have been laid out and would give—

$$\text{Area} = \frac{h}{6}(1a + 4y + 1b) + \frac{h}{6}(1b + 4z + 1c) + \frac{h}{3}(1c + 4d + 1e)$$

If we were to halve the multipliers instead of the interval then we would get—

$$\text{Area} = \frac{h}{3}(\tfrac{1}{2}a + 2y + \tfrac{1}{2}b) + (\tfrac{1}{2}b + 2z + \tfrac{1}{2}c) + (1c + 4d + 1e)$$

Note that in the above series b and c, the boundary ordinates, are repeated and the expression may be more conveniently written—

$$\text{Area} = \frac{h}{3}(\tfrac{1}{2}a + 2y + 1b + 2z + 1\tfrac{1}{2}c + 4d + 1e)$$

Example. Given the following ordinates from the part waterplane in figure 42, calculate its area using Simpson's First Rule.

Station	Ordinate	S. M.	Product Area	
a	5·5 m	$\tfrac{1}{2}$	2·75	
y	7·5 m	2	15·0	
b	10·5 m	1	10·5	The waterplane length
z	13·5 m	2	27·0	was 48 m and a
c	16·0 m	$1\tfrac{1}{2}$	24·0	common interval of
d	19·5 m	4	78·0	12 m was chosen to
e	21·0 m	1	21·0	give the correct
				number of ordinates.

Sum of the products of area   178·25

$$\text{Area} = \frac{h}{3}(\text{Sum of the products of area})$$

$$= \frac{12}{3} \times 178\cdot25$$

$$= 713 \text{ m}^2$$

Combined Rules. There are occasions when we are presented with a problem where the number of ordinates given cannot be covered by either of the above rules. Examples would be 6, 8 and 12 ordinates and in these cases both rules must be used together. Figure 43.

In the figure there are six ordinates and the rules have been laid out ready for use.

We cannot in this case combine our multipliers as before because the constant for h is different in each rule.

$$\text{Area} = \frac{h}{3}(1a + 4b + 1c) + \frac{3h}{8}(1c + 3d + 3e + 1f)$$

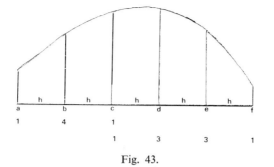

Fig. 43.

Example. Given the following ordinates from the waterplane in figure 43 calculate the area using the combined Simpson's Rules.

Station	Ordinate	S.	M.	Product	Area
a	7·0 m	1		7·0	
b	14·5 m	4		58·0	The common interval
c	19·0 m	1	1	19·0	19·0 chosen to give the
d	20·0 m		3	84·0	60·0 correct number of
e	15·5 m		3		46·5 ordinates was 8 m.
f	4·0 m		1		4·0
					129·5

$$\text{Area } 1 = \frac{h}{3} \times (\text{Sum of the products of area})$$

$$= \frac{8}{3} \times 84 \qquad = 224 \text{ m}^2$$

$$\text{Area } 2 = \frac{3h}{8} \times (\text{Sum of the products of area})$$

$$= \frac{3}{8} \times 8 \times 129 \cdot 5 \qquad = 388 \cdot 5 \text{ m}^2$$

Total area = Area 1 + area 2 = 224 + 388·5 = 612·5 m²

The Centroid of Areas and Volumes. The method used to find the centre of both areas and volumes is directly analogous to that employed earlier for the centre of gravity. Moments must be taken about some specified point, the bow, stern, amidships, the waterplane or keel, and then their sum divided by the total area or volume.

Consider figure 39 and the use of Simpson's First Rule to establish its area. If we take moments about the first ordinate (*a*) the lever here will be zero, at the second ordinate (*b*) the lever will be $1 \times h$, the third (*c*) $2 \times h$ and so on. As *h*, the common interval, is a constant throughout we may ignore it at this stage. The levers are applied to the products for area as these are the values we are using to establish the area.

Example. Given the following ordinates of the waterplane, calculate the position of the C of F with respect to station a. The common interval is 10 m.

Station	Ordinate	S. M.	Prod. Area	Lever	Moment Area
a	6 m	1	6	$0 \times h$	0
b	12 m	4	48	$1 \times h$	48
c	16 m	2	32	$2 \times h$	64
d	18 m	4	72	$3 \times h$	216
e	17 m	2	34	$4 \times h$	136
f	13 m	4	52	$5 \times h$	260
g	8 m	1	8	$6 \times h$	48
			252		772

$$\text{Centre of area} = \frac{\text{Sum of the moments of area}}{\text{Sum of the products of area}}$$

As both the sum of the moments and the sum of the areas have been subjected to the Simpson's Rule then the $\frac{h}{3}$ constant must be applied.

In addition, to save unduly large numbers when dealing with the moments, the value of h has been considered a constant and this must be allowed for in the final statement.

$$\text{Centre of area} = \frac{\frac{h}{3} \, (\text{Sum of the moments of area}) \times h}{\frac{h}{3} \, (\text{Sum of the products of area})}$$

$$= \frac{\frac{10}{3} \, (772) \times 10}{\frac{10}{3} \, (252)}$$

$$= 30 \cdot 63 \text{ m from station a.}$$

In a similar manner the centre of a volume may be calculated.

Example. Given the following areas at each station below the waterline, calculate the position of the LCB with respect to station g. The common interval is 10 m.

Station	Area	S. M.	Prod.	Volume Level	Moment Vol.
a	12 m²	1	12	$6 \times h$	72
b	24 m²	4	96	$5 \times h$	480
c	32 m²	2	64	$4 \times h$	256
d	36 m²	4	144	$3 \times h$	432

Station	Area	S. M.	Prod. Volume	Lever	Moment Vol.
e	34 m²	2	68	$2 \times h$	136
f	26 m²	4	104	$1 \times h$	104
g	16 m²	1	16	$0 \times h$	0
			504		1480

Centre of volume

$$= \frac{\frac{h}{3} \text{ (Sum of the moments of volume)} \times h}{\frac{h}{3} \text{ (Sum of the products of volume)}}$$

$$= \frac{\frac{10}{3}(1480) \times 10}{\frac{10}{3}(504)}$$

$$= 29 \cdot 36 \text{ m from station g.}$$

Example. Given the waterplane areas at the following drafts from the waterline to the keel, calculate the KB.

Draft	Area	S. M.	Prod. Volume	Lever	Moment Vol.
7·50 m	2150 m²	1	2150	$6 \times h$	12900
6·25 m	2090 m²	3	6270	$5 \times h$	31350
5·00 m	2030 m²	3	6090	$4 \times h$	24360
3·75 m	1960 m²	2	3920	$3 \times h$	11760
2·50 m	1870 m²	3	5610	$2 \times h$	11220
1·25 m	1700 m²	3	5100	$1 \times h$	5100
keel	100 m²	1	100	$0 \times h$	0
			29240		96690

Centre of volume

$$= \frac{\frac{3h}{8} \text{ (Sum of the moments of volume)} \times h}{\frac{3h}{8} \text{ (Sum of the products of volume)}}$$

$$= \frac{\frac{3}{8} \times 1 \cdot 25 \times 96690 \times 1 \cdot 25}{\frac{3}{8} \times 1 \cdot 25 \times 29240}$$

$$= 4 \cdot 13 \text{ m above the keel.}$$

Area or Volume of a single section. When it is required to calculate the area or volume of a single section from a waterplane or body then a series of multipliers derived from half of the Simpson First Rule can be used.

In order to define any curve a minimum of three ordinates are required, in figure 44 four have been used although *a*, *b* and *c* or *b*, *c* and *d* would have sufficed.

The multipliers are 5, 8 and −1 and are shown in the correct position to derive the area between ordinates *b* and *c*. The area in question uses the multipliers 5 and 8 on its bounding ordinates, that using the −1 is discarded. The constant for the common interval is $\dfrac{h}{12}$

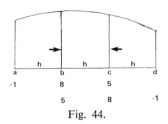

Fig. 44.

Example. Using ordinates *b*, *c* and *d* in figure 44, calculate the area between stations b and c.

Station	Ordinate	S. M.	Product Area	
b	12 m	5	60	
c	11 m	8	88	The length of the figure
d	8 m	−1	−8	was 20 m giving a
			———	common interval of 5m
			140	

$$\text{Area} = \frac{h}{12} \times (\text{Sum of the products of area})$$
$$= \frac{5}{12} \times 140$$
$$= 58 \cdot 33 \text{ m}^2$$

Example. Given the following areas at stations *a*, *b* and *c* in figure 44, calculate the volume between stations b and c.

Station	Area	S. M.	Product Volume	
a	90 m²	−1	−90	
b	108 m²	8	864	The length of the figure
c	99 m²	5	495	was 20 m giving a
			———	common interval of 5m
			1269	

$$\text{Volume} = \frac{h}{12} \times (\text{Sum of the products of volume})$$
$$= \frac{5}{12} \times 1269$$
$$= 528 \cdot 75 \text{ m}^3$$

The Centroid of a single section. To calculate the centre of a single area or volume requires the use of a special set of levers unique to this problem. The levers always have the values 3, 10 and -1, the 3 and 10 being applied to the bounding ordinates and the -1 to that discarded. In addition, the levers act directly on the ordinate or area and not on their products as in previous examples.

The constant for the common interval is $\dfrac{h^2}{24}$ and the centre is with respect to the first ordinate.

Example. Using ordinates *b*, *c* and *d* from figure 44 calculate the centre of the area between ordinates *b* and *c* with respect to ordinate *b*. Common interval 5 m.

Station	Ordinate	S. M.	Prod. Area	Lever	Moment Area
b	12 m	5	60	3	15
c	11 m	8	88	10	110
d	8	-1	-8	-1	-8
			140		117

$$\text{Centre of area} = \frac{\dfrac{h^2}{24} \times (\text{Sum of the moments of area})}{\dfrac{h}{12} \times (\text{Sum of the products of area})}$$

$$= \frac{\dfrac{5^2}{24} \times 117}{\dfrac{5}{12} \times 140}$$

$$= 2{\cdot}09 \text{ m from station b.}$$

CHAPTER XIV

MISCELLANEOUS

The Shipping Industry is no different from other industries in that it must comply with the various Acts of Parliament which are passed from time to time. Many of these Acts apply to other industries as well as shipping, but in nearly ninety years, starting with the Merchant Shipping Act 1894, over thirty Acts have been passed which solely concern merchant shipping and the fishing fleet. A number of these Acts have been passed to satisfy the British Government's responsibilities following agreement at International Conventions concerned with such subjects as Loadlines, Tonnage, Safety, Oil pollution, etc. In the early Acts all the details were contained in the sections of the Act itself, but modern practice seems to be to pass an Act which states the broad outline of the legislation, and contains enabling sections which allow the responsible minister to make detailed Rules and Regulations in the form of Statutory Instruments which are laid before Parliament for approval. In order to be fully acquainted with a particular law it is necessary to examine the Act itself and any Rules which have been made. The Acts and Rules can be obtained from Her Majesty's Stationery Office or Government Bookshops. The Government Department mainly concerned with the administration of the Merchant Shipping Acts is the Department of Transport.

The Department of Transport (DTp) has sections which deal with the following: Foreign Shipping relations, Marine Safety, Marine Crews, Navigational Aids, and General Shipping Policy. The Department draws up rules and regulations on safety for submission to Parliament, and employs surveyors with specialist knowledge, e.g. masters, engineers and naval architects, to check by inspections that the rules are being complied with. It is also responsible for H.M. Coastguard, the Mercantile Marine Offices and for the inspection of ship's provisions.

Examinations are held at regular intervals to enable officers, seamen and cooks to obtain certificates of competency as required by law. The department is responsible also for the investigation of shipping casualties which involve British ships. If thought necessary, officers who have been found guilty of negligence may have their certificates withdrawn or a certificate of a lower grade issued for a limited period.

As a result of such investigations the Department may wish to warn other owners, masters, shipbuilders, etc., of dangers which had not previously been apparent to prevent them occurring again. This is usually done by issuing a ministry notice called an M. Notice, copies of which can be obtained at Mercantile Marine Offices. M. Notices are also used to inform the shipping industry of other information of a technical nature.

H.M. Customs and Excise is the Government department responsible for the control of goods entering and leaving the U.K., and for the collection of duty which may have to be paid on them This control is exercised by Preventative Officers who board the ship on arrival to search the ship and check the ship's stores, and crew's property. The master reports the ship's arrival by lodging a declaration and a list of cargo called a manifest, at the Custom House. Cargo is checked against the manifest as it is landed, and any duty payable is collected. Before sailing the ship must declare the nature and length of its proposed voyage so that duty free stores can be obtained. The cargo is loaded under the control of Customs Officers and when this is completed, the master (or his agent) obtains clearance to sail by submitting the ship's Register and Safety Certificates so that they can be checked. A manifest of the cargo is also handed in.

Lloyd's. The Corporation of Lloyd's, known usually simply as Lloyd's, owes its origin and name to Edward Lloyd who owned and ran a coffee house in the City of London in the 17th century. Shipowners, insurers and merchants found it convenient to meet there because of the shipping information, such as ship's arrival and departure dates, which Lloyd obtained from shipmasters and made available to his customers.

The present day activities of Lloyd's still include the collection and publication of shipping information through the daily printing of Lloyd's List and Shipping Gazette. The main function of the corporation is to provide facilities, such as buildings and staff, that enable the underwriting members to carry out their business of insuring shipowners and others against loss or damage caused to their ships or property by an insured peril.

Classification Societies. The majority of the world's ships are registered with the national authority of each shipowner's country. Apart from this, and in addition, most shipowners register their ships with one or other of the recognised Classification Societies such as:

Lloyd's Register of Shipping (U.K.)
Bureau Veritas (France)
American Bureau of Shipping (U.S.A.)
Norske Veritas (Norway)
Germanischer Lloyd (Germany).

These societies perform three important functions. Firstly they make and publish rules for the construction of ships which are to be registered with the individual society to enable designers to know the sizes (scantlings) of component parts that will be acceptable and safe. Secondly, their rules require the plans of a ship to be submitted for approval, and then for the materials used to be made, and the ship itself to be built, under the supervision of the society's surveyors, thus ensuring a good standard of workmanship, and a properly designed ship. The rules also require periodical surveys to be carried out to maintain the ship in good condition, i.e. "in class", during its working life. Thirdly, they publish a register book which contains in abbreviated form details for all classed ships such as dimensions, hold capacities, derrick capacities and equipment etc., which might be of interest to charterers, underwriters, bankers, shippers and others interested in shipping. There is no legal requirement for any ship to be classed with a classification society, but most are as the owner of an unclassed ship may find difficulty in insuring it or find that premiums are higher than for a classed ship, and charterers may avoid employing an unclassed ship if a classed one is readily available. The society employed by most British shipowners, and many foreign owners is Lloyd's Register of Shipping.

Lloyd's Register of Shipping must not be confused with the Corporation of Lloyd's underwriters. The latter is often referred to as "Lloyd's of London" and, as has been described, is concerned with the insurance of ships, aircraft, motor cars, etc. It is Lloyd's Register which is behind the expression "A1 at Lloyd's" which is sometimes heard. Lloyd's Register is an independent non-profit making authority which relies for its income on fees charged for surveys and services rendered. The notation 100 A1 against the name of a ship in Lloyd's Register Book is assigned to sea-going ships built in accordance with the Society's Rules and Regulations for the draught required, the figure 1 in the notation indicating that the ship's anchors and cables are in accordance with the Rules.

International Maritime Organisation (IMO). This organisation came into being in 1958 when it was called the Inter-Governmental Maritime Consultative Organisation (IMCO). Its present name was adopted in May 1982. It is one of the specialised agencies of the United Nations, and its members include the traditional maritime countries and also those countries which rely on the shipping services of others.

The first objective of IMO is to improve co-operation among governments in technical matters of all kinds affecting shipping. It has a special responsibility for the safety of life at sea and arranges for a wide exchange of maritime technical information between nations.

Another purpose of IMO is to discourage discriminatory, unfair and restrictive practices affecting ships in order to promote the freest possible availability of shipping services to meet the world's transport needs. The organisation is also required to give advice on shipping matters to other international bodies including agencies of the United Nations. Another important responsibility has been, and continues to be, the prevention of pollution of the sea by oil.

The functions of the organisation are consultative and advisory, and it has a permanent staff at its headquarters in London.

Registration and Certification of Ships. The **Certificate of British Registry** of a British ship is issued to the owner of the ship after he has applied to the registrar, who is a Chief Officer of Customs at the port of registry. All British ships, except those of less than 15 tons nett trading coastwise must be registered, and before registration the owner must make a declaration that he is entitled to own a British ship on the grounds that it is wholly owned, either by a British company subject to British laws, or by persons who are British subjects. The certificate contains the ship's name, official number, when and where built, a description of the ship and engines and its principal dimensions, gross and register tonnage, signal letters, the master's name and certificate number and the owner's name, address and number of shares held in the ship. The first master's name is endorsed on the front of the certificate, and any subsequent master on appointment must take the certificate to a Registrar, or Consul if in a foreign port, so that his name can be endorsed on the back of the certificate by the official. This endorsement shows that the master is lawfully appointed, and he is the proper person to hold the certificate while he remains master. He must produce it on demand to various authorities, for example to the Customs when reporting and clearing the ship in and out. Before the certificate is issued the ship must be marked with its name on each bow, its name and port of registry on the stern, draught marks in decimetres, or metres and decimetres, at stem and stern, and have its official number and register tonnage cut in on the main beam.

If the ship is lost or sold to foreign owners, the certificate must be delivered to a registrar or consul after notifying the registrar at the port of registry.

International Tonnage Certificate (1969). Any British ship of 24 metres in length or over, constructed on or after 18th July 1982, must be measured by a surveyor appointed by a Certifying Authority such as the DTp. or Lloyd's Register of Shipping, and the ship's gross and net tonnages determined in accordance with the provisions of the International Convention on Tonnage Measurement of Ships (1969).

The total volumes of all enclosed spaces and of all cargo spaces are measured. The gross tonnage (GT), which is a measure of the ship's size is then calculated using the formula:—

$GT = K_1 V$ where:—

V = total volume of all enclosed spaces in cubic metres; and

$K_1 = 0.2 + 0.02 \log_{10} V$.

The Net Tonnage (NT), a general indication of the ship's earning capacity, is calculated using the formula:—

$$NT = K_2 V_c \left(\frac{4d}{3D}\right)^2 + K_3 \left(N_1 + \frac{N_2}{10}\right) \text{ where:—}$$

V_6 = total volume of cargo spaces in cubic metres,

$K_2 = 0.2 + 0.02 \log_{10} V_c$,

$K_3 = 1.25 \dfrac{GT + 10,000}{10,000}$ (GT=gross tonnage);

D = moulded depth and d=moulded draught, amidships, in metres;

N_1 = number of passengers in cabins with not more than 8 berths;

N_2 = number of other passengers.

The factor $(4d/3D)^2$ is not to be taken as greater than one, and the first term is not to be taken as less than $0.25GT$. N_1 and N_2 are to be taken as zero when $N_1 + N_2$ is less than 13 (i.e. the ship is not classed as a passenger ship) and net tonnage shall not be taken as less than $0.30 \times$ gross tonnage.

On completion, an International Tonnage Certificate (1969), showing the gross and net tonnages and the spaces included in each, is issued to the owner.

All British ships less than 24 metres in length will continue to have their tonnages ascertained in accordance with the regulations previously in force, as will, until 17th July 1994, existing ships, 24 metres in length and over, constructed before 18th July 1982.

A Certificate of British Tonnage is issued to the owner of such a ship after it has been measured by surveyors of the DTp. or an authorised classification society such as Lloyd's Register of Shipping. For this purpose a ton is taken to be 100 cubic feet. The *Gross Tonnage* is first obtained by measuring the internal volume up to the tonnage deck, i.e. the upper deck in single deck ships, and the deck next below the upper deck in other ships, to give the Under-deck tonnage; to this is added the 'tween deck tonnage, the tonnage of any closed in spaces on or above the upper deck which are not exempted by the rules, the "excess of hatchways" and spaces above the upper deck providing light and air for the engine room (if the owner requests their inclusion). Spaces on or above the upper deck which are exempted from gross tonnage include the wheelhouse, chartroom, radio room, galley, bakery, crew washing and sanitary accommodation, workshops, storerooms and lamp room, which must be marked that they aie exempt. The *Register tonnage* is then calculated by deducting the tonnage of many non-earning spaces such as the master's and crew's accommodation, chain lockers, workshops and storerooms below the upper decks, and water ballast tanks, together with the propelling machinery allowance which is either 32% of the ship's gross tonnage, or if the engine room tonnage is 20% or more of gross tonnage, is 1¾ times the tonnage of the space. The detailed tonnages of all the deducted spaces are shown on the certificate.

Owners may apply to the DTp. to have the tonnage of the upper 'tween deck space exempted from tonnage measurement after requesting that greater than minimum freeboards are assigned to the ship. If permission is granted the smaller tonnages assigned are called the

Modified Gross and register tonnages. To indicate to the authorities that the ship has an exempted space which may contain cargo which must be measured to temporarily increase the ship's tonnage, a **Tonnage Mark** 15 inches (38 cm) long and surmounted by a 12 inch (30 cm) equilateral triangle apex down, at the centre, is marked on each side of the ship 21 inches (54 cm) abaft the centre of the loadline disc and level with the tropical fresh mark. (see fig. 1)

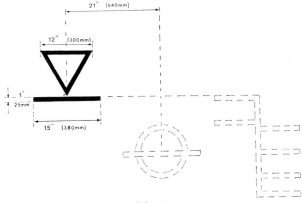

Fig. 1.

The owner of a ship with modified tonnages will benefit by not having to pay as much in dues when in ballast, but he will not be able to load as much deadweight of cargo as a ship with simply gross and nett tonnages, because of the limited draught. An owner can apply to the DTp. for modified tonnages to be assigned to his ship as an alternative to the tonnages ascertained in the normal way. If permission is granted the ship is assigned two sets of tonnages, i.e. gross and nett, and modified gross and nett. Such a ship must also have marked on each side a tonnage mark 21 inches (54 cm) abaft and lower than the loadline disc, in a position obtained by reference to tonnage mark tables. (see fig. 2)

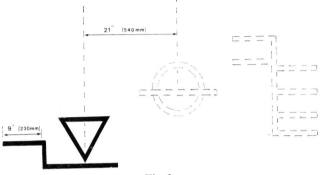

Fig. 2.

The tonnage mark on such a ship serves to indicate which of the two tonnages apply at any particular time. When the ship's waterline is below the upper edge of the tonnage mark, the modified tonnages apply, but when the tonnage mark is submerged the ordinary gross and nett tonnages will be used for calculating dues etc.

Whenever any goods or stores are carried on deck or in any covered space which is not included in the register tonnage, for example in fo'c'sles, poops, bridge spaces, double bottom tanks, the tonnage of the space occupied must be measured and declared to the Customs on arrival in the U.K. This so called Deck Cargo temporarily increases the ship's register tonnage when paying dues.

Suez and Panama Canal Tonnage Certificates. Ships which are to transit these two canals must be supplied with a Suez Canal tonnage certificate and/or Panama Canal tonnage certificate. Either certificate can be obtained in the United Kingdom from the D.o.T. or Lloyd's Register of Shipping. When a ship is measured for British tonnage, the measurements are taken for these other tonnages at the same time. Generally the two sets of rules produce gross and nett tonnages which are similar, but there are differences in detail in the treatment of exempted and deducted spaces, so that they are not usually numerically equal.

Passenger and Safety Certificate. (P. & S. 1.) These two certificates are combined into one document which must be put up in a conspicuous place on board before the ship goes to sea so that it is legible to any person who wishes to see it. They are issued to the owners of any ship carrying more than twelve passengers after it has been surveyed and passed by DTp. Ship, Nautical, Engineer and Radio Surveyors. Such a survey is carried out annually in drydock so that the surveyors can examine the hull, structure, engines, boilers, boats, fire appliances, radio equipment and any other safety equipment, to satisfy themselves that it is as required by the rules and that the ship is safe to carry the stated number of passengers. During the survey the crew will have to demonstrate that they can close the watertight doors, use the ship's fire appliances and launch safely the boats and liferafts into the water. The Passenger Certificate certifies the number of passengers of different classes that may be carried, and the Safety Certificate states the freeboards associated with sub-division loadlines (where marked), the number of boats, liferafts, lifebuoys, lifejackets, etc., the number of radio operators carried and their hours of duty, together with a statement that the ship has been duly surveyed.

Cargo Ship Safety Construction Certificate. A certificate issued to the owner of a cargo ship of 500 gross tons and upwards after a survey of its hull, machinery and equipment by DTp. surveyors or, more likely, by the surveyors of one of the classification societies authorised to carry out such surveys, i.e. Lloyd's Register of Shipping, and the British Committees of Det Norske Veritas, Bureau Veritas and American Bureau of Shipping. The certificate is valid for 5 years provided the following intermediate surveys are passed:—

(*a*) hull and sea connection fastenings, overboard discharge valves to be examined in drydock every $2\frac{1}{2}$ years and sea connections and overboard discharge valves thoroughly examined in drydock at intervals not exceeding 5 years.

(*b*) all main propulsion steam generators and water-tube boilers to be examined internally and externally at 2 year intervals;

(*c*) all other boilers to be examined internally and externally at 2 year intervals until they are eight years old and then annually;

(*d*) tail end shafts to be surveyed every 5 years or 2 years according to type.

Further, every tanker of ten years of age and over, must have an intermediate survey of hull, machinery and equipment $2\frac{1}{2}$ years after the certificate is issued, and all cargo ships must be surveyed annually. Guidelines as to the conduct of these surveys are specified in Merchant Shipping Notice No. M.964.

Cargo Ship Safety Equipment Certificate. This certificate is issued after DTp. Nautical surveyors have surveyed and passed a ship's lifesaving appliances consisting of lifeboats, liferafts, lifeboat radio, lifebuoys, lifejackets, lifeboat and liferaft equipment; also its line-throwing apparatus, fire extinguishing appliances and fire control plans, echo sounder, gyro compass, navigation lights and shapes, pilot ladder, sound signals and distress signals. The certificate remains in force for 24 months, subject to passing an Annual Survey in accordance with guidelines specified in Merchant Shipping Notice No. M.963.

A **Cargo Ship Safety Radio-telegraphy Certificate** is issued to cargo ships fitted with a radio-telegraph installation, which includes its D.F. and a **Cargo Ship Safety Radio-telephony Certificate** covers small cargo ships of under 1600 gross tons fitted with a radio-telephone apparatus. Both the above certificates are in force for one year.

International Loadline Certificate (1966). This certificate is issued to the owners of ships of not less than 24 metres in length trading on international voyages after they have been surveyed to see that they comply with the conditions of assignment stated in the Loadline Rules, 1968. For British ships the survey is usually carried out by Lloyd's Register of Shipping who are authorised by the DTp. to issue the certificate on completion of the survey and after the ship has been marked on each side with a deck line and loadlines. It is also a requirement of these Rules that the ship is issued with sufficient stability information to enable the master to safely load or ballast the ship. The certificate remains in force for 5 years subject to annual surveys of hatches, closing appliances, etc., and the loadline marks.

All of the above documents must be produced to H.M. Customs at the time when the master or his agent applies for the ship's clearance to sail. If any certificate is not in force the ship may be detained.

A **Deratting Certificate** is issued by the medical officer of a Port Health Authority after a ship has been de-ratted by fumigation or otherwise It is valid for 6 months. A ship which is inspected by such an officer and found to be clear of rats so that there is no need for it to be fumigated, will be issued with a **Deratting Exemption Certificate** which is also valid for 6 months.

The Deck and Engine Room logs are used to keep a record of activities during the voyage. The deck "scrap log" or rough log book is kept by the officers of the watch. The exact form will vary according to the shipping company but information recorded usually includes courses steered, compass errors, engine movements, daily distances, times of passing important headlands, noon positions, weather and sea conditions and sounding of tanks. When the ship is in port information concerning the loading or discharging of cargo and the draughts forward and aft will also be included. Important details concerning emergencies or accidents must be recorded.

The Chief Officer's Log Book is a fair copy of the deck scrap log book which is written up by the chief officer and sent to the shipping company at the end of the voyage. It is signed by both the master and the chief officer at the bottom of each page.

All log book entries should be made in ink or indelible pencil and any alterations should be initialled. Both log books may have to be produced in court following an accident but it is the scrap log book which is considered more important for this purpose.

The Official Log Book is supplied by the Department of Transport and must be kept by the master of a British ship, although there are some exceptions. The information to be recorded in the official log book includes: particulars of the ship, list of crew, details of crew changes, births, deaths, records of boat and fire drills, examinations of lifesaving appliances and details of collisions and other accidents.

All entries in the official log book must be signed by the master and by the chief officer or some other member of the crew.

LOADLINES

The United Kingdom accepted and signed an International Convention on Loadlines in 1966 and to give effect to it the Merchant Shipping (Loadlines) Act 1967 was passed by Parliament and came into operation in 1968. The Act provides for the making of Loadline Rules which state the conditions of assignment which have to be complied with, and which concern the ship's structural strength and stability, superstructures, hatchways and covers, machinery space openings, ventilators, air pipes, scuppers, side scuttles, freeing ports, and protection and access for the crew.

The Rules contain two tables which show the minimum permitted freeboards for two types of ship each of which is assumed to be of a standard form, the freeboards being given in millimetres against ship's length in metres.

One table covers ships designed to carry bulk liquid cargoes, i.e. tankers, and the other covers all other ships. Adjustments are made by the assigning authority when calculating the freeboard for a ship by modifying the basic freeboard to take account of differences in block coefficient, sheer, depth, bow height and superstructures, beween the actual ship being considered and the standard ship assumed for the tables.

The Assigning Authority, usually Lloyd's Register of Shipping for British Ships, assigns freeboards to a ship on the satisfactory completion of the loadline survey and states which loadlines are to be marked on the ship's sides and their positions. This information is shown on the International Loadline Certificate (1966) issued to the ship's owner, which must be framed and posted up in some conspicuous place on board as long as the certificate remains in force and the ship is in use. The Act lays down penalties to which the master is liable if the ship proceeds or attempts to proceed to sea without the certificate and without it being posted up. It is also an offence for a ship to be overloaded by submerging the appropriate loadline and such a ship may be detained. The master may be fined for overloading the ship, and for a further offence if he takes an overloaded ship to sea.

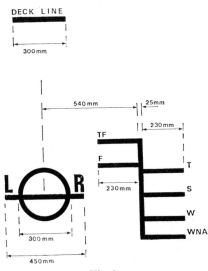

Fig. 3.

A ship must be marked on each side with a deck line, loadlines and a loadline mark as shown in figure 3. The marks must be plainly visible and cut in, centre punched or welded if a steel ship or cut into the planking of a wooden ship, they must be painted white or yellow on a dark background or black on a light background, and their dimensions are as shown in the figures. The thickness of all marks is 25 millimetres.

The **freeboard** of a ship at any time is the vertical distance between the upper edge of the deck-line and the waterline. **Statutory freeboard** means the vertical distance between the upper edge of the deck-line and the upper edges of the respective loadlines as stated on the load-line certificate.

The Deck Line is marked amidships and indicates the position of the freeboard deck. Its upper edge passes through a point where, if continued outwards, the upper surface of the freeboard deck would meet the shell, as shown in figure 4.

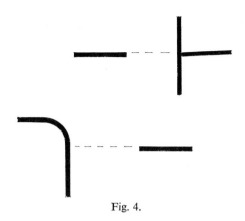

Fig. 4.

On ships with rounded sheer strakes the deck line is marked below the freeboard deck as shown in the figure, its location being stated on the loadline certificate.

The Loadline Mark is marked amidships vertically below the deck-line and consists of a ring with the upper edge of a horizontal line passing through its centre as seen in figure 3. The vertical distance between the centre of the ring and the upper edge of the deck line is called the Summer freeboard which is deduced from the freeboard tables as described previously. A letter marked on each side of the loadline mark indicates the name of the assigning authority e.g. LR indicates Lloyd's Register of Shipping.

A Summer Loadline marked S, is placed forward of, and on the same level as the loadline mark.

The Winter Loadline marked W, is placed one forty-eighth of the summer loadline draught below S and the **Tropical Loadline** marked T, is placed the same distance above S.

A Fresh Water Loadline marked F, is placed above the summer load-line a distance equal to $\dfrac{\triangle}{4T}$ millimetres where:—

$\triangle$ is displacement in salt water at the summer loadline in tonnes, and T is the tonnes per centimetre immersion in salt water at the water-line.

The Tropical Fresh Water Loadline marked TF is placed the same distance above F as T is above S.

The Winter North Atlantic Loadline marked WNA is placed only on ships of 100 metres or less in length, at a distance of 50 millimetres below W.

Timber Loadlines. The owners of ships which are regularly to carry timber cargoes on deck may apply to have timber loadlines assigned to them. Such ships must have a standard height forecastle of length at least 7% of the ship's length, longitudinally sub-divided double bottom tanks over the ship's midships half length to assist stability, and specially strong bulwarks or rails at least one metre high. The calculations which determine the summer timber freeboard assume that a compactly stowed timber deck cargo offers reserve buoyancy, so that the summer timber freeboard is less than the summer freeboard. This allows the ship to load to a deeper draught if required, provided the deck cargo of timber is at least the height of the fore-castle, and is stowed and secured as required by the Deck Cargo Regulations 1968.

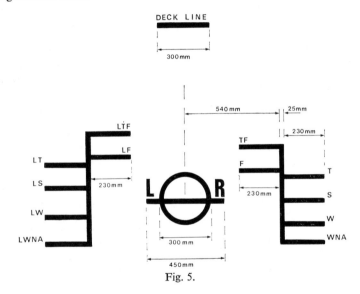

Fig. 5.

The Timber Loadlines when marked are as shown in figure 5. The position of the Summer Timber Loadline is determined by calculation using the freeboard tables and is marked LS. The other timber loadlines are marked as follows:—

LW   is one thirty-sixth of LS draught below LS.

LT   is one forty-eighth of LS draught above LS.

LWNA is marked on all ships which have timber loadlines, either on the same level as the W mark (for ships more than 100 metres in length) or on the same level as the WNA mark for other ships.

LF   is $\frac{\triangle}{4T}$ mm above LS where $\triangle$ is the salt water displacement in tonnes at the LS draught and T is the tonnes per centimetre immersion at that draught.

LTF   is one-forty eighth of LS draught above LF

Zones, Seasonal Zones and Seasonal Areas. The maximum depths to which ships are entitled to load at different seasons and in different parts of the world is laid down in Schedule 2 of the Loadline Rules 1968. After considering the frequency at which gales and storms occur in different parts of the world, an official chart (An extract of which is shown in figure 6) has been drawn up, showing the sea areas of the world divided up into zones and areas in such a way that a ship's master is able to decide his limiting loadline at any time of the year and at any place. A master must ensure that his ship is loaded to a loadline at his departure port such that as his voyage progresses the ship will at no time be overloaded, after taking account of fuel, water and stores consumed, ballast, fuel, water, cargo and stores loaded, and also changes of season and zone en-route.

There are three permanent zones shown on the chart. One, the tropical zone, straddles the equator, and when within it a ship may be loaded to its tropical loadline at any time. The other two are summer zones which lie on each side of the tropical zone and when within them a ship is limited to its summer loadline at any time of the year.

Between the tropical and summer zones in certain areas e.g. Caribbean Sea, Arabian Sea, Bay of Bengal, South Indian Ocean, China Sea, and North and South Pacific, there are seasonal tropical areas in which a ship may be ioaded to its tropical loadline in the fine weather part of the year and only to its summer loadline during the storm season for the area concerned, e.g. North Atlantic Seasonal Tropical Area:— Tropical: 1st Nov. to 15 July; Summer:— 16 July to 31 Oct., during the hurricane season.

On the polar side of each of the Summer Zones lie Winter Seasonal Zones within which a ship may be loaded to its winter loadline between the winter dates and to the summer loadline during the remainder of the year. The North Atlantic Ocean is divided into two Winter Seasonal Zones, with the winter loadline the limiting line in Zone I from 16 Oct to 15 April, and in Zone II from 1st Nov. to 31 March. During the remainder of the year the summer loadline applies in each zone.

Ships 100 metres, or less in length making a passage through the North Atlantic Seasonal Zone I or through the area between 15°W and 50°W in Zone II, must be loaded no deeper than their WNA loadline during the winter season. There are other small seasonal

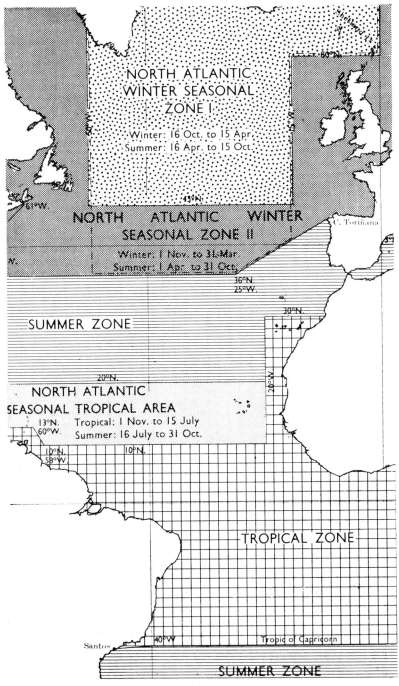

Reproduced from B.A. chart with the sanction of the Controller H.M.
Stationery Office and of the Hydrographer of the Navy.

Fig. 6.

areas which apply to these small ships for details of which reference must be made to the chart, i.e. Eastern coast of U.S.A. and Canada, Baltic Sea, Gulf of Lyons, Black Sea, and Russian Pacific Coast.

Before sailing from every port the master or an authorised officer must enter in the official logbook details of the ship's draught forward and aft, her freeboard each side and mean freeboard, together with any allowances claimed for density of water or fuel consumed before reaching the sea. A notice (FRE 13) showing these details must be posted up before sailing in a place where it is accessible to the crew and kept posted while the ship is at sea.

CLASSIFICATION SURVEYS

New Ships

Plans of a new ship must be submitted to the Society for approval before construction commences. A Special Survey is carried out during construction and the Society's surveyors examine the materials and workmanship from the commencement of the work until the ship's completion. The date of completion of the Special Survey is normally taken to be the date of build and entered in the Register Book.

Periodical Surveys

Annual Surveys. All steel ships are to be surveyed at intervals of approximately one year.

Docking Surveys. Ships should be examined, if possible, in drydock at intervals not exceeding 2 years, except for ships with approved paint and cathodic protection, the interval may be extended to $2\frac{1}{2}$ years by the Society. There are rules that enable an "In-water survey" to be carried out on suitable ships less than 15 years old having a beam greater than 30 metres, by employing divers.

Special Surveys are to be carried out at four yearly intervals, the first one four years from the date of build, and thereafter four years from the date of the previous special survey.

Continuous Surveys. The Society may approve, at the owner's request, a Special Survey to be progressed on a continuous survey basis, so that each compartment is examined and tested once in rotation with an interval of five years between successive examinations.

Survey Requirements

Annual. The annual survey should, if possible, be held at the same time as the statutory annual or loadline survey. The surveyor is to ensure that the following are in good condition:—

Hatchways, ventilator and air pipe coamings, exposed casings, fiddley openings, skylights, deckhouses, superstructure bulkheads, side, bow and stern doors, side scuttles and deadlights, shoots and other openings, together with all closing appliances. Means of ensuring that steel hatches are watertight. Scuppers, sanitary discharges with valves, guard rails and bulwarks, freeing ports, gangways and lifelines, and fittings for timber deck cargoes.

Steering arrangements are to be examined, and auxiliary steering gear, if supplied, is to be assembled and found in good order. A forward and after hold or tank are to be examined internally at the second or third annual survey after each Special Survey held on dry cargo ships 16 years old and over, and tankers 10 years of age and over. A general examination of machinery and boiler spaces is to be carried out and the arrangements for fire protection, detection and extinction are to be examined.

Special Surveys—Hull requirements.

(A) **For ships under five years old.** All the requirements of the annual survey are to be complied with and the ship examined in drydock. The holds, 'tween decks, peaks, deep tanks, engine and boiler spaces are to be cleared and cleaned as necessary and examined. Bilges and limbers are to be cleaned, engine and boiler room floor plates lifted and close and spar ceiling is to be removed as necessary and the structure examined. Sufficient ceiling is to be removed from bilges and inner bottom to allow the condition of steel to be ascertained. If the steel is in good condition the remainder of the ceiling may be left in position. Heavy reinforced compositions coating the steel may be left in position at the Surveyor's discretion if there is no evidence of leakage, cracking or other faults in the composition.

The steelwork is to be exposed and cleaned as required by the Surveyor and he is to carefully examine parts of the structure particularly liable to corrosion and wear due to chafing, lying on the ground and handling cargo.

Openings in the shell plating such as bow, stern and side doors, shoots and other openings are to be carefully examined. The surveyor may require the thickness of any part to be measured by drilling or other method where there are signs of wastage, and defective and wasted parts are to be renewed. Where the inner surface of the bottom plating is covered by cement, asphalt or other composition, it may be left in position provided it is inspected, tested by beating or chipping, and found sound and adhering satisfactorily to the steel.

Double bottom, peak and all other tanks are to be tested by a head which gives the maximum pressure that can be experienced in service; the tests may be done afloat as long as the following examination is also carried out afloat. Main structural tanks are to be cleaned and examined internally, except that tanks used exclusively for oil fuel or for oil fuel and fresh water ballast, need not be examined internally, if after test and external examination they are found to be satisfactory. Special attention is to be given to tanks under boiler spaces. Double bottom tanks used for oil fuel and which are ballasted with salt water when the oil has been consumed need not all be examined internally provided that the Surveyor finds the condition satisfactory after an external examination and an internal examination of the after end of one forward tank.

All decks, casings and superstructures are to be examined with special attention to the corners of openings and other discontinuities in strength decks.

Wood decks or sheathing are to be examined, and renewed where rot or excessive wear is found. Special attention is to be given to the plating under wood decks, sheathing or other deck coverings, sections of which are to be removed if necessary. Masts, standing rigging and anchors, also cables if ranged, are to be checked.

The steering gear, its connections and main and alternative control systems are to be examined together with the auxiliary steering gear which should be assembled. The windlass, hand pumps, suctions, watertight doors, and air and sounding pipes are to be examined. The Surveyor should see that striking plates are fitted under sounding pipes.

Limbers and hatches are to be removed in holds insulated for carrying refrigerated cargoes to allow examination of the frames and plating. If the hull had not been examined by Surveyors before the insulation was fitted, additional insulation is to be removed as necessary to ascertain the condition of the structure. The Surveyor must see that the following are in an efficient condition:—

(a)   Means of escape from machinery spaces, passenger spaces, and crew living and working spaces

(b)   Communication links between bridge and engine-room, and bridge and alternative steering position

(c)   Helm indicator, protection of aft steering wheel and gear.

(B)   Special Survey of Ships between 5 and 10 years old. All the requirements of (A) together with the following:—
Sufficient ceiling in the holds is to be removed from bilges and inner bottom to examine the structure in the bilges, inner bottom plating; pillar feet, and the bottom plating of bulkheads and tunnel sides. If the surveyor considers it necessary the whole of the ceiling is to be removed.

Oil fuel tanks or fresh water ballast tanks (not peak tanks), need not all be examined internally provided that after an external examination and test, and an internal examination of the aft end of one forward double bottom tank, and of one selected deep tank, the Surveyor is satisfied with the condition. Lubricating oil tanks need not be examined internally.

Chain cables are to be ranged and anchors and chains examined. When the reduction in mean diameter of any length at its most worn part is 11 % or more from its nominal diameter, the length is to be renewed. The chain locker is to be cleaned and examined internally.

(C) **At each Special Survey of Ships over ten years old** all the requirements of (A) and (B) are to be complied with, together with the following:—
The steelwork is to be cleaned and rust removed. Casings of air, sounding, steam, and other pipes, spar ceiling and lining round scuttles are to be removed as required by the Surveyor. If steelwork is found to be in good condition, free from rust and coated, after portions of hold ceiling have been removed, the Surveyor may dispense with removal of the whole ceiling.

Parts of the structure in the way of boilers and areas where local wastage and grooving occurs (e.g. shell plating along the heels of frames) are to be carefully examined.

For ships of 10 to 15 years old all tanks are to be cleaned as necessary to permit internal examination if required. Internal examination of tanks used exclusively for oil fuel, oil fuel or fresh water ballast, or lubricating oil need not be carried out as long as they have passed the test and external examination and the Surveyor is satisfied with the internal examination of selected double bottom and deep tanks.

These tanks should be selected so that as many tanks as possible are examined internally before the ship is 20 years old.

For ships 20 years old or over, all tanks should be examined internally. Cement chocks at bilges and decks, and wood sheathing on decks to have portions removed so that the steel condition can be ascertained. Sufficient insulation is to be removed in refrigerated compartments to enable the Surveyor to see the condition of framing and plating.

For ships between 15 and 20 years old, the thickness of the plating between the light and load waterlines, and the strength deck plating, outside the line of openings, is to be gauged by drilling or other means. Gauging is to be done in at least two places in each strake of plating on each side within the midship half-length.

(D) **At the first Special Survey after the ship is 20 years old and at every Special Survey thereafter,** in addition to (A), (B) and (C):—
Within the midship's half length, the thickness of shell plating and

strength deck plating is to be gauged by drilling or other means in at least two places in each strake of plating on each side; also any remaining ungauged plates between the light and load waterlines and strength deck are to be gauged. All paint and rust to be entirely removed before gauging.

The thickness of bottom plating in way of cement is to be measured unless the Surveyor, after making an internal and external examination, considers it unnecessary. Selected portions of cement to be removed if required.

Special Surveys—Tankers. In addition to (A), (B), and (D) above:— At all Special Surveys all cargo tanks and cofferdams to be cleaned out, gas freed and examined. Particular attention to be given to ensure that there is no excessive pitting of bottom plating.

Strums of cargo suction pipes to be removed to allow inspection of the structure in the vicinity. Anodes and anode attachments in tanks to be examined.

At Special Surveys each cargo tank bulkhead is to be tested by filling alternate tanks with water to the top of the hatchway, including permanent ballast tanks. Tanks may be tested when the ship is afloat as long as the internal examination is carried out afloat. Where extensive repairs have been carried out to shell plating, tanks are to be tested.

The gauging of plating thickness required in (D) is to be carried out at every Special Survey after the ship is 5 years old, and the thickness of every deck plate within the midships half length is to be gauged. All gaugings are to be taken in way of tanks.

Screwshafts and Tube Shafts are to be drawn periodically for examination. Shafts fitted with continuous liners or approved oil glands, or made of approved corrosion-resisting material are normally due for survey at three year intervals for single screw ships, and four year intervals for ships having two or more screws. For shafts with approved keyways the above intervals are increased by one year. All other shafts are to be drawn at two year intervals.

DRYDOCKING

A Graving Dock is one which is excavated from the land and has access to the sea, a river or a wet dock. The dock entrance is closed by a caisson gate which is floated into position after the ship has entered. The water is pumped out of the dock to leave the ship supported by a row of keel blocks along the centre of the dock, and other bilge beds, bilge shores and side shores each side to keep it upright.

A Floating Dock consists of a long shallow steel sub-divided tank with high vertical side tanks built on each edge, but no ends. The side tanks must be wide enough apart to allow the largest ship for which the dock is designed to enter. Such a dock is moored in one position and then has its tanks flooded to sink the dock sufficiently to allow a vessel to be moved into position over the keel blocks along the centre of the dock. The water is then pumped out of the tanks which regain their buoyancy and lift the ship clear of the water.

A Slipway consists of a cradle on wheels which can be eased down into the water on an inclined railway track. The ship approaches bow-on and when resting securely on the cradle, is hauled out of the water by winches and wire purchases.

Drydocking. Classification Societies require ships to be drydocked or slipped at intervals of 2 years ($2\frac{1}{2}$ years if special paint used). A ship is normally docked upright with a slight trim by the stern, and with sufficient stability to dock safely. Boats and derricks, etc., should be swung inboard before docking. As the water recedes the ship's plating is scrubbed and cleaned to remove any fouling, before re-painting with suitable anti-corrosive and anti-fouling paint. Draught marks at stem and stern are re-painted.

Surveyors examine the rudder and propeller and measurements to ascertain wear down are taken to decide whether bearings need re-bushing. The tail end shaft may be withdrawn for inspection. All underwater valves, intakes and discharge outlets are examined after being opened up. Cathodic protection anodes are examined and re-newed if necessary.

If it is necessary to drain any of the ship's tanks, plugs are removed from them and kept in a safe place so that they can be replaced before undocking. Plate indentations are noted by the Surveyor and if neces-sary repaired. Anchors and cables are sometimes ranged in the dock for inspection and two or three lengths next to the anchor may be moved to the locker end of the cables to enable wear to be spread evenly.

When all work in the dock is completed the Chief Officer and Chief Engineer check that all plugs and ship's side fittings have been re-placed and that all staging and trestles have been removed before the dock is re-flooded or the ship re-floated.

Drydocking a loaded ship. Normally a ship is drydocked when it is empty and at its lightest working displacement. It is sometimes necessary after an accident to drydock a loaded ship for inspection and repair.

The drydock manager will require more information about the ship than would normally be required. He will ask for a docking plan which shows the positions of bulkheads and other main structural members, the rise of floor (if any) and plug positions. A cargo plan showing weights in each hold will also be required. He will use this information to prepare extra support for the ship in the dock, in the form of bottom or bilge beds built up to the level of the bottom plating before the ship docks. The ship will be docked on an even keel or trimmed to the slope of the dock, or as nearly as possible so, to reduce the thrust on the after keel blocks during docking. After the ship has been docked an extra row of side shores may be put in as well as bilge shores to give extra support. If possible water to above the level of the ship's bottom will be left in the dock, or run back in the dock after inspection has been carried out, to give further support to the ship.

HEALTH AND SAFETY AT WORK, ETC., ACT 1974
DOCKS REGULATIONS

Employers and employees have responsibilities under the Dock Regulations 1934, to try to ensure the safety of all personnel involved in the processess of loading, unloading, moving and handling goods in or at any dock, wharf or quay. These regulations apply in the United Kingdom under the supervision of the Health and Safety Executive but similar regulations apply in other countries wherever loading and unloading is carried out.

The regulations require broadly that workers shall be provided with safe means of access to the dock and ship, that the derricks, blocks, shackles etc., used in loading shall have been tested and examined, and that a safe method of working shall be used. A Register of Machinery, Chains, etc., and Wire Ropes must be kept on board ready for inspection by a Factory Inspector when one boards the vessel. This contains test certificates for the derricks, shackles, blocks, etc., and wire rope, also examination certificates for steel gear, and annealing and examination certificates for wrought iron gear where carried. Examinations of derricks and attached running gear must be recorded in the appropriate sections of the register.

Ship's officers should be conversant with the following requirements as action may be required of them in order to prevent an accident or comply with the regulations.

Gangways. When a ship is loading or discharging cargo or bunkers at a wharf, a gangway shall be provided for the safe means of access of authorised persons, and when alongside other vessels or barges the ship with the higher freeboard shall provide the gangway.

The gangway has to be at least 22 inches (56 cms) wide, properly secured and fenced throughout on each side to a clear height of $2\frac{3}{4}$ feet

(84 cms) by means of upper and lower rails, taut ropes or chains, or by other equally safe means.

Access to holds, unless permanent footholds are fitted according to prescribed regulations, shall be by means of ladders, and these are only to be deemed safe when the cargo is stowed far enough from the ladder to have at each of its rungs sufficient room for a man's feet. All parts of the ship to which persons employed may be required to proceed in the course of the employment shall be sufficiently lighted, subject to the safety of the ship, her cargo, navigation, or to bye-laws or regulations of Harbour Authority.

Hatches. Portable hatch beams to have suitable gear for lifting them. Hatch beams and covering to be plainly marked for the position they belong, and adequate handgrips to be fitted on all hatch coverings. A hatch is defined as an opening in the deck used for the purpose of handling cargo, for trimming, or for ventilation, and if the coamings are less than two feet six inches (76 cms) in height such hatches shall either be fenced to a height of three feet (91 cms) or be securely covered. Hatch coverings shall not be used in the construction of deck or cargo stages, or for any other purpose which may expose them to damage.

No person shall, unless duly authorised or in case of necessity, remove or interfere with any fencing, gangway, gear, ladder, hatch covering, life-saving means or appliances, lights, marks, stages or other things whatsoever required by these Regulations to be provided. If removed such things shall be restored at the end of the period during which their removal was necessary by the persons last engaged in the work that necessitated such removal.

The fencing required by the Regulations shall not be removed except to the extent and for the period reasonably necessary for carrying on the work of the dock or ship, or for repairing any fencing. If removed it shall be restored forthwith at the end of that period by the persons engaged in the work that necessitated its removal.

Every *person employed* shall use the means of access provided in accordance with the Regulations, and no person shall authorise or order another to use means of access other than those provided in accordance therewith.

No person shall go upon the fore and aft beams or thwartship beams for the purpose of adjusting the gear for lifting them on and off nor shall any person authorise or order another to do so.

LIFTING GEAR

All *lifting machinery* shall have been tested and examined by a competent person in the manner set out in the Schedule to these Regulations before being taken into use.

(i) All derricks and permanent attachments, including bridle chains, to the derrick, mast and deck, used in hoisting or lowering shall be inspected once in every twelve months and be thoroughly examined once at least in every four years.

(ii) All other *lifting machinery* shall be thoroughly examined once at least every twelve months.

(iii) For the purposes of this Regulation thorough examination means a visual examination, supplemented if necessary by other means such as a hammer test, carried out as carefully as the conditions permit, in order to arrive at a reliable conclusion as to the safety of the parts examined; and if necessary for the purpose, parts of the machines and gear must be dismantled.

No chain, ring, hook, shackle, swivel or pulley block shall be used in hoisting or lowering unless it has been tested and examined by a competent person in the manner set out in the Schedule to these Regulations.

All chains, other than bridle chains attached to derricks or masts, and all rings, hooks, shackles and swivels used in hoisting or lowering shall, unless they have been subjected to such other treatment as may be *prescribed*, be effectually annealed under the supervision of a competent person and at the following intervals:—

(i)   13 mm and smaller chains, rings, hooks, shackles and swivels in general use, once at least in every six months.

(ii)   All other chains, rings, hooks, shackles and swivels in general use once at least in every twelve months.

Note: Steel gear is exempted from annealing but must be thoroughly examined once every 12 months.

(*a*)   No rope shall be used in hoisting or lowering unless—

(i)   it is of suitable quality and free from patent defect, and

(ii)   in the case of wire rope, it has been examined and tested by a competent person in the manner set out in the Schedule to these Regulations.

(*b*)   Every wire rope in general use for hoisting or lowering shall be inspected by a competent person once at least in every three months, provided that after any wire has broken in such rope it shall be inspected once at least every month.

(*c*)   No wire rope shall be used in hoisting or lowering if in any length of eight diameters the total number of visible broken wires exceeds ten per cent. of the total number of wires, or the rope shows signs of excessive wear, corrosion or other defect which, in the opinion of the person who inspects it, renders it unfit for use.

(d) A thimble or loop splice made in any wire rope shall have at least three tucks with a whole strand of the rope and two tucks with one half of the wires cut out of each strand. The strands in all cases shall be tucked against the lay of the rope. Provided that this Regulation shall not operate to prevent the use of another form of splice which can be shown to be as efficient as that laid down in this Regulation.

No *pulley block* shall be used in hoisting or lowering unless the safe working load is clearly stamped upon it.

Means shall be provided to enable any persons using a chain or wire rope sling to ascertain the safe working load for such chain or sling under such conditions as it may be used.

(a) As regards chain slings, such means shall consist of marking the safe working load in plain figures or letters upon the sling or upon a tablet or ring of durable material attached securely thereto.

(b) As regards wire rope slings, such means shall consist of either the means specified in paragraph (a) above or a notice or notices, so exhibited as to be easily read by any person concerned, stating the safe working loads for the various sizes of wire rope slings used.

Chains shall not be shortened by tying knots in them; and suitable packing shall be provided to prevent the links coming into contact with sharp edges of loads of hard material.

SAFETY PRECAUTIONS

All motors, cog-wheels, chain and friction gearing, shafting, live electric conductors and steam pipes shall (unless it can be shown that by their position and construction they are equally safe to every *person employed* as they would be if securely fenced) be securely fenced so far as is practicable without impeding the safe working of the ship.

Adequate measures shall be taken to prevent exhaust steam from and so far as is practicable live steam to, any crane or winch obscuring any part of the decks, gangways, stages, wharf or quay where any person is employed in the *processes.*

Appropriate measures shall be taken to prevent the foot of a derrick being accidentally lifted out of its socket or support.

Precautions shall be taken to facilitate the escape of the workers when employed in a hold or on 'tween decks in dealing with coal or other bulk cargo.

When the working space in a hold is confined to the square of the *hatch*, hooks shall not be made fast in the bands or fastenings of bales of cotton, wool, cork, gunny bags or other similar goods, nor shall can hooks be used for raising or lowering a barrel when, owing to the construction or condition of the barrel or of the hooks, their use is likely to be unsafe.

Nothing in this Regulation shall apply to breaking out or making up slings.

When work is proceeding on any skeleton deck, adequate staging shall be provided unless the space beneath the deck is filled with cargo to within a distance of 600 mm of such deck.

Where stacking, unstacking, stowing or unstowing of cargo or handling in connection therewith cannot be safely carried out unaided, reasonable measures to guard against accident shall be taken by shoring or otherwise.

The beams of any *hatch* in use for the processes shall, if not removed, be adequately secured to prevent their displacement.

When cargo is being loaded or unloaded by a fall at a *hatchway*, a signaller shall be employed, and where more than one fall is being worked at a *hatchway*, a separate signaller shall be employed to attend to each fall.

Provided that this Regulation shall not apply in cases where a barge, lighter or other similar vessel is being loaded or unloaded if the driver of the crane or winch working the fall has a clear and unrestricted view of those parts of the hold where work is being carried on.

When any *person employed* has to proceed to or from a ship by water for the purpose of carrying on the *processes*, proper measures shall be taken to provide for his safe transport. Vessels used for this purpose shall be in charge of a competent person, shall not be overcrowded, and shall be properly equipped for safe navigation and maintained in good condition.

PEST CONTROL IN SHIPS

Insects and rodents are objectionable for various reasons. Some annoy persons but cause no appreciable harm; some spread disease and infection, while others contaminate food during stowage and preparation in galleys. Some may cause damage to cargoes causing commercial losses. Very few pesticides are suitable for use against all kinds of pests and so the use of them must be considered separately.

Insects in holds and cargoes. Insect and mite pests of plant and animal products may be carried in with goods, move from one product to another, or may be left behind after discharge of cargo to attack later cargoes. Control is required to prevent spread of pests or to prevent commercial damage to cargo.

Maintenance of the ship and cleanliness are important factors in preventing insect infestation. The repair of holds and ceilings to make sure that they are kept in a grain tight condition and thorough cleaning during and after discharge, of box beams, stiffeners, deck girders, pipe casings, etc., to ensure that no cargo residue is left, are important. Any material collected should be burnt or treated with a pesticide or if at sea, dumped.

If preventative action does not succeed and a hold becomes infested with insects, a chemical toxicant must be used to kill them. There are two main classes, contact insecticides and fumigants, and choice depends upon the type of commodity, the extent and location, the habits of insects and climatic and other conditions. The work is best carried out by professional firms, but the crew might carry out small or "spot" treatments. The master should be told the names of the active ingredients used, and great care must be exercised in choosing chemicals to be used with foodstuffs to avoid breaking the law of the country of discharge, or the contract of carriage terms.

Contact insecticides can be space sprayed to deal with flying insects, or sprayed onto surfaces to produce a toxic coating; smokes are the most convenient for use by a ship's crew, and work well against insects in the open. Surface sprays are laborious, but safest and do not require the ship to be evacuated.

Fumigants may be applied as solids or liquids but act as gases. The spaces to be fumigated must be made air-tight before treatment and fumigants must be used only by specialists and NOT ship's personnel, as they can kill a man. The crew may need to be sent ashore during treatment. Care is needed in selecting a suitable fumigant for treatment of particular commodities on loaded or partially loaded holds, and no pesticide should be applied to human or animal food without professional advice to avoid leaving excessive toxic residues.

Examples of pesticides which may be used are:—

Contact Insecticides.

In empty holds and accommodation:—Pyrethrins or malathion or dichlorvos or others.

Against particular pests not in holds:— Dieldrin and aldrin in lacquers against ants and cockroaches. Diazinon as a spray or lacquer against ants, cockroaches and flies. Methoprene bait, for control of Pharaoh's ants.

Fumigants against insects.

In empty holds:—Methyl bromide or hydrogen cyanide or hydrogen phosphide or carbon dioxide and nitrogen.

In loaded or partially loaded holds:—Methyl bromide. Hydrogen phosphide. Methyl bromide and carbon dioxide mixture. Carbon dioxide and nitrogen.

Rodents. The International Sanitary Regulations require ships to be kept in a rat free condition to avoid the spread of disease. The plague can be transferred to man by a flea carried by the rat and there are other rat-borne diseases which are dangerous. Rats may also damage cargoes, stores and even the ship's equipment, causing commercial losses.

Control takes the form of first trying to prevent rats boarding the ship, and then if this is not successful, keeping down numbers by trapping or putting down where the rats move, baits incorporating chronic poison which kills slowly over several days. If after this treatment a Port Medical Officer inspects the ship and finds that the number of rodents on board is negligible, he will issue to the owner on request, a Deratting Exemption Certificate. If control is unsuccessful or nothing is done a ship's rat population can increase rapidly. The ship's owner would then have to obtain a Deratting Certificate from a Port Medical Officer after the ship had been cleared of rats by the use of baits incorporating acute poisons or by fumigation. Fumigation should be avoided if possible because of the expense of having to lodge the crew ashore and keeping the ship idle for several hours.

Precautions which can be taken in port to try to prevent rats boarding a vessel are to fit rat guards or two feet long pieces of tarred canvas round the mooring lines at each end. Painting the gangway white, keeping it well lighted and removing overside cargo nets at night may also help to deter rats from boarding a ship. Ship's refuse should not be allowed to collect on board.

Chronic poison baits can be put down by ship's personnel by following the manufacturer's instructions and being careful when handling them. The poison used is usually an anti-coagulant which acts slowly as the rat eats the bait which is usually a cereal treated to prevent it going mouldy. Rats die due to hæmorrhages from small blood vessels which have been damaged in everyday life. Baits should be placed in rat runways and be protected from accidental consumption by man or other animals, and from contact with human and animal food. A record should be kept of where baits are placed and they should be searched for and removed from cargo spaces prior to loading of bulk food and livestock cargoes. Cereal baits should be replaced within 30 days to avoid insect infestation.

Acute poisons in baits or liquids must only be used in port and then only by qualified personnel. In many ports the Port Health Authorities will now issue a Deratting Certificate following treatment by one of the acute poisons which cause less disruption to the ship's working than does fumigation. For example sodium fluoroacetate may be put out at the end of a day as a liquid in several hundred plastic pots which are left out overnight and collected in the morning, this treatment being continued for several days. The poison acts within a few minutes. Baits must be collected and disposed of when treatment is complete.

A Port Health Authority may insist on the ship being fumigated before issuing a Deratting Certificate. Fumigation must be carried out by qualified personnel and if hydrogen cyanide gas is used in U.K. ports, is subject to the Hydrogen Cyanide (Fumigation of Ships) Regulations 1951. It should be carried out, if possible, when the ship is empty. These regulations lay down a good basis for fumigation carried out everywhere.

All compartments, accommodation etc., should be made available to the fumigator, with limbers, cabins, and store rooms open internally, but with outside doors and hatches closed and ventilators covered. The master must ensure by searching that *all* persons have left the ship after the crew have shut down the engine-room and generators. Foodstuffs must be removed unless permission is given for them to be fumigated. A notice marked "DANGER POISON GAS: KEEP AWAY" with a skull and crossbones symbol on it, and lighted at night, is to be placed on each side of the ship and all gangways are to be raised. When this is completed the master must sign a Safety Statement certifying that he has searched the ship and carried out the requirements specified above, which is then countersigned by the fumigator after he has carried out a similar search. The fumigant is then released and the ship kept under gas for at least two hours for an empty ship, and four or more if loaded. The fumigator then ventilates the ship with all means at his disposal, and for this purpose ship's engineers with respirators may be allowed to return to the ship to operate the ventilating fans before the ship has been officially cleared. When he considers it safe and after tests have been made, the fumigator issues an Entry Permit to allow the owner to have bedding, blankets, pillows, clothing, cushions, etc., to be thoroughly aired until they are free from any trace of the fumigant. A Certificate of Clearance is then issued by the fumigator, which allows free access to the ship for normal working. Both certificates must be countersigned and the date and time of receipt noted, by the master.

Rodenticides which may be used.

Chronic poisons in baits:— Anti-coagulants—hydroxycoumarins (e.g. warfarin) or indandiones.

Acute poisons in baits or liquids:— Fluoroacetamide or sodium fluoroacetate or zinc phosphide or barium fluoroacetate.

Fumigants:— Methyl bromide or hydrogen cyanide or hydrogen phosphide or carbon dioxide and nitrogen or methyl bromide and carbon dioxide mixture.

Summary of Safety Precautions.

(a) Read label on containers and follow instructions.

(b) Never store pesticides of any kind in accommodation, where people sleep, or prepare, store or eat food.

(c) Never eat or smoke while using pesticides.

(d) Never re-use empty containers.

(e) After using pesticides always wash hands.

(f) When spraying insecticides wear protective clothing, gloves, respirators and goggles appropriate to the pesticide being used and do NOT remove while working under hot conditions.

(g) If clothing becomes contaminated, stop work immediately and leave area, remove clothing, take a shower, wash skin thoroughly and wash clothing.

(h) After work, remove and wash clothes and other equipment, and take a shower using plenty of soap.

(i) Follow strictly the requirements of the fumigator before fumigation, and do not enter a fumigation area until it has been certified that it is safe to do so.

(j) If fumigation has been commenced in port with aeration to be carried out while on passage, the master must be provided by the fumigator with written instructions, which must be carefully followed, regarding ventilation and tests to be carried out before crew are allowed to re-enter spaces fumigated. If it is necessary in an emergency for crew members to enter a hold containing gas or containers under gas, not less than two men must enter together and they must be adequately protected with approved breathing apparatus lifeline and harnesses, ready for use where appropriate.

CHAPTER XV

THE INTERNATIONAL CODE OF SIGNALS

THE International Code of Signals is translated into nine languages, English, French, German, Greek, Italian, Japanese, Spanish, Norwegian and Russian. The book consists of one volume devoted to all means of communication at sea, namely, Visual Signals by Code Flags, Flashing Light Signals using Morse symbols, Sound Signalling using Morse, Voice over a loud hailer, Radiotelegraphy, Radiotelephony, Signalling by hand-flags or arms in Semaphore or Morse.

The Code is intended to cater for situations related to safety of navigation and persons, especially where language difficulties arise between ships and aircraft or authorities ashore, such as harbour authorities, quarantine authorities, agents, etc.

THE CODE FLAGS

The set of Code flags consists of 26 alphabetical flags (one for each letter of the alphabet), 10 numerical pendants (one for each unit 1, 2, 3, 4, 5, 6, 7, 8, 9, 0) 3 substitutes and the answering pendant—40 flags in all. The flags shown on the coloured plate should be memorised so that they may be recognised at a glance. The substitutes are intended to indicate a repeat of a flag or pendant, in a hoist, so that double or even treble letters or figures may be conveyed in the same hoist by one set of flags only.

SINGLE-LETTER HOISTS

Single-letter signals relate to phrases which are very urgent, important or of very common use.

358

Single-letter Signals

May be made by any method of signalling.

A   I have a diver down; keep well clear at slow speed.

*B   I am taking in, or discharging, or carrying dangerous goods.

*C   Yes (affirmative or "The significance of the previous group should be read in the affirmative").

*D   Keep clear of me; I am manoeuvring with difficulty.

*E   I am altering my course to starboard.

F   I am disabled; communicate with me.

*G   I require a pilot. When made by fishing vessels operating in close proximity on the fishing grounds it means: "I am hauling nets".

*H   I have a pilot on board.

*I   I am altering my course to port.

J   I am on fire and have dangerous cargo on board: keep well clear of me.

K   I wish to communicate with you.

L   You should stop your vessel instantly.

M   My vessel is stopped and making no way through the water.

N   No (negative or "The significance of the previous group should be read in the negative"). This signal may be given only visually or by sound. For voice or radio transmission the signal should be "NO".

O   Man overboard.

P   *In harbour.* All persons should report on board as the vessel is about to proceed to sea.
At sea. It may be used by fishing vessels to mean: "My nets have come fast upon an obstruction."

Q   My vessel is "healthy" and I request free pratique.

*S   I am operating astern propulsion.

*T   Keep clear of me; I am engaged in pair trawling.

U   You are running into danger.

V   I request assistance.

W   I require medical assistance.

X   Stop carrying out your intentions and watch for my signals.

Y   I am dragging my anchor.

*Z   I require a tug. When made by fishing vessels operating in close proximity on the fishing grounds it means: "I am shooting nets."

NOTES:

1. Signals of letters marked * when made by sound may only be made in compliance with the requirements of the International Regulations for Preventing Collisions at Sea.
2. Signals *K* and *S* have special meanings as landing signals for small boats with persons in distress. (International Convention for the Safety of Life at Sea.)

Single-letter Signals with Compliments

Single letters when followed by numerals have a special significa-
tion and may be made by any method of signalling.

A with three numerals.	*AZIMUTH* or *BEARING*.
C with three numerals.	*COURSE*.
D with two, four or six numerals.	*DATE*.
G with four or five numerals.	*LONGITUDE* (the last two numerals denote minutes and the rest degrees).
K with one numeral.	I wish to *COMMUNICATE* by (method in Complements Table 1).
L with four numerals.	*LATITUDE* (the first two denote degrees and the rest minutes).
R with one or more numerals.	*DISTANCE* in nautical miles.
S with one or more numerals.	*SPEED* in knots.
T with four numerals.	*LOCAL TIME* (the first two denote hours and the rest minutes).
V with one or more numerals.	*SPEED* in kilometres per hour.
Z with four numerals.	*GMT* (the first two denote hours and the rest minutes).

Two-letter Signals

Two-letter signals cover the general section to the "International Code" which deals with Distress; Emergency; Casualties; Damage; Aids to Navigation; Manoeuvres; Miscellaneous; Meteorology; Weather; Communications and International Health Regulations. In certain cases the meaning of a two-letter signal may be varied by including a numeral pendant, for example:

KR   means "All is ready for towing."
*KR*1   „   "I am commencing to tow."
*KR*2   „   "You should commence towing."
*KR*3   „   "Is all ready for towing?"

Three-letter Signals

The three-letter signals cover the Medical Section of the "International Code" and the first letter is always *M*. There are three medical tables of complements which consist of two numeral pendants which relate to Regions of the Body; List of Common Diseases and List of Medicaments.

Four-letter Signals

Four-letter groups refer to the identity of ships for the purpose of making a ship's name known at sea. The Signal letters and the ship's radio call sign are the same. The first letter or number and in some cases the first two letters indicate the nationality of the ship.

USE OF SUBSTITUTES

Substitutes are used when a Code group or a Numeral group contains a repetition of a letter or a figure.

The rules to be followed when deciding which substitute to use are:

1. The *first substitute* always repeats the uppermost signal flag of the class of flags which immediately precedes the substitute.

2. The *second substitute* always repeats the second signal flag counting from the top of that class of flags which immediately precedes the substitute.

3. The *third substitute* always repeats the third signal flag counting from the top of that class of flags which immediately precedes the substitute.

4. No substitute can ever be used more than once in the same group.

5. The answering pendant when used as a decimal point is to be disregarded in determining which substitute to use.

Example. Letters *MMW* mean "Patient has boil in ear", and would be hoisted.

M

1st sub

W

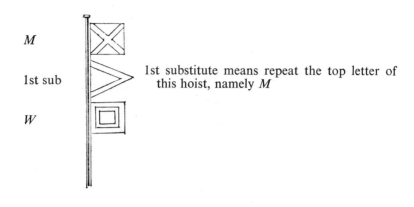

1st substitute means repeat the top letter of this hoist, namely *M*

NOTE: It might be a useful lesson in flag identification if the student were to put in the colourings of the respective flags in the several illustrations given here.

Example. Letters *MAA* mean "I request urgent medical advice", and would be hoisted.

M

A

2nd sub

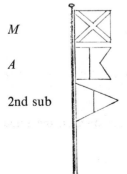

2nd substitute means repeat the second-top letter of this hoist.

NUMERAL HOISTS

Example. Numeral signals are made without reference to the Code book. If it were required to signal the number 2266, then the hoist would appear:

No. 2 pend't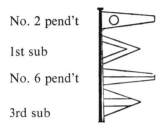

1st sub

No. 6 pend't

3rd sub

1st substitute means repeat the top numeral of the hoist, which is 2, and 3rd substitute means repeat the third numeral of the hoist, which is 6, thus making the signal 2266.

Example. Signal the number 5555.

No. 5 pend't

1st sub

2nd sub

3rd sub

1st substitute means repeat the top numeral.
2nd substitute means repeat the second numeral just as if No. 5 pendant had been hoisted instead of 1st substitute.
3rd substitute means repeat the third numeral from the top, just as if No. 5 pendant had been hoisted instead of 2nd substitute, thus making the signal 5555.

This is the extreme limit to which the use of the substitutes can go, and no substitute can be used more than once in the same group.

Example. To signal the fishing vessel registration number *YH* 344, we would hoist:

Y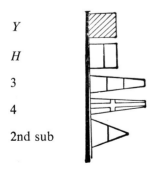

H

3

4

2nd sub

The 2nd substitute, in this sense, means repeat the second numeral, viz. No. 4 pendant, because the 2nd substitute is in the numeral part of the hoist, thus completing the signal *YarmoutH* 344.

LATITUDE AND LONGITUDE

Letter *L* refers to latitude and is at the top of the four numeral pendants when signalling latitude. Similarly the letter *G* above four or five numeral pendants indicates that the hoist refers to longitude.

Example. To signal latitude 05° 30′ N., longitude 70° 05′ E.

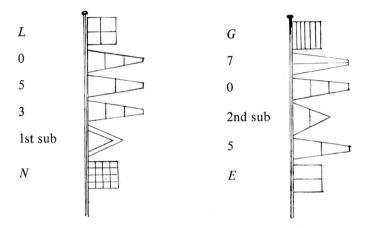

L	*G*
0	7
5	0
3	2nd sub
1st sub	5
N	*E*

Means Lat. 5° 30′ N.,   Means 70° 05′ E.,
a six-flag hoist.   a six-flag hoist.

When the longitude is 100° or more the first figure need not be hoisted unless to prevent misunderstanding as to whether the degrees are under or over the 100, thus longitude 176° 40′ W. may appear as *G* 17640 W. or as *G* 7640.

The letters *N* or *S* (North or South) in latitude signals, or the letters *E* or *W* (East of West) in longitude signals need not be hoisted unless to avoid confusion when latitude is near the Equator or when longitude is near the 180th meridian.

TIME SIGNALS

Times are expressed in four figures of which the first two denote the hour (from 00=midnight up to 23=11 p.m.), and the last two denote the minutes (from 00 to 59). The figures are preceded by the letter *T* to indicate local time or by the letter *Z* to indicate Greenwich Mean Time.

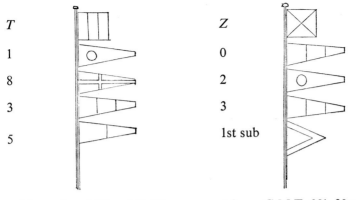

Means Local Time 18h 35m.   Means G.M.T. 02h 30m.

AZIMUTH BEARINGS, COURSES AND DISTANCES

When signalling Azimuth or Bearing three figures are used to denote the degrees from 000° to 359°, measured clockwise. The bearings are True unless stated otherwise and if there is any possibility of confusion about what the figures mean, they should be preceded by the letter A to form a single group. Bearings made by a ship to indicate an object are to be reckoned from the ship making the signal, thus $A270$ signifies Bearing 270° T.

When signalling Courses three figures are used to denote the degrees from 000° to 359° measured clockwise from true north unless otherwise stated, thus $MG155$ indicates "You should steer 155° T".

Figures preceded by the letter R indicate distance in nautical miles, and figures preceded by the letter S indicate Speed in knots.

FLAGS TO BE FLOWN BY BRITISH MERCHANT SHIPS

The Merchant Shipping Act provides as follows:

1. A ship belonging to a British subject shall hoist the proper national colours:

   (a) On a signal being made to her by one of Her Majesty's ships (including any vessel under the command of an officer of Her Majesty's Navy on full pay; and

   (b) On entering or leaving any foreign port; and

   (c) If of 50 tons gross tonnage or upwards, on entering or leaving any British port.

2. If default is made on board any such ship in complying with this section the master of the ship shall for each offence be liable to a fine.

3. This section shall not apply to a fishing boat duly entered in the fishing boat register, and lettered and numbered as required by the fourth part of this Act.

MORSE SIGNALLING

The following Tables give a list of the Morse symbols used for Visual and Sound signalling.

MORSE SIGNALLING BY HAND-FLAGS OR ARMS

The "dot" and "dash" characters can be made by hand-flags by raising both hand-flags or arms vertically above the head for "dot" and spreading out both hand-flags or arms at shoulder level for "dash". Separation of "dots and dashes" is indicated by bringing the flags before the chest, and separation of letters, groups or words by hand-flags or arms kept at 45° away from the body downwards. A circular motion of hand-flags over the head indicates erase if made by the sender, and request for repetition if made by the receiving station.

INTERNATIONAL MORSE CODE

Alphabet

Meaning	Symbol	Meaning	Symbol	Meaning	Symbol
A	. —	J	. — — —	S	. . .
B	— . . .	K	— . —	T	—
C	— . — .	L	. — . .	U	. . —
D	— . .	M	— —	V	. . . —
E	.	N	— .	W	. — —
F	. . — .	O	— — —	X	— . . —
G	— — .	P	. — — .	Y	— . — —
H	. . . .	Q	— — . —	Z	— — . .
I	. .	R	. — .		

Numerals

Meaning	Symbol
1	. — — — —
2	. . — — —
3	. . . — —
4	. . . . —
5	. . . . .
6	— . . . .
7	— — . . .
8	— — — . .
9	— — — — .
0	— — — — —

Punctuation

Meaning	Sign	Symbol
Fullstop (.) and decimal point	AAA	. — . — . —

PROCEDURE SIGNALS AND SIGNS

Meaning	Signs	Symbol
Call for unknown ship and general call	$\overline{AA}$ $\overline{AA}$, etc.	·—·— ·—·—, etc.
Answering sign	$\overline{TTTTTTT}$, etc.	—————————, etc.
Erase sign	$\overline{EEEEEEEE}$	········, etc.
Repeat sign	RPT	·—···—·—·—
All after ⎫	AA	·—·—
All before ⎪	AB	·—···
Word or group between ⎬ used in conjunction with RPT	BN	—···—·
Word or group after ⎪	WA	·——·—
Word or group before ⎭	WB	·———···
Ending sign	$\overline{AR}$	·—·—·
From	De	—·· ·
Yes, or previous group should be read in the affirmative	C	—·—·
Message received	R	·—·
Word or group received	T	—
International code groups follow	YU or spoken word INTERCO	—·——··—
Full stop and decimal point	$\overline{AAA}$ or spoken word either STOP or DECIMAL	·—·—·—
Call for unknown ship and general call by R.Tel.	CQ	—·—· ——·—

PROCEDURE SIGNALS AND SIGNS (continued)

Meaning	Signs	Symbol
No, or previous group should be read in the negative	N	▬ ▪
Interrogative, or the previous group should be read as a question	RQ	▪ ▬ ▪ ▬ ▬ ▪ ▬
Waiting signal or period	$\overline{AS}$	▪ ▬ ▪ ▪ ▪
I wish to communicate with you, or invitation to transmit	K	▬ ▪ ▬
It is correct	OK	▬ ▬ ▬ ▬ ▪ ▬
What is the name or identity signal of your vessel	CS	▬ ▪ ▬ ▪ ▪ ▪ ▪

Use of Procedure Signals and Signs
General Call

The general call or the call for an unknown ship $\overline{AA}$ $\overline{AA}$, etc. (▪ ▬ ▪ ▬ ▪ ▬ ▪ ▬, etc.) is used to attract attention when wishing to signal to a ship whose name is not known. It is the normal method of calling up at sea, and is to be continued until the ship addressed answers.

Answering Sign

The answering sign $\overline{TTTTTTT}$, etc. (▬ ▬ ▬ ▬ ▬ ▬ ▬, etc.) is used to answer the call. It is to be continued until the transmitting ship ceases to make the call.

De (▬ ▪ ▪ ▪)

The signal "De" used in the identity signifies: "From . . . ." Thus: De GHZU means "From ship Mahout" whose signal letters are GHZU.

T (▬)

The letter T is used to indicate the receipt of each word in the text of a plain language message.

$$R (\cdot - \cdot)$$

The letter R signifies that the *message* is received.

$$\overline{AS} (\cdot - \cdot \cdot \cdot)$$

The signal AS, meaning "wait", would be used by a ship or shore station who were not ready to receive a message, probably due to other traffic on hand at the time.

$$K (- \cdot -)$$

The letter K, meaning "I wish to communicate with you" or "Invitation to transmit", would be used to indicate that the ship was now ready to transmit or to receive signals.

Erase Sign ($\overline{EEEEEEEE}$, etc. $\cdot \cdot \cdot \cdot \cdot$, etc.)

The erase sign is used to indicate that the last word or group was signalled incorrectly. It is to be answered with the erase sign. When answered, the transmitting ship will repeat the last word or group which was correctly signalled, and then proceed with the remainder of the message.

If the mistake was not discovered until after the message has been completely signalled, a new message must be made.

If it is desired to cancel the whole of a message while in process of transmission, the erase sign must be made, followed by the ending sign, viz. $\overline{EEEEEEEE} \ A\overline{R}$.

Repeat Sign RPT ($\cdot - \cdot \cdot - - \cdot -$)

The repeat sign is used to obtain a repetition of the whole or part of a message.

To obtain the repetition of the whole message.

The repeat sign made singly signifies: "Repeat the last message." The repetition is signalled by making the message through in exactly the same form as it was originally transmitted.

To obtain a repetition of a part of a message.

The repeat sign is used in conjunction with the signs AA, AB, BN, WA or WB, and an identifying word or group.

"$\overline{RPT}$ $\overline{AA}$ VESSEL"—signifies: "Repeat *all after* the word VESSEL."

"$\overline{RPT}$ $\overline{AB}$ MBP"—signifies: "Repeat *all before* the group MBP."

"$\overline{RPT}$ $\overline{BN}$ BOAT-SUNK"—signifies: "Repeat between BOAT and SUNK."

"$\overline{RPT}$ $\overline{WA}$ MN"—signifies: "Repeat the group after MN."

"$\overline{RPT}$ $\overline{WB}$ WRECK"—signifies: "Repeat the word before WRECK."

If a message is not understood, or if a coded message, when decoded, is not intelligible, the repeat sign is *NOT* used. The receiving ship must then make the appropriate signal from the Signal Code.

Ending Sign

The ending sign $\overline{AR}$ (• — • — •) is used in all cases to end a message.

International Code Group Indicators "YU" and "YV"

In messages transmitted by means of the Morse Code, the International Code group indicator "*YU*" is to be used as the first group of the coded text to indicate that the message which follows consists of Code groups from the International Code of Signals and not plain language. If plain language has to be used in the message for names and places this is preceded by "*YZ*". Group indicator "*YV*" is then used to indicate a return to Code groups.

SIGNALLING BY FLASHING

Component Parts of a Message

A message made by flashing is divided into the following components:

1. Call. 2. Identity. 3. Text. 4. Ending.

How to Signal

Component 1. *The Call.* The transmitting ship will commence signalling by making the call, which will be flashed continuously until answered.

The call consists of:

(i) The general call ($\overline{AA}$ $\overline{AA}$ $\overline{AA}$), etc., or

(ii) The signal letters of the ship to be called, or name of the ship.

On observing the call, and when ready in all respects to read and write down, the receiving ship will answer by making the answering sign.

Component 2. *The Identity.* It will not always be necessary for two ships to establish their identity; should such necessity exist the two ships will carry out the following procedure: when the call has been answered the transmitting ship will make "*De*" (from), followed by her signal letters or name. This will be repeated back. The receiving ship will then signal her own signal letters or name, which the transmitting ship will repeat back. If either ship fails to repeat back immediately or repeats back incorrectly, the other will make her signal letters or name again until they are correctly repeated back.

Component 3. *The Text* consists of plain language or of code groups. Each word or group is signalled separately. The receiving ship will:

Acknowledge the receipt of each plain language word or group with "*T*". If the receiving ship does not acknowledge the receipt the transmitting ship should immediately signal again the last word or group.

Component 4. *The Ending* consists of the ending sign $\overline{AR}$. The ending is answered by "*R*".

Omitting the Call and Identity

When two ships are signalling and several messages are passed between them, the call and identity need be signalled in the *first* message only, in order to avoid delay.

Example 1. **A Plain Language Message.**

Ship *Falaba* (signal letters *GHZZ*) wishes to signal to ship *Benvalla* (signal letters *GIAM*) the following message: "Can I transfer rescued persons to you?"

Component	*Falaba* transmits	*Benvalla* receives and makes
Call	$\overline{AA}$ $\overline{AA}$ $\overline{AA}$, etc.	*TTTTTTTTTT*, etc.
Identity	Dc *GHZZ*	
		De *GHZZ*
	OK	T
		GIAM
	GIAM	
		OK
	T	
	Can	T
	I	T
	transfer	T
Message	rescued	T
	persons	T
	to	T
	you	T
Ending	$\overline{AR}$	R

NOTE. The interchange of signal letters is always repeated in acknowledgement, but when identity has been established they are not repeated in further communication between ships.

Example 2. **A Coded Message.**

Messages may be morsed by transmitting the appropriate letters from the Code book.

The letters *YU* mean "I am going to communicate with you by International Code", *RV* means "You should proceed to the place indicated" and *UW* means "I wish you a pleasant voyage".

Component	Transmitting ship makes	Receiving ship makes
Call	$\overline{AA}$ $\overline{AA}$ $\overline{AA}$	$\overline{TTTTTTTTT}$, etc.
Identity	*De GHZZ*	
		De GHZZ
	OK	*T*
		GIAM
	GIAM	
		OK
	T	
Groups from	*YU*	*T*
International	*RV*	*T*
Code	*YZ*	*T*
Plain language	LONDON	*T*
Groups from	*YV*	*T*
Int. Code	*UW*	*T*
Ending	$\overline{AR}$	*R*

Example 3. **Ship "X" to Ship "Y".**

NOTE. *The replies of ship " Y" are the signals within the brackets.*

```
- - - -    - - - -    - - - -    (- - - - - - - -)
- - -    - - - -    - - -    -    (-)   - -    - - -    (-)   -    - - - -    -
(-)    - - -    -    - -    -    - - - -    -    - - -    (-)   - - - -
- - -    - - -    -    - - - -    - -    - - -    -    (-)   - - - -
- - -    - - -    (-)   -    - - -    - -    - -    - -
- - -    - - -    - - -    - - -    (-)   - - - -    (- - -)
```

Call (Answer) What (*T*) is (*T*) the (*T*) weather (*T*) forecast (*T*) for (*T*) tomorrow (*T*) Ending (Received).

Ship "Y" to ship "X". An example of repeat "all after".

NOTE. *The replies of ship "X" are the signals within the brackets.*

```
▬ ▬ ▬    ▬ ▬ ▬    ▬ ▬ ▬    (▬ ▬ ▬ ▬ ▬ ▬ ▬)    ▬ ▬ ▬ ▬
▬ ▬ ▬ ▬  ▬ ▬ ▬ ▬  ▬ ▬ ▬ ▬  ▬ ▬ ▬   ▬ ▬   ▬   (▬)   ▬ ▬
▬ ▬ ▬ ▬  ▬ ▬ ▬ ▬  ▬ ▬ ▬   ▬ ▬ ▬   ▬ ▬   ▬ ▬ ▬ ▬   ▬ ▬ ▬ ▬
▬ ▬   ▬ ▬   ▬ ▬ ▬   (▬)   ▬ ▬ ▬ ▬   ▬ ▬ ▬   ▬ ▬ ▬   (▬)
▬ ▬ ▬   ▬ ▬ ▬ ▬   ▬ ▬ ▬   ▬ ▬ ▬   ▬ ▬ ▬ ▬   ▬ ▬ ▬   (▬)   ▬ ▬ ▬ ▬
▬ ▬ ▬   ▬   (▬)   ▬   ▬ ▬ ▬   (▬)   ▬ ▬ ▬   ▬   ▬ ▬   (▬)
▬ ▬ ▬   ▬ ▬ ▬   (▬)   ▬ ▬ ▬   ▬   ▬ ▬ ▬   ▬   ▬ ▬   ▬ ▬ ▬
▬   ▬ ▬ ▬ ▬   ▬   ▬ ▬   (▬)   ▬ ▬   ▬ ▬ ▬   ▬ ▬ ▬   ▬ ▬ ▬
▬ ▬   ▬ ▬   ▬ ▬ ▬   ▬ ▬ ▬   (▬ ▬ ▬ ▬ ▬ ▬ ▬ ▬ ▬   ▬ ▬ ▬ ▬
▬ ▬ ▬   ▬ ▬ ▬)   ▬   ▬ ▬ ▬   ▬   ▬ ▬ ▬   ▬   ▬ ▬
▬ ▬ ▬   ▬   ▬ ▬ ▬ ▬   ▬   ▬ ▬   (▬)   ▬ ▬   ▬ ▬ ▬
▬ ▬ ▬   ▬ ▬ ▬   ▬ ▬   ▬ ▬   ▬ ▬ ▬   ▬ ▬ ▬   (▬)   ▬ ▬ ▬ ▬
(▬ ▬ ▬)
```

Call (Answer) Cyclone (*T*) approaching (*T*) you (*T*) should (*T*) put (*T*) to (*T*) sea (*T*) or (*T*) strengthen (*T*) moorings (Repeat all after the word or) *T* strengthen moorings (*T*) Ending (Received).

SIGNALLING BY SOUND (Whistle, Siren, Foghorn)

Caution. The misuse of sound signalling being of a nature to create serious confusion in the highways at sea, the captains of ships should use these signals with the utmost discretion. Owing to the nature of the apparatus used sound signalling is necessarily slow, and it is for this reason that it is necessary for ships to reduce the length of their signals as much as possible.

Sound signalling in fog should be reduced to a minimum. Signals other than single-letter signals should be used only in extreme emergency and never in frequented navigational waters.

QUARANTINE SIGNALS

The following signals are to be shown on arrival by vessels requiring or required to show the state of health:

In the Daytime.

Q flag—*signifying* -   -   -   "My ship is 'healthy', and I request free pratique."

or

ZS flags—*signifying*   -   -   "My ship is 'healthy', and I request free pratique."

Q flag over first substitute (*QQ*)—

signifying   -   -   -   -   "I require health clearance."

By Night.

Red light over a white light—

signifying   -   -   -   -   "I require health clearance."

Only to be exhibited within the precincts of a port. The lights should be about two metres (6 feet) apart and visible all round.

PILOT SIGNALS

The following signals are signals for a pilot:

In the Daytime.

The International Code Signal *G signifying* "I require a pilot."

At Night.

(1) The pyrotechnic light, commonly known as a blue light, every fifteen minutes.

(2) A bright white light, flashed or shown at short or frequent intervals just above the bulwarks for about a minute at a time.

(3) The International Code Signal *G* by flashing.

GALE WARNING SIGNALS

The Meteorological Office sends to certain Signal Stations a warning telegram on any occasion when a gale is expected to occur in the vicinity of the station. The fact that one of these notices has been received at any station is made known by hoisting a black canvas cone, 1 m high and 1 m wide at the base, which appears as a triangle when hoisted.

The South Cone (point downwards) is hoisted for gales commencing from a Southerly point; such gales often veer, sometimes to as far as North-west.

For gales commencing from East to West the South Cone will be hoisted if the gale is expected to change to a Southerly direction.

The North Cone (point upwards) is hoisted for gales commencing from a Northerly point; for gales commencing from East or West the North Cone will be hoisted if the gale is expected to change to a Northerly direction.

QUESTIONS AND ANSWERS

1. How many hoists should be shown at a time?

Usually one hoist, but if more than one group of hoists are shown they should be kept flying until answered by the receiving ship.

2. Name the order in which several hoists should be read when displayed simultaneously.

(i) Masthead, (ii) triatic stay, (iii) starboard yardarm, (iv) port yardarm.

3. Suppose more than one group is shown on the same halyard, how are they separated and read?

They are separated by a "tack" line about 2 m. long, and the groups are read in their order from the top group downwards.

4. A vessel is flying several groups of signals on different halyards at the same yardarm; in what order should they be read?

From the outboard yardarm hoist inwards.

5. Several hoists are shown from different halyards on the triatic stay; in what order should they be read?

From forward aft.

6. Define what is meant by superior and inferior signals.

Signals take their superiority from the order and position in which they are hoisted, the follow-up groups being called inferior signals. The first signal hoisted is superior in point of time to the second one hoisted, and so on.

Similarly, they take superiority from the position in which they are hoisted, viz.: (i) masthead, (ii) triatic stay, (iii) starboard yardarm, (iv) port yardarm.

7. Describe the procedure of signalling to another ship.

I would hoist her signal letters above the signal with a tack line, if necessary, or I would just hoist the signal.

After completing the signal I would hoist my answering pendant close up. The receiving ship would do the same.

8. A vessel is flying your signal letters and flags K9 what would you do?

She wants to communicate with me by VHF on Channel 16. I would hoist my answering pendant close up. When she hauled the signal down I would lower my answering pendant, set watch on Channel 16 and await her call.

9. How can one tell if the Code pendant is at the dip?

Unless it is lowered well down it is sometimes difficult to see whether it is close up or not, especially if flown from the triatic stay, so it is better to hoist the answering pendant at the masthead or yardarm.

10. You cannot distinguish the signal made by another ship, or cannot decode them intelligibly; what would you do?

Keep my answering pendant at the dip and hoist:

ZK—I cannot distinguish your flags. *Or,*

ZL—Your signal has been received but not understood.

11. How can you tell when a man-of-war is communicating with a merchant ship?

She flies the Code pendant in a conspicuous position during the whole time the signal is being made.

12. How is a numeral signal made?

By means of the numeral pendants, simply by bending them together in the order to make up the number, introducing substitutes when double figures appear in the groups.

13. What is a substitute?

A substitute is a triangular flag. There are three substitutes, 1st, 2nd and 3rd, and they are used when a letter or a figure is repeated in a group thus, 7755 would appear when hoisted as 7, 1st substitute, 5, 3rd substitute.

14. What are the functions of the Code pendant?

(*a*) When hoisted by a warship preliminary to signalling it means that the International Code is to be used.

(*b*) When hoisted at the dip by a receiving ship it means signal seen, and when hoisted close up it means signal understood.

(*c*) It is used as an answering pendant to acknowledge each hoist as received.

(*d*) It indicates the decimal point in a numeral signal.

(*e*) Flag signalling completed.

15. When and by whom must National colours be shown?

By all British vessels when entering or leaving foreign ports, and on a signal being made from a Government ship. Vessels under 50 tons gross are exempted when entering or leaving British ports, so also are registered fishing vessels.

INDEX